Confessions of an Animal Rights Terrorist

CONFESSIONS OF AN ANIMAL RIGHTS TERRORIST

KAREN LEVENSON

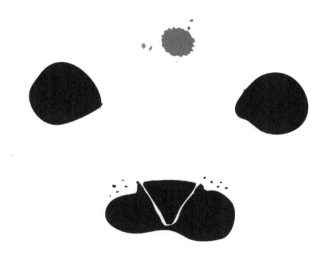

Lantern Publishing & Media • Brooklyn, NY

2021

Lantern Publishing & Media

128 Second Place

Brooklyn, NY 11231

www.lanternpm.org

Printed in the United States of America

Library of Congress Cataloging-in-Publication Data

Names: Levenson, Karen, 1957- author.
Title: Confessions of an animal rights "terrorist" / Karen Levenson.
Description: Brooklyn, NY : Lantern Publishing & Media, [2020]
Identifiers: LCCN 2020023292 (print) | LCCN 2020023293 (ebook) |
ISBN 9781590566213 (paperback) | ISBN 9781590566206 (ebook)
Subjects: LCSH: Levenson, Karen, 1957- | Animal rights activists—Biography.
| Sealing—Moral and ethical aspects—Canada. | Animal welfare.
Classification: LCC HV4716.L48 A3 2020 (print) | LCC HV4716.L48
(ebook) | DDC 179/.3092 [B]—dc23
LC record available at https://lccn.loc.gov/2020023292
LC ebook record available at https://lccn.loc.gov/2020023293

DEDICATION

I DEDICATE THIS book, first, to Canada's harp seals, living and dead. I wish I could have done more for them. Then there is my mother, who will feel, at the same time, on top of the world and frightened about what her friends will think when they find out that the only book dedicated to her has the word "terrorist" in the title. Such is life.

There is also the math professor who gave me a D in analytic geometry. I know you tried to explain why algebra had a right to participate in my analytic geometry class, but you were speaking a language that doesn't belong on my planet. No matter, thanks for introducing me to the seals.

Of course, I also must dedicate this book to Karma, who is looking down from heaven (yes, it really is a place) and saying, "woof, woof, wooooooooof."—roughly translated: "I thought you'd never finish that darn book. Now start writing about husky-malamutes."

Levi and Bella, my kitties, deserve dedications, since they have shown extreme dedication and forbearance throughout the many, many, many hours I took to write this book. That said, I do believe Bella should be able to eat by herself and not demand I sit with her at every meal. Levi is also in heaven now, but I assure him he will always have a dedicated place on my lap when I write, not on the computer keyboard.

The one animal above all others to whom I dedicate this book is Murray, the love of my life. You give me your love every day and have turned devotion into an art. I wish you were a vegan, but there's still time, and you are almost there, thanks to Marmite. Nonetheless, you make every word I write better and every day I live the best. *Je t'aime.*

AUTHOR'S NOTE

DEAR READER,

Thank you for buying this book. Proceeds will go to my chiropractor, who warned me not to sit so long in front of my computer.

Sarcasm is a dish better served cold. Humour can be served lukewarm, so you can save on hydro. I have attempted to use humour in this book, unless you don't find anything funny. In that case, I have never attempted to use humour in this book. There is nothing humorous about violence, however, whether it is perpetuated on a nonhuman animal or a human one. And that's no joke.

Life can be painful, for instance if you're stuck in a zoo, or on a factory farm, or when a friend drives his Honda Civic over your foot, although one of those examples is not like the others. Life can also be absurd, like when some people call fishermen bashing days-old seal pups over the head with a baseball bat *humane* and not *blunt-force trauma*. It's probably because the fishermen only suffer carpal tunnel syndrome, though some doctors don't even think there is such a thing, which means some fishermen are hypochondriacs. Nevertheless, there is not one thing, or even a half a thing, or a quarter or an eighth or a sixteenth of a thing that is humane about killing animals: be they seals, cows, pigs, chickens, horses, dogs, cats, mink, sheep, weasels, gophers, beavers, coyotes, kangaroos, mice, rats ... or any other animal, even human ones. Though some people wonder if we could make an exception for people like Hitler and maybe the Grinch.

Times are changing. I for one no longer eat canned peas, wear braces, or believe the Monkees was a real boy band. As a species, humans are adapting all the time, whether we like it or not. Thanks to science—we now know definitively that coffee is good for you, no, bad for you, no, good for you, and Earth rotates like a top. Climate change and pandemics have pushed us to the brink, forcing us to jump without a parachute. Some people don't believe in climate change, but that's because they're in the destroying-the-environment business, and have three homes, one of them in Fort McMurray, Alberta, and the other two on stilts.

Science and technology are changing our understanding of the world and our participation in it. We've discovered that humans are mammals of the primate species, the same as chimpanzees and bonobos, of whom we share 99 percent of our DNA, whether the chimps and bonobos want to share it or not. We also know wild animals are wild and do not make good pets. And if you have a wild animal like a baby chimpanzee, lion cub, or python, it's because you paid someone to steal them from their families, often by shooting their mothers. This is the original drive-by shooting. Anyone who does this should be shot with a water pistol full of simulated seal blood, though it wouldn't be funny (see second paragraph).

Humans are noted for our tool use. Our major accomplishments are climate change, global pandemics, and virtual warfare, though not on a PlayStation. Crows and ravens are also known for their tool use. Their major accomplishments are their ability to amaze us and their ability to prove humans are generally ignorant of the animal kingdom. It's because we're too busy binge-watching Netflix or a racist former US president, whom I won't mention by name.

I should mention that some of the names and places in the book have been changed to protect the guilty and innocent, unless I've gotten their permission, or it would be too awkward to rename them because you'll know who they are anyway. Some people I interviewed were remarkably brave (and likely still are). They provided firsthand information when they weren't supposed to, according to their bosses in the Canadian government.

I've compressed time and moved some conversations out of chronological order to leave out the boring bits, focus on my evolving level of knowledge, and because life is a mash-up. The seal hunt is like a kaleidoscope. Each time you turn around, it looks different. There's so much to it, in fact: the philosophy, the politics, the laws, the economics, the politicians, the leaked documents, the underhandedness, the comedians, Morrissey and Pamela Anderson, the documentary filmmaker who called her sealing ancestors *rogues* and *murderers* right in the title, the history, all the death, all the life, snow, ice, Anthony Bourdain, even a song I wrote about the seal hunt to the tune of the "The Wreck of the Edmund Fitzgerald," which I didn't include so Gordon Lightfoot wouldn't sue me.

Then there's the idiocy, which makes me sometimes speak like a Newfoundlander—*Oh me nerves, ya got me drove*—because of all the lies and the truths, and the lies about the truths, and the truths about the lies. Sometimes, I found myself rolling my eyes so much I thought they might roll out of my head. I couldn't write about it all. If I had, the book would have been a thousand pages and never would have found a publisher.

My last message to you dear reader is if you love animals don't eat them. Don't even taste them or wear them or visit them in zoos, aquariums, or on trophy hunts. If you're a teacher, please do not bring your class to a zoo to enlighten them about wild animals. There are no wild animals in zoos; there are only imprisoned animals, who are depressed nervous wrecks with Stockholm syndrome. Think of this: when it's -30°C and you're sitting at home with the heater turned up binge watching *Outlander* or *Star Wars*, zoo animals are in tiny stalls, on cement floors, getting arthritis, and an elephant hook. (It's like a hakapik for zookeepers.)

And my last, last message to you is: vote. Make sure the candidate you vote for has a strong history of animal and environmental protection and is a vegan. Or run as a candidate yourself. The list of animal protection parties is growing. In countries outside of Canada, there are animal protection parties that hold seats in government. I'd like to see my old boss, Liz White, the leader of the Animal Protection Party of Canada, hold one. She'd make a great prime minister and she isn't paying me to say that.

That's all for now, Dear Reader. Let's grab a coffee soon,

Karen

I don't belong to Al-Qaeda, Boko Haram, or ISIS.
But I do belong to a long line of junk collectors.

CONTENTS

1
BOMBS, ANYONE?

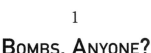

November 2009

"WE WORK FOR CSIS," the woman says, flashing her badge at me in the 24-hour Tim Hortons coffee shop. With a quick sweep of her head, she indicates the woman beside her. "We want to ask you some questions."

CSIS! What does CSIS want with me? Are they here to arrest me? For what? CSIS, pronounced *ceesis*, stands for the Canadian Security Intelligence Services. It investigates terrorists. Think CIA, but polite. How did I get to this point?

It begins on a breezy, leaf-tossing day in November 2009. My office window rattles with the one-two punch of wind as the ominous grey sky sucks in any remnants of sun. Hunched over my computer, I'm filling in the cells of an Excel spreadsheet that charts the courses of the 2006 and 2007 Canadian commercial seal hunts. I've already been tucking the data into their own nest-like rectangular cells for three hours when the phone rings.

A woman's voice stumbles into the receiver. "Are you the Karen Levenson who's involved with public safety and animals?"

"Public safety"? I don't do public safety, unless the public has four legs and a tail. Who is this woman? What does she want?

"In parks? Public safety and animals?" she says.

I lean back in my office swivel chair and sigh. It's not that I don't care about public safety. It's just the things done in the name of public safety make the world less safe for animals. However, I know what she's referring to. Four years ago, I successfully lobbied for a trapping ban in Guelph after a wildlife trap meant for raccoons strangled a Jack Russell terrier in a popular off-leash dog park.

"May I help you?"

"I was hoping to meet with you."

"What about?"

"Errr . . . uhmmm."

"Has an animal been caught in a trap?" I ask. Although Guelph is the only Canadian city where animals are safe from throat-crushing or leg-breaking traps, animals not living in Guelph still suffer excruciating deaths in them. Perhaps she knows about one.

"I'd rather not say any more on the phone. I'm at work." Her voice is hushed, as if she were trying to stuff all her words into the phone receiver without spilling any of them. "Can I meet you somewhere?"

Is the woman a whistleblower? I imagine an envelope full of confidential information—I can't fathom what about. It could be so many things: hunting . . . trapping . . . poaching . . . research . . . the seal hunt.

"Where do you work? Can I meet you nearby?"

"Toronto," she says. "No, I'd rather come to you."

"There's a Tim Hortons off Stone Road," I suggest. Tim Hortons is a Canadian coffee chain that's as ubiquitous as the beaver on the Canadian nickel. Every town has at least one, selling fresh coffee and donuts. Guelph has nine.

We agree to meet at 3 p.m. She describes herself as tall, thin, and blond; she'll be wearing a navy jacket. Not much to go on, but I'm sure I'll find her.

I pull into the parking lot a few minutes before three. The wind whips my feet and blows me inside the Tim Hortons. Construction workers, retirees, and mothers with strollers block the aisles, waiting in line. I squeeze through, scanning for a tall, thin, blond woman. I locate a couple of women with light blue jackets, but no one in navy is sitting alone. I consider calling out the woman's name but realize I don't know it.

Close to the entrance, two females—both blond, both thin—sit at a table in identical navy jackets. They look like girls from a Catholic high school. Every thirty seconds, their eyes flit to the entrance. As I step closer, one leans forward.

"Are you Karen?"

I nod.

"I'm Andrea. And this is my colleague, Andrea." Both women stand simultaneously.

My head jolts in surprise. Wow! What are the odds of two whistleblowers being named Andrea? The first woman offers me her hand—a grip so firm it hurts. The second offers hers, too. I squeeze it hard. They look professional, although I can't imagine professional *what*. As we sit, I notice it's not just their identical navy jackets and navy pants that make them look alike—although the first (whom I shall call Andrea One) wears her hair in a bun while the second (Andrea Two), who is taller and a little too skinny, wears hers in a ponytail. For a quick moment, I imagine the latter hunched over the toilet, with her fingers down her throat. I toss the image aside.

"You want coffee?" Andrea Two asks.

I reach for my faux-leather purse and am about to pull out my wallet when Andrea Two stands and gestures dismissively, indicating coffee is on her. She strides to the end of the ordering line with such pole-up-her-back posture and brisk efficiency that she could put them on her résumé.

Once Andrea One and I are alone, my eyes search for a file folder or an envelope bursting with telltale animal-cruelty evidence. But there's nothing on top of or beneath the table. As I ponder where the evidence could be, Andrea One extracts something from her pocket and flashes it in my face. It's a blue and silver badge in a protective plastic holder. Why is a whistleblower carrying a badge? I squint but the light filtering through the windows makes the words cresting the insignia hazy.

"We work for CSIS," Andrea One says. "We want to ask you some questions."

She slides her badge back into her pocket as Andrea Two returns with the coffees, setting mine in front of me.

"Do you know any animal rights terrorists?" Andrea One asks, raising both eyebrows.

"Do you?" Andrea Two echoes.

My eyes dart from one to the other. Are they kidding? At first, I'm flattered. Being questioned by CSIS is a rite of passage in the animal protection movement. I always thought it was glamorous (like in the movies where the big-hearted protagonist eventually prevails, earning the actress who plays her an Oscar that she waves in the air at the Academy Awards). Now I'm not so sure. Andrea One interrogates me.

"Do you know any terrorists?"

"Do you?" Andrea Two parrots.

"Do you know anyone with bombs?"

"Do you?"

"Do you know anyone who can make a bomb?"

"No. No. And no!" I say.

After fifteen minutes, I've had enough. I search for my purse, ready to huff with matronly defiance out the door, but I decide against it. Getting on CSIS's bad side doesn't seem prudent. So I refocus, just as Andrea One asks, "Do you know anyone you may not think of as a terrorist but who might break into a lab or use violence?"

Andrea Two leans forward, elbows on the table. "Do you know any terrorists who might act alone—not in your group, but maybe someone who hangs out with your group?"

The truth is I don't. The people I work with are among the kindest I know. They don't believe in violence (neither do I)—toward either a sealer, an animal researcher, or a slug on the side of the road. In fact, after it rains, I move snails and worms from the sidewalk and put them in the grass so they won't get stepped on.

There are probably lots of legitimate terrorists at work in Canada who know all about timers, fuses, and incendiary devices, or how to nurture anthrax. Maybe they live in Guelph; maybe they don't. I'm not one of them. But it becomes clear to me, after forty-five minutes under their burning glares, that the Andreas want a name, any name. If I don't provide one, I might be spending the next twenty-four hours on a hard plastic chair at Tim Hortons.

So I give them names. "The only terrorists I know are . . ." I pause, building suspense. Now both Andreas are leaning forward.

"The only terrorists I know . . ." I repeat, before downing the rest of my coffee to give the illusion I'm struggling with my conscience. Andrea Two inches to the edge of her seat. I hope she falls off.

"Are . . ." I say, letting the word wander off for effect.

"Are . . . ?" Andrea Two urges, inclining closer, the table bisecting her stomach.

"Stephen Harper and Loyola Hearn."

The two Andreas fall back in their seats, as if they'd been blasted by a grenade. They give each other dazed, deflated glances. Andrea One *sighssss*. Andrea Two *SIGHSSSS*. I shrug my shoulders and smile sweetly. Stephen Harper is prime minister of Canada and Loyola Hearn is his obedient Department of Fisheries and Oceans (DFO) minister. Both are responsible for the slaughter of over a million harp seals between the years 2006 and 2008.[1]

Andrea One wearily hands me her business card. "If you hear anything, call me." The card is white and has her name and phone number embossed in shiny black letters. There's no CSIS logo, or CSIS address, or even a CSIS employee title.

As I drive out of the parking lot, I wonder if the Andreas will follow me. I scan my rear-view mirror. Both are leaning against a silver two-door Acura. Andrea Two's ankles splay and her head hangs. A fin of hair breaks free of Andrea One's bun, masking one side of her face. She flips off her black pumps. Neither is looking in my direction, but they probably know where I live. I turn onto Stone Road and step on the gas. I ache to call Liz White, my boss at Animal Alliance of Canada, but decide against making the call from my home phone. It might be bugged. I reach for my cellphone, then think better of it. CSIS might be tapping my cellphone.

I head for the Zehrs Supermarket several blocks away, zooming past shaded single-family homes, narrow woodlots, and new housing developments. I skid to a stop in front of the supermarket, rush inside to find a pay phone—one of the last pay phones in Guelph—and insert a handful of quarters. The rotary dial is oddly comforting.

"If CSIS wants information, they can call our office," Liz shouts into the receiver once I've debriefed her. "They have no right to contact you."

I've never heard Liz so angry. She's been described by Toronto's *NOW Magazine* as being as warm as apple pie; she's also been characterized by an outwitted politician as the most dangerous woman in Canada. Normally though, she resists outbursts even when confronting the worst animal abusers—not like me, who can go from calm to rankling in under two seconds. I give Liz Andrea One's phone number, but it's almost five o'clock. I doubt she'll be reachable. Liz promises to call her in the morning.

It's noon the next day when Liz telephones me about her phone confrontation with Andrea One.

"Do you know any terrorists? Do you work with any terrorists?" Andrea One asked her.

"Do *NOT* call our staff again," Liz warned. "If you want to know anything, come to our office. We'll have our lawyer present and we'll tape the conversation."

"So you *do* have terrorists working in your office," Andrea One said.

"That's not what I said. I said: 'Any time you want information, you come to our office.' Don't you dare intimidate our staff! We've nothing to hide." Then, Liz tells me, she slammed down the receiver.

Several weeks after my meeting with the Andreas at Tim Hortons, a man I have been dating ends our relationship. He says he doesn't want to live with fur—referring to my dog, Karma, a woolly, white, shedding husky-malamute with a front-loader mouth and a penchant for putting his front paws on strangers' shoulders. To emphasize the fact, my date picks off a strand of white fur from the shoulder of his navy jacket and holds it up for me to see. Have the Andreas gotten to him? Was he a plant all along? Has he bugged my phone? I have visions of a tiny, wireless transmitter embedded in a dust mite under my desk and of CSIS operatives huddling over a receiver in the low-rise rental apartment building across the street.

After my date has left that evening, I throw myself onto the sofa and expel a wail, transforming it into loud, heaving sobs. I want someone to love me, and Karma, and my two cats, Levi and Bella, and my Fauna Foundation rescue chimp, and the horse I haven't rescued yet but one day will, and the seals. Could anyone love me with the seals? I cry from a place so deep I didn't know it exists.

Then a horrible thought occurs to me. What if CSIS really is listening? I'll never be able to show my face in espionage circles again. I have visions of CSIS agents rolling their eyes and saying, "If she's all we have to worry about, let's move on to those radical Mothers Against Drunk Driving." Even if CSIS is listening, I know I must carry on. After all, if you can't stand up for baby seals, whom can you stand up for?

2

Dogs of the Sea

YOU MAY BE mesmerized by baby harp seals for their white-puffball adorableness. I'd never want to take that away from you. But there's so much more to harp seals than being cuddlable capsules of cuteness.

In French, harp seals are called *loups marins*—"sea wolves." In English, they're known as *dogs of the sea*, *dog mermaids*, or *sea puppies*. But unlike dogs, harp seals can dive 183 m beneath the surface of the ocean, and they can swim better than any Olympic gold medalist on steroids. Every spring, pregnant harp seals migrate from the west coast of Greenland, going on an 8,046 km journey that brings them to the ice floes off the coasts of Newfoundland and Labrador, where each of them gives birth to one baby. The female harp seal's pregnancy will last about eleven months. Her pup will arrive sometime in February or March, slipping out of her womb at 80 cm long and weighing about 11 kg. A mother seal will protect and nurse only her baby. Should an infant lose his mother, no other mother will step in to nurse and nurture him. His fate is set. He will starve and die.

Seals weren't always sea dogs. Charles Darwin suggests in *On the Origin of Species* that twenty to twenty-five million years ago, seals were land mammals who occasionally dipped their toes into shallow water to reach a water-dwelling snack. No one can tell us definitively what those first land-loving seals looked like. Did they have legs, floppy ears, long and slender bodies, maybe even wagging tails? Did they have small heads, sharp teeth, and snouts—as they do today? Despite their fun dogs-of-the-sea nickname, seals are not even closely related to dogs. Chances are you'll be surprised whom they are related to: bears, weasels, raccoons, skunks, and red pandas. But there is a tenuous canine connection. Pinnipeds belong to a suborder called Canoidea, which literally means "dog-like."

Over time, seals decided to forget the snacks near the shore and head for the entire delicatessen—for not only was the sea bountiful but it also provided safety from land predators. Thus, they made the sea their home. To do so, however, seals had to reinvent themselves to survive in their new underwater habitat.

Next time you're near the ocean, stick your toe in. It's cold, right? Even a temperature of 21°C (70°F) can feel cold to the unaccustomed foot. Imagine having to swim in temperatures below freezing. Seals didn't imagine it. They did it. They had to adapt their bodies to the frigid temperatures of their new environment. Instead of maintaining their elongated shape, they became rounder, adding a layer of brown-yellow fat for extra warmth and buoyancy. No longer needing to maintain a sleek physique, a healthy adult harp seal today can weigh from 113 to 160 kg.

Now we come to the real reason people love baby harp seals aside from their cute snouty faces and teary dark eyes. Baby seals have an outburst of white, flossy, makes-you-want-to-touch fur. But wait! It's not really fur. It's hair! Technically, harp seals are hair seals and it's the newborns' hair that gives them their white, light-reflecting, photogenic pizzazz. Their coats are made up of dense bundles of fine, water-repellent hair serving as a thick, felty undercoat to prevent heat loss. Each of these bundles is attached to a single strand of coarse, deeply rooted hair—an amazing biological solution to the seal's evolutionary problem of living in glacial temperatures. But here's the rub: when you combine felty, flossy, and warm, you have a perfect opportunity for high-fashion winter wear. All you need is a sealer.

Before commercial sealing began in the late 1700s, a Newfoundland sealer recorded in his journal that harp seals "filled the sea from the landwash seaward to the limit of [his] vision and took ten days and nights to pass." For the next two centuries, commercial sealers slaughtered seventy million harp seals. One sealer, Captain Abram Kean, who began sealing at age twelve, had killed one million seals by his retirement at age seventy-nine. Sir Wilfred Grenfell, a British missionary and medic, wrote of his time in Labrador in the 1830s that the harp seal hunt was "the greatest, most protracted mass slaughter ever inflicted upon any wild mammal species" and that "no class of mammals on earth [had] ever, or [could] ever, withstand such onslaught."[1]

In Grenfell's day, one could see nearly 14,000 Newfoundland sealers jumping off hundreds of barques and brigantines onto expansive hippodromes of ice that stretched past the horizon. Sealers brought home 680,000 pelts in 1831 and 686,000 in 1844. By the 1950s, landings had diminished by half. The Canadian federal Fisheries and Oceans Department recorded that between 1952 and 1956, only 1,302,753 were landed in Canada, with just 15–25 percent being over the age of one, and the rest being under two weeks of age.[2]

3

JUST BREATHE

I AM BORN on December 1, 1957—a Sunday. The temperature outside is 29°F (-2°C), with wind blowing 22 miles (35 km) across Framingham, Massachusetts. Dwight D. Eisenhower is the US president and John Diefenbaker the Canadian prime minister. Elvis Presley shakes up the radio and Buddy Holly and the Crickets debut on *The Ed Sullivan Show*. Cars resemble ocean mammals with silvery tail fins. That year, Laika, the Soviet dog, becomes the first animal in space. Viet Cong guerrillas attack South Vietnamese villagers, and federal troops march into Little Rock, Arkansas, to enforce anti-segregation laws. I, of course, know nothing about this. At the time, my lips are firmly attached to a bottle of milk formula that has been expressed from a grieving cow, whose baby has been wrestled from her.

My mother's father has hoarded every issue of *Look* and *Life* magazines since the 1940s. His attic is filled with records, children's books, Sears catalogues, stuffed animals, and broken dolls—a lifetime of family memories he can't bear to throw out. His hardware store, like his attic, bursts with stuff—towers of discontinued wallpaper catalogues, paint rollers, measuring cups, wooden rulers, straw-bristle brooms in white protective sleeves, and chainless toilets—all smelling of machine oil, wood shavings, and cigars.

My father's father is a junk metal trader. He wheelbarrows through demolition sites for rusty screws, bent nails, abandoned gears, thin coils of copper wire, half of a pair of pliers, the face of a watch, and small rectangles of sheet metal with the aroma of diesel. He peddles them street to street, knocking on doors, his felt hat in his hand.

"Your husband home?" he asks, tilting his head in the direction of his full green cart. If he's lucky, a man in denim overalls, his fingernails clogged with grease, will come to the door and pull some doubtfully workable widget out of the cart. "Wait here while I get some change."

These are the dollars and cents of my grandfathers' lives, and also of my father's, mother's, and mine. After Grandpa Levenson dies, my father takes over the junk business and grows it like an obsession, eventually switching nuts, bolts, and strands of rusty wire for shiny, well-oiled hoists and cranes.

Before my father's father dies, however, he kills someone. It's a secret tossed into the wastebasket of family accomplishments and is not spoken of until long after my grandfather's death. The story, I learn, is that he runs a red light and KER-BAMs the oncoming car, then hightails it home before the police arrive, and only learns about it from the newspapers. Between 1957 and 1960, 701,434 baby seals are killed, most of them KER-BAMMED in front of their mothers.[1]

Once, when I'm four, a neighbour's black Labrador presses his nose against our living room window and leaves a moist print in the frost. I demand my mother put my snowsuit on me. By the time I'm zipped and booted and high-stepping across the snowy yard, the dog has vanished.

"DOG!" is one of my first words, then "I want dog!"

"I'm not having muddy paw prints on the floor or a puppy teething on my armchairs," my mother would tell my father in her don't-hold-your-breath voice. Instead, she buys me faux critters: Lambie, my wool sheep with glass eyes; Monkey, a fleshy, rubber-faced chimp; and Brownie, the fawn-coloured mutt with the black plastic nose—the one I love most.

* * *

Adult harp seals can hold their breath underwater for fifteen minutes and dive one hundred metres to find food. They create breathing holes in the ice, using their front flippers to claw an opening large enough to stick their noses through. During sleep, their bodies float vertically beneath the ocean's surface, their nostrils closing and opening automatically as they bob up for air. In 1961, 187,866 harp seals are killed during the commercial seal hunt. Strategically placed nets trap the seals underwater, preventing them from coming up for air; or pots, primarily used in the lobster fishery, are baited to lure the seals inside. Once they are trapped, without the ability to surface for air, their lungs will burst, but not before a thrashing, panicked attempt to extricate themselves.

* * *

My grandmother Evelyn won't get out of bed. I follow my father into her bedroom and watch from behind a bedpost as he spreads open the drapes, letting a green, gauzy, seawater light into the dark cave of her room.

"Come on, Mom, sit up," Dad says, levering her up and swishing her sideways, so her legs dangle off the cliff of her bed. Her hair is rolled like a carpet; wisps of white flail amid the bobby pins. I can see, through her flimsy nightgown, her beluga stomach and the orbs of her seaweed-coloured nipples.

"I'm sorry," she sobs. "I'm so sorry."

"Mom. Stop saying you're sorry." He turns to me and points to the bed. "Karen, stay with your grandmother." He helps me up onto the bed before disappearing into the hall. I cuddle myself into my grandmother and breathe in her aroma of linseed oil, gefilte fish, and the smelly cream she slathers on her face from the blue jar. She wraps me in her brown-spotted arms, as if I were a life preserver in a boatless ocean. Her floral hat with the lovely pink ribbon waits on top of her dresser; her paint-stained smock droops from the bedpost; and turpentine—a live-in guest—wanders forlornly through the house.

"Where's Grandpa?" I ask.

"You don't understand, do you?" she says.

I stare at her drooping eyelids and kick my heels against the bedframe.

"No. Of course you don't. So much death. So much sadness. One can barely breathe."

"I can breathe." I inhale and exhale, again and again.

Dad pokes his head into the bedroom. "I've called the hospital. They're on their way."

"You should shoot me instead."

"Mom. It's just electricity. The doctors know what they're doing."

"Where's Grandpa?" I ask again, but before she can answer, men in white coats, the kind the mean dentist wears, lift Grandma off her bed and onto a cot with wheels. They swaddle her in straps, so she can't fight, and wheel her to the ambulance.

"So much sadness," she cries as the men wheel her past me. "Don't forget to breathe."

"I won't," I promise. It's the last time I see her alive. By the end of the year, 277,350 harp seals have stopped breathing. Nearly all are under two weeks old.

* * *

Baby harp seals are not born white; they slide out of the womb yellow. Scientists suggest that the newborn's yellowness is the stain of amniotic fluid, which her mother quickly licks off.

Seal pups are categorized by age class. And each age class is given a name. Our just-born pup is a *yellowcoat*, but she doesn't stay yellow for long. In a day or so, she becomes the world's most adored and photographed baby, with a full head (and body) of luxurious white silk hair. She is now a *whitecoat*, and her image will appear on more magazine covers than those of 99 percent of the world's animals, including humans. Twelve to fourteen days later, our baby begins to moult. Each soft, flamboyant, white strand of hair makes way for a shorter, darker one. The whitecoat's hair doesn't fall out at once, but in tufts—a not-so-comely effect. It's this patchiness that gives the moulting whitecoat a new name: *raggedy jacket*.

"What! Not so comely?" our raggedy jacket might harrumpf, if she could speak her mind. Her incoming pewter-coloured coat, dappled with spots, is more than beautiful, and beneath it is a thick layer of blubber to keep her warm. Fully moulted after about four weeks, her coat is a darker, shadowy colour, with splotches of even darker, impressionist-like dabs. She is now a *beater*. (Put those images of sealers beating the skulls of baby seals aside.) The name *beater* refers to the sound the baby's tiny back and front flippers and tail make during her clownish first attempts to swim. Our pup is now roughly three months old—still a baby. She can't swim or feed herself yet, but she's trying. Eventually, she succeeds. By the time she moults again, at about fourteen months, she is a gregarious water acrobat—looping, gyrating, and somersaulting in all her grey-black sleekness. Her world is no longer the ice but the sea. She is now a *bedlamer*. You can recognize her by her much larger spots. Eventually, these spots will meet and form a harp-shaped pattern. It's what gives the harp seal her name.

The harp seal is not yet on any endangered list, but that doesn't mean she shouldn't be. Endangered lists can be political and slow to respond to quickly intensifying human activities and climate conditions. In the Grand Banks, for instance, politicians and industrial cod fisheries once held fast to the belief that wild cod would continue feeding the world forever. As they assured the inland fishermen there was no need to worry, the cod species crashed. As for pinnipeds, archeologists have identified more than fifty extinct species from excavated fossils. At one time, those seal populations were healthy and abundant . . . until they weren't. As for the harp seal, her home is the Northwest Atlantic, from Greenland to the Gulf of St. Lawrence. As the oceans warm and the sea ice melts, there's no telling what her future holds. Will she be the fifty-first, fifty-second, or fifty-third pinniped to go extinct?

* * *

I am five when my parents buy a US$12,500 ranch-style house on Hanna Road in Framingham, bringing attention to my father's success and our upward mobility. My mother enrolls me at Anita's Kiddie Lodge, a nursery school several blocks from our house. She walks with me all the way to school and when she leaves, I cry. Because the Soviet Union is testing atomic bombs, we practice climbing under our desks and putting our hands over our heads to keep them from exploding. Our fate is in the hands of Russians, our teacher tells us. It's 1962 and 319,989 harp seals' heads explode under the force of non-atomic clubs with hooks on one end, their fates in the hands of Canada's fishermen who seal. Similarly, on November 22, 1963, a high-speed projectile penetrates President John F. Kennedy's skull. I hear about it from schoolmates on the way home from school.

"President Kennedy's head got blown off," says a girl in my class in an awed voice.

"To smithereens," says another.

When I get home, I ask my mother if it's true. She points to the black-and-white TV screen, nods, and blows her nose. Newspapers later report that it was a single shot through the right temple. What I don't know is that between the beginning of 1963 and the end of 1964, 683,705 harp seals, mostly nursing pups, are killed by high-speed clubs with hooks penetrating their skulls. In May 1964, a documentary film about the killing of a pup airs on TV. *Les Grands Phoques de la Banquise (Seals of the Floes)*, narrated by Québécois singing sensation and self-styled environmentalist Serge Deyglun, publicizes the ugly hunt and creates a public relations nightmare for the sealing industry by focusing public attention on the annual slaughter.

In early March 1965, right before Canada's commercial seal hunt, the first US Marines land in Da Nang. A battalion of them—3,561 in total— is massacred in the thirty-four days of the campaign. In about the same amount of time, 234,253 harp seals are killed in Canada.[2]

4

I WILL ALWAYS PROTECT YOU

IN 1966, CHINA'S Cultural Revolution began. Historians estimate that millions of people were killed over ten years, although exact numbers are not known. Between March and June 1966, about 323,139 harp seals were killed, although exact numbers are not known.

When I turn ten, my father brings home a black poodle puppy from the pet store. I name him Inky. Within weeks, dry crusts of skin pimple his body. Inky has eczema.

"We should return him," my mother says, folding her arms tightly across her chest. "We should demand our money back."

"No!" I cry. Inky sleeps with his head on my pillow and his legs tangled in my arms. "No," I say, every time the conversation veers toward the awful subject.

Finally, my mother relents. One afternoon, while I am in school, she plucks Inky off my bed, plops him in the car, and drives to Framingham Animal Hospital. The veterinarian shaves Inky's fur and rubs ointment on his skin. Every night, my mother massages the goo down his naked legs, onto his belly, and into the skin of his furless back.

Once Inky's skin clears up, my father spreads the *Boston Globe* out on a corner of the kitchen floor and dribbles Inky's pee onto the headlines about race riots in Roxbury so Inky will know where to squat. On Sunday mornings, I like to stay in bed and read, although hunger often coaxes me downstairs into the kitchen, where I fill up a bowl with Froot Loops and sneak it back to my room. I am halfway down the spiral staircase on my way to the kitchen one Sunday morning when I hear Inky yelp. Down I speed and listen behind the kitchen doorway.

"I'm gonna kill that dog," my father shouts to himself. Metal chairs scud across the floor. A rolled-up newspaper thwacks against something solid. Inky yelps again, his paws scuttling on the linoleum. From the doorway, I see the cords of my father's neck, thick as columns, holding up his enflamed face. His mouth chews and spits out *goddammits* as if they were pistachio shells. I scan the room and find Inky shivering under the kitchen table, his eyes wide as beach balls.

"Stop!" I screech as I step into the kitchen and a warm puddle no bigger than a pancake squishes between my bare toes. Just beyond the puddle are my father's damp slippers.

"Out of my way," my father says, lunging. He thrusts out the rolled-up *Boston Globe* like a fencing sword, ready to skewer Inky, who lurches right, then left, then trips over the prongs of the table base.

"Stop it!" I scream as Inky scrambles from under the table and leaps into my arms. The edge of my pajama leg is moist against my heel.

"Put him down," my father orders, thumping the air with the newspaper, attempting to hit Inky. I turn my back to shield Inky and feel the heft of the newspaper whack my shoulder. "*Aouwww!*" I yell. Inky vibrates with fear.

"Give him to me. He has to learn."

I spin on the balls of my feet and catapult back upstairs. Morning sun beckons from the window of the bathroom at the far end of the hall. I hurtle in and shove the door shut, pressing the clinch to lock it. Leaning against the doorframe, I listen for my father's footsteps. But with Inky pressed against my chest, all I can hear is the thrum of our hearts beating together.

"I will always protect you," I say *sotto voce*, as I settle Inky on the bathroom counter. I open the cabinet under the sink and feel my way to the hidden spines. I tilt one on its edge and pull it out from behind the Ajax and Mr. Clean. Hoisting myself up onto the counter, I shift Inky onto my lap, lean *The Secret of Shadow Ranch* by Carolyn Keene against my knee, and contemplate life as a girl detective.

While I am saving Inky and reading Nancy Drew, increasing numbers of soldiers are trooping into Vietnam, the Atomic Energy Commission is launching nuclear tests in Nevada, and 334,356 baby seals are bludgeoned to death in front of their mothers. I'm as painfully unaware of these events as I am of the start of a Save the Seals campaign in 1968, led by New Brunswick Humane Society employee Brian Davies, in response to the mass baby seal killings (192,696 whitecoats are butchered on the ice floes of Newfoundland that year). The campaign prompts Davies to leave his job to found the International Fund for Animal Welfare (IFAW).

The next year, 288,812 baby seals are killed; their murders hardly register because the Manson family's murder of seven rich and famous Californians, referred to as the Tate-LaBianca murders, overwhelms every other killing. In 1970, I turn thirteen. I love horses and dogs but have not yet latched onto seals. While President Richard Nixon orders the invasion of Cambodia, and 257,495 seal pups die in the killing fields of the North Atlantic, I'm learning the words to "In the Summertime" by Mungo Jerry. The next year, 1971, the government of Canada institutes a quota designed to reduce the numbers of seals killed and curb fishermen's propensity to massacre all seals in sight. Now they must abide by an annual catch limit, called a Total Allowable Catch (TAC), and compete with other boats to catch as many seals as they can before the hunt shuts down. The TAC is a designated allocation that determines how many seals can be taken by fishermen and is determined by region and size of fishing vessel. The first TAC is set at 245,000 pups and fishermen-sealers catch 230,966 of them. What I don't know, because I'm still mourning the Beatles' breakup in 1970, is the harp seal population has plunged to slightly over 1.1 million.

By the time I'm a high school freshman, the National Women's Political Caucus is mobilizing to encourage females to enter politics. The news reports the blasphemy on TV. "The idea of a woman running for elected office," my father says, "is more ludicrous than a Jewish pope." *Who cares?* I think. I want to be like Twiggy, the super-skinny British model on the cover of a 1971 *Vogue* magazine. To prove it, I put on lots of makeup in the high school girls' bathroom.

While I tape-measure my waistline and stick fingers down my throat over the toilet after dinner, Canada's East Coast fishermen have an ocean of seafood, including whales and seals, to gorge themselves on. Canada bans East Coast whaling in 1972, and Ottawa introduces unemployment insurance to help whalers through the economic turmoil. Many whalers turn to fishing cod, causing scientists to warn of a future cod collapse.[1] Canadian former whalers and fishermen also turn to killing baby seals.

Canada's national broadcasting company, CBC, celebrates the seal hunt by interviewing Nova Scotia sealer Ulf Snarby, who reports that during "a good day on the ice," one sealer can kill and skin between 150 and 200 whitecoats and young seals.[2] South of the border, events are less fortuitous for sealers. The US congress also passes the Marine Mammal Protection Act in 1972, banning the importation of seal products. It's a crushing blow to Canadian sealers, who depend on the US market. Even so, Newfoundland sealers wallop 116,810 baby seals, as well as 13,073 seals over one year old, with their own crushing blows.

In 1973, US Military Fatal Casualty Statistics record that 58,220 American military personnel have died in the Vietnam War; many more are presumed dead because their bodies are not recovered. Between 1973 and 1974, 213,160 dead seal pups under the age of one are recorded, plus 58,307 older seals—though many more are presumed dead because their bodies are not recovered.

5

A GREENER SHADE OF PALE

BRANDEIS UNIVERSITY IS an unlikely place to encounter Canada's commercial seal hunt. Waltham, Massachusetts is more than 1,500 miles from St. John's, Newfoundland. The closest bodies of water are a pond on campus and the Moody Street Dam a few miles away. Instead of docks, harbours, and Paleozoic rocks, there are turnpikes and tacky strip malls. My dorm is a medieval castle with towers and turrets, and rooms shaped like pie pieces. In one of those pie pieces, I study psychology, history, and literature. A boy with a Florida twang and pocket watch asks me out; 1975 is the year I lose my virginity. Months earlier, 174,363 harp seals (mostly newborns) have died. They will never lose their virginity.

I hate math, but I'm great at analyzing things, so I choose analytic geometry for my sophomore year math credit. Determined to master this mathematical monster, I sign up for weekly tutoring sessions with my professor. My first glimpse of Canada's harp seal hunt occurs while I am waiting in line outside his office. Taped to the wall adjacent to his door is a large poster of a white baby seal staring up at me from a bed of turquoise ice, her black eyes offering depths I can fall into. I stop breathing as my finger outlines the white edges of her fur. In the poster, two men in orange survival suits stand behind the seal pup, clutching cans of green spray paint. Behind them, a zigzag of seal pups, with splotches of green dotting their white fur, stretches to the horizon.

"What's that about?" I ask as I step into my professor's office.

"That's Greenpeace, on the ice off Newfoundland, trying to sabotage the seal hunt."

"What seal hunt?"

He tells me about Canada's fishermen, who kill hundreds of thousands of newborn seals for their fur each year, and how the guys in the orange survival suits try to save those seals.

"Wow! I wish I could do that."

"Me too," he says. He takes me outside his office and we stand in front of the poster, even though students are waiting impatiently in line. "That's Paul Watson and Bob Hunter," he points out. "You could say they're heroes of mine."

"Can you go with them?"

"Well, it's dangerous. Sealers have threatened their lives.[1] For right now, I think I'll keep my job."

"Why do they paint the seal pups green?"

My professor chuckles. "No one wants a green fur coat."

The students in line fade away. Snow crunches under my feet. Cold blisters my nostrils. I hurry across the ice, my fingers wrapped around a can of spray paint. My thumb presses the nozzle; a funnel of green sprays across white fur.

"Don't use so much," someone says.

I half-turn on the bunchy snow as the bliss around me fades, and I turn to see two students huddled over a notebook, the one with glasses scrubbing a brick-sized eraser across a piece of graph paper; turquoise crumbs fall on the floor like snowflakes. I turn to my professor, wanting to share my poster-entering experience, but he is no longer beside me. The door to his office is closed. I take a last look at the seal pup, then head to my next class, clueless that this year's class of newborn seal pups will not yet have had their first moult before the sealers' clubs smash their growing brains. None of the 165,002 killed will move up to the next age class. More than 38,000 of them will die unnecessarily because the sealers exceed their quota of 127,000.

At the start of 1977, double murderer Gary Gilmore dies by firing squad. Unlike the US, Canada has abolished the death penalty for humans, but not for 155,143 seals. A freshman boy in my poetry class calls me "babe" and discourses on male superiority before class begins.

"You can be whatever you want," my boyfriend tells me as I sit on the edge of his bed, ranting that evening. "If I'm elected president, I'll make you vice president. How about that?"

"Business and politics are men's games."

"Screw it," he says. "Make them women's games."

The next day, I switch my major to women's studies, and because there is no real women's studies program, I create one. Empowered, I hold my head a little higher and my back a little straighter as I walk to the library. *I am woman. Hear me roar!*

Walking past an aisle of books toward my study carrel, I notice a folded *New York Times* abandoned on a table. I glance at it. "In Defense of Canadian Seal Hunting," the headline flashes.[2] I take a step back and grab the paper. Who left it? Will they be coming back? I look up and down the aisle. I scan the first few paragraphs, quickly fold the paper, and slide it between *The Second Sex* and *The Feminine Mystique* (Simone de Beauvoir and Betty Friedan won't mind).

At my carrel, I sit, stretch out the paper, and read: "Seals eat fish—up to a ton and a half per seal per year. There are twice as many seals as Newfoundlanders. [. . .] A balanced ecology means seals must be hunted." Is it true? And if so, is the killing of 165,002 harp seals, mostly babies, justifiable to prevent them from eating?

I know nothing about Canada. When I ask my American studies professor, he tells me that Canadians live in igloos and traverse the snow in shoes that look like tennis rackets. My mother tells me Canadians kiss by rubbing their noses together.

By the end of my junior year, in 1978, my Florida-born, pocket watch–carrying boyfriend begins dating a girl in his political history class. I'm heartbroken. As for the 161,723 dying harp seals, their heartbeats are silenced.

With only a year of university left, I weigh my post-graduation options. My connection to the vice presidency seems less certain, as I catch my former boyfriend kissing his new girlfriend in front of the student centre. My classmates are applying to law schools and medical schools. The thought makes my brain ready to jump ship. Stopping the seal hunt seems the most glamorous, exciting, worthwhile thing I can do. But how will I get there? What will it cost? And where is *there* exactly?

"Don't be ridiculous," my mother says, stirring a pot of canned chicken soup on the stove in our kitchen. My father grunts from downstairs in his reading chair, the Sunday *Boston Globe* spread open on his lap. "What about the real world, young lady?" he asks. "How are you going to put a roof over your head?"

The truth is I don't know. By the time I figure it out and realize I have no way of getting to the seal hunt, 160,541 harp seals are killed.

I graduate with high honours, *magna cum laude*, missing out on the prestigious *summa cum laude* distinction by one point. Damn analytic geometry! Had I not taken it, I'd be a genius. Now I'm only smart. But if I'd dropped the class, I might have never learned about the seal hunt.

After university, I head off to the prestigious Medill School of Journalism at Northwestern University in Illinois. My mother is apoplectic when I drop out. My father—in his *Globe*-reading chair—looks at me as if I had spiraled onto a highway and caused a fatal car crash. I spend 1980 depressed in bed, wondering how I could have hit bottom. I'm not alone: 169,526 harp seal carcasses also hit bottom, though their bottom is the floor of the Northwest Atlantic. I don't rack up any points the next year either. In 1981, I go back to Brandeis as an alumni communications assistant. When I tell my supervisor that the sixty-year-old campus photographer put his hands between my legs, she says, "What world do you come from? The moon?" I quit. At the same time, 202,169 harp seals are not so fortunate. The only way they can quit the seal hunt is to die.

Being a woman sucks, I tell myself. Brandeis is supposed to be a top-tier social justice university, but apparently not for women. And given the fact that animals aren't even discussed on campus, it sucks for them, too. As

I compare myself to the models in *Vogue*, I notice an ad for seal fur coats. The message is that to be beautiful, women have to wear beautiful things, like the fur of a dead whitecoat harp seal pup. I tear all the fur ads out of my copies of *Vogue*, and I read *Warriors of the Rainbow: A Chronicle of the Greenpeace Movement* by Robert Hunter.

I spend the next two years, 1982 and 1983, working at my father's company, assembling 20,000 engineering catalogues for a direct mail campaign for the latest cranes and hoists. Although 20,000 seems like a lot, it's not nearly as many as 224,628—the number of harp seals killed during those two years.

IFAW launches a boycott of Canadian seafood in Britain that threatens the livelihoods of Canadian fishermen-sealers. The little I know of it comes from TV, before my father turns the channel to *M*A*S*H*.

One night, as I'm getting into bed, my mother sticks her head into my room.

"Enough moping and talking about seals. Find a job."

The next day, I begin my job search, doubtful of what a women's studies degree can get me. I drive to Boston and lumber uncertainly up and down Washington Street, looking for job-applying inspiration. At the same time, 31,544 baby and young harp seal pups lumber across the ice, unable to out-lumber fishermen-sealers swinging their clubs.

6

FANATICS AND SANITARY NAPKINS

AT THE END of 1982, I accept a job with Procter & Gamble selling female sanitary napkins to grocery stores' paper-products buyers, who smirk as I prop up my demonstration kit on their desks and pour simulated menstrual fluid to exhibit our product's unrelenting absorbency.

Unrelenting, too, is IFAW's Canadian Seafood Boycott campaign. Britain's top supermarkets, Tesco and Marks & Spencer, boycott Canadian cod, flounder, halibut, haddock, and sole, as activists across Europe dress in seal costumes and play dead in front of Canadian embassies. Outside the European Parliament in Strasbourg, activists take the next step in their pay-attention-this-is-serious campaign: they drench their white seal costumes in simulated blood. Stephen Best, a young IFAW activist, delivers one million signed petitions to Prime Minister Margaret Thatcher, demanding the United Kingdom stop purchasing Canada's baby-seal products. Three to four million additional petitions are trucked and offloaded into the foyer of the European Parliament building. The boxes form a 6 ft. high, 6 ft. wide, 30 ft. long cordillera of anti-sealing outrage. During a press conference held in the foyer, journalists, thinking the cartons may hold nothing more than blank paper, claw them open and mine handfuls of petitions, each bearing twenty-five signatures. Reality fracks through the members of the fledgling European Parliament: their constituents want Canadian baby-seal products banned. On March 14, 1982, the European Parliament votes to outlaw the importation of baby-seal skins from Canada.[1] In screw-you defiance, Canada's fishermen-sealers kill 91,006 whitecoats, 30,565 beaters, and 20,920 harp seals over one year.

The vote in Parliament is only the first step in the long process of signing the ban into law. The neophyte Parliament must wade through bureaucracy and uncertainty. Does it have a right to ban Canada's baby-seal skins? After all, it has an international trade agreement with Canada. What would a ban of baby-seal skins do to the agreement? While chewing the sides of its collective cheeks, the European Parliament comes up with a solution. Pornography! The trade agreement has an anti-pornography clause that prevents each nation's smut from crossing the others' borders. Like nude pictures or erotic novels, Canada's baby-seal skins are a blight on Europe's public morality. The ban slaughters Canada's fishermen-sealers' hope for unfettered European markets.

Trying to lessen the post-ban trauma for sealers, the Canadian government begins to exploit the vague specifications of what constitutes a baby seal pup. Is a harp seal pup still a baby if she no longer has her full white coat? Or is she an adult and fair game for seal hunters? Canada's federal fisheries department settles the question. Once a seal begins to moult even a few strands of hair, she is no longer a baby, despite her not having learned to feed herself or swim. Fishermen-sealers continue slaughtering seal pups of questionable ages and peddle them to seal processors. In 1983, 57,889 harp seal skins and accompanying body parts land on the docks of Newfoundland fishing ports.

I continue to peddle female protection pads with their super-absorbency and nonslip side-flippers across Massachusetts. With my Fortune 500 sales job, I can afford to move out of my parents' house and into the second-floor apartment of a cockroach-infested, crumbling, redbrick walk-up on the ragged edges of Boston.

On March 10, 1984, as I enter the convenience shoppe near my apartment for a pack of gum, I glance at the rack of newspapers just inside the sliding doors. What I don't see is the article inside *The New York Times*, "Ottawa Rejects Ban on Seal Hunt."

One may think that Ottawa rejecting a seal hunt ban would be good news for Canada's sealers. It's not. The heft of negative attention the seal hunt has received over the years has deformed the fishermen-sealers' resolve to kill baby seals. In an about-turn, they beg the federal government to call a baby-seal hunt moratorium in order to silence their critics. They'll resume hunting when the ruckus has died down. Cabinet ministers rebuff the proposal, refusing to acquiesce to activist pressure. Federal Fisheries and Oceans Minister Pierre de Bané admonishes sealers for suggesting the moratorium.

"Let's not forget who we are dealing with," he states. "We're dealing with blackmailers, with liars, with fanatics, so obviously no rational argument can convince fanatics, people that I would call fascists."[2]

Only 31,544 harp seals are killed that year, 23,922 of them under the age of one year.

❋ ❋ ❋

That July, amid blinding sun, I step into my first job as a Boston advertising copywriter. Over time, I forget about the seals and focus on writing ads for Dunkin' Donuts, Swarovski crystal, and a new carwash in Brookline. Cooking for myself has presented its own set of problems. Grocery stores abound with so many unfamiliar products: I stand dumbfounded before shelves and cases of fresh rosemary, real maple syrup, and coffee you can brew. I am no less dumbfounded when, while driving to the supermarket for my weekly shop, I notice an animal-transport truck stopped beside me at a red light. Cows' eyes peek through the truck slats, their pupils pinpoints of terror.

The truck moves on, but the image doesn't. In front of the meat case, my brain feels muzzy. When I lift a package of cube steak out, I begin to think. *Who was this chopped-up being? Where had she lived? When was she slaughtered?* The eyes of terror stare back at me. I lay the cube steak back into position and head for the fruits and vegetables.

In February 1985, Kirk Smith, executive director of the Canadian Sealers Association, tells *The New York Times* in an article entitled "Days of Clubbing Seal Pups Appear to be Over in Canada": "There will be no commercial clubbing of whitecoats in the foreseeable future, perhaps never again. It is quite evident that this is something that cannot be resold."[3] Despite the capitulation, 1,419 raggedy jackets and 11,915 beaters are killed, most under three months of age.

7

BOOKSTORE DAVE

"KAREN, COME HOME; I need you," my mother says into the phone on an early evening in June in 1986.

"What's wrong?" I ask, sprawled out on my apartment sofa, having just returned from work, dead tired.

"Come home. Bring clothes."

As I drive down the highway to Framingham, I reassure myself that tragedy happens to other families, not ours. It was my father's secretary's scream that had alerted my uncle, not the thud of my father's body hitting the floor between his swivel chair and office desk. By the time the paramedics arrived, my father's face had turned blue. Before the ambulance could reach the hospital, his heart had flatlined.

The remaining months of 1986 are flea dirt on the towel of my memory. What I remember most is calling in sick, coughing and rasping at my creative director on the phone. Popping sleeping pills, pulling blankets over my head, descending into a memory-nullifying sleep, I call in sick once too often and am sacked from my first advertising job. I take up temporary work in a shoebox factory, until boredom makes me want to hold my head underwater. Next, I waitress, until drinks fly from my tray and nosedive onto a table of regulars.

My career as a waitress is shot, and at times it seems my future is shot along with it. In Canada, meanwhile, government records show 25,934 harp seals are shot or clubbed to death in the 1986 seal hunt.

The year 1986 finally slides into 1987. I secure an advertising job in Canada. To celebrate, I splurge on a new wardrobe and vow to swim up to the surface of life and stay there. I pay a therapist eighty dollars a visit to help me. He tells me to breathe. I'm skeptical. Is that it? Is that all I need to know? I think of my grandmother handcuffed to her ambulance cot, being wheeled to electricity hell. I cancel my next appointment and buy a new sweater.

My company-paid apartment is on the seventeenth floor of an expensive downtown-Toronto high-rise. I walk to work, past fashionable window displays of Burberry coats and Davids footwear, and past small-plate delicacies at the luxurious Park Avenue Hotel. I write headlines and copy for Export "A" cigarettes, Nabob Coffee, and a radio jingle for Close-Up toothpaste. If I'm lucky, I may even get a bank. I can breathe.

* * *

It's a banner year for cod fishers, I learn from the *Globe and Mail*, as I look for clever newspaper advertisements to cut out and paste in my inspiration notebook. The inshore cod fishery employs 28,830 registered fishermen.[1] There are 231 fish-processing plants with 27,567 plant workers. Cod landings jump to C$126 million. With so much cod-catching, one may think fishermen would give up catching seals as small potatoes. Not so: 42,574 harp seals are killed, 32,156 under three months old.

I meet Dave in the elevator of my apartment building. We get out on the same floor.

"Are you new?" he asks.

"Huh?"

"New. Did you just move in?"

"Yuh." I nod.

"You're American," he concludes. His hair is the colour of a rusty can and touches the ceiling of the elevator.

"How do you know that?"

"Your accent."

I furrow my brow. "Huh?"

"We don't say *huh*. We say *eh*." He smiles.

Later in the week, he invites me out. Then again. And again. Once to a movie. Once to a concert. Once to an expensive restaurant. On December 30, he invites me over for dinner. Books form a maze on the floor of his apartment and stack up on chairs. Stephen King is next to Kazuo Ishiguro and Alice Munro. There are books on history, poetry, science fiction crammed together.

"I thought *I* had a lot of books. Does your family own a bookstore?" I joke.

"A chain!"

My jaw drops. "A whole chain!"

He nods. "I do the marketing." He shrugs. "I have to read."

We're sitting on his floor, drinking wine and discussing the books, the TV on low hum in the background. Out of the corner of my eye, I catch sight of a seal, then a journalist standing on a dock and pointing to the unmanned fleet of boats bobbing in the water.

"Would you mind turning the volume up?" I ask, repositioning myself in front of the television. Dave does so, just in time for me to hear: "A just-announced ban of baby-seal products in Europe has put an end to Canada's commercial seal fishery, some fisheries experts say forever."

My head whips from the TV to Dave, then back to the TV. "What!?"

"The government just ended the seal hunt."

"Really!" My eyes become plates. Thrill, and then something else, geysers through me. A hot spray of anguish shoots out of a dormant volcano of longing. Why have I let the fight go on without me? What has been so important to keep me away? But relief jets out, too. It's over! The seals have been saved without me, but at least they've been saved.

"It's really, really ended?"

Dave confirms. "The fishermen aren't happy, but the activists are. They pressured Europe to stop buying seal fur. And they won."

How have I not known? On the TV screen, moody boats sulk in the gloomy sea. Dry-docked fishermen stare out at a bitter horizon. When the interviewer sticks a microphone in their faces, they are speechless, even teary.

I tell Dave I had wanted to be a seal hunt activist, but life got away from me.

I raise my wine glass. "Here's to the end of the seal hunt." Dave clinks his glass on mine.

What I do not realize is that the seal hunt has not ended. Despite forlorn sealers standing on splintered docks, watching their fishing vessels tug restlessly at their anchor chains, and despite my celebratory glass clink with Dave, only two parts of the seal hunt have ended: the large-vessel hunt for seals far out from shore, and the inshore killing of days-old seal pups. A total of 42,574 harp seals are slaughtered, though none of them are whitecoats.

Nor do I know how the baby-seal hunt ended. I don't know that Brian Davies, the founder of IFAW, gave the government an ultimatum, or that then-Federal Minister of Transport John Crosbie, a descendant of one of the first and wealthiest Newfoundland sealing families, announced the government's response during a press conference in St. John's, Newfoundland: "Anything that's going to affect the livelihood of 35,000 fishermen and all the processing workers has to be taken seriously. We've seen what they can do."[2]

* * *

The next time I'm downtown, I visit one of the bookstores Dave's family owns. After browsing the recently published books, I climb the stairs to the second floor to look at the out-of-print titles on decorating, knitting, and riding horses, which surround a book with a baby harp seal on the front cover: *Seal Song* by Brian Davies, the founder of IFAW. I gasp. *At least I can read about the campaign I missed*, I tell myself as I pull it off the half-price table and head downstairs to the cash register.

"Pinnipeds," I mouth as the subway train rumbles along the track. I flip through the pages of *Seal Song* and marvel at the clusters of diaphanous baby seals cushioned on a bassinet of ice.[3] My hand caresses a close-up of one with her chin resting on a pillow of snow, her nostrils mid-sniff, a ray of sun buttering her back. I read the text on the opposite page: "To stand up against pain, shame and waste in this time is often to stand alone, often to be mocked, sometimes to be threatened." Maybe it's the subway cold or the fact that I skipped lunch, but as I reread the quote a snake of chill wraps up and down my spine.

I turn the page and see a glacial cemetery of seal pup carcasses that have bled out and deadened the once-glittering snow. I turn the page again as the ceiling lights flicker, as the gears screech into the tunnel. Then, the lights flash off and a glow of white luminescence beams from nowhere. I look down at my lap and find that instead of the book, the whitecoat seal pup who was resting her chin on the snow pillow is now cradled in my arms, her chin balanced on my breast as if it were a pillow. The gears shriek again; the ceiling lights flicker on. The seal pup is gone from my lap, but the book is there and my hands are cradling it. Thick black words pulse from its page: "No one who seriously subscribes to the faith of 'Don't Hurt' can go very far along the road dictated by his conscience without encountering the risks." I close my eyes again, and when I open them the words have receded and returned to their twelve-point Bodoni typeface.

8

THE DICTATES OF CONSCIENCE

YOU CAN'T GO "very far along the road dictated by conscience without encountering the risks."

I repeat Brian Davies's words as I walk down the hall to my creative director's office. Framed award-winning magazine advertisements hang to attention on the walls. In glass cubicles, art directors pencil in graphics on tracing paper and writers slam keys against the rubber platens of their typewriter carriages. When I step inside my creative director's office, he grunts, without raising his head from the copy paper he is grease-penciling.

I shift my feet and cough. "I can't work on the Ontario pork campaign," I tell him.

"Why not?" he says, still not raising his head.

"I'm a vegetarian."

His head shoots up. "I'm Jewish and I got the damned client," he scowls.

"Can't you give it to someone else?"

"You don't get to pick and choose campaigns." (I know this isn't true. The men in the office often get to pick and choose the campaigns they want at their liquid lunches at Filmores Gentlemen's Club.)

I frown and chew my bottom lip, buying time until I can think of what to do next. My first thought is to eye-laser him into oblivion. Instead, I look out the window above his head. I can just see the roof of the slaughterhouse several blocks away. I stand firm.

"All right, this *one* time," he caves. He pushes a manila file folder at me. "Take it."

I open the folder and stare down at the client sheet outlining the project for a multi-billion-dollar pharmaceutical client and its new pain medication. I take the file, walk back to my desk, and begin to read the monograph inside. An hour later, I'm back in my creative director's office.

"This drug has been tested on cats."

"So?" my creative director growls.

"They strand cats on turned-over flowerpots in tubs of water."

"Your point?"

"They shoot electricity through them."

"What do you want this time, Levenson?"

"I can't work on this." I slide the file back across his desk.

His eyes bulge as he pushes it back toward me. "Just do it."

"Just do it" is what the federal fisheries minister tells commercial sealers who balk at hunting seals older than whitecoats, claiming there is no market for them. But they do just do it, coaxed on by the government, and in 1988 they kill 94,046 harp seals, the majority under one year old.

But I can't just do it. I brainstorm pain-relieving headlines with myself but always come up with the same line: *If you want to relieve pain, don't fucking put cats on flowerpots, in tubs of water, and shoot electricity through them to see how much pain they'll endure before jumping into the water.* I stick with the job, until I find myself hiding on the mezzanine balcony of the Royal York during lunch hour and bribing myself with a new book if I can force myself back to the agency. I love books, so it works every time. But clearly, I need to put my advertising career on hold. I take a course in film continuity instead.

* * *

Come spring, the bulk of Canadians are not thinking about cat- or baby seal-pain relief. Likely, they won't know that 65,304 young harp seal pups will have their thick coats skinned off in 1989, and also 112,751 in 1990 and 1991 combined.

My next job is at a boutique advertising agency, where I work on campaigns for Kodak, the Ontario Lottery and Gaming Corporation, and CTV, one of Canada's largest TV stations.

I walk across the crumbling asphalt of a nearby parking lot and enter a tin can–sized sound-recording studio, right on time to meet Bruce, the agency's account executive, in the lobby. The receptionist guides us to the sound-editing room where our client and a pair of unwelcoming chairs wait. For two hours, we redistribute our weight on the unrelenting plastic as we listen to the soundtrack of a TV spot I wrote for Kodak. At noon, we break for lunch and order sandwiches. While we wait, the sound technician turns on the radio. It's July 2, 1992: John Crosbie, now Canada's federal fisheries and oceans minister, is declaring a two-year moratorium on the 400-year-old Grand Banks cod fishery, the world's largest and most lucrative fishery.

"I didn't take the fish from the goddamned water, so don't go abusing me," Crosbie tells the fishermen and plant workers enraged over the cod moratorium.[1] He offers a fishing licence buyback program to coax cod fishers out of the industry, but the program leaves the thousands who refuse to sell their licences out of work. Nearly 40,000 fishermen and plant workers, more than a third without high school educations or job prospects, lose their jobs.[2]

While Newfoundland fishermen blame Crosbie, the federal fisheries minister blames harp seals.

"We will either control the seals or the Northern cod fishery will be gone," he says.

IFAW and Greenpeace reply: "Only one percent of a harp seal's diet is made up of cod or capelin, the fish cod love to eat."

To drive the message home, IFAW takes out a two-page newspaper advertisement headlined "Who had cod for dinner?" A dozen cartoon harp seals each reply: "Not me."

The cartoon seals are right. Harp seals didn't cause the cod crisis. Specifically, they ate the cod the fishermen didn't want.[3] Still, Crosbie allows cod fishermen to club 68,668 harp seals with their homemade spike-ended hakapiks.[4]

* * *

In the sound studio, when the radio journalist calls the moratorium "one of the greatest environmental disasters of all time," I feel the room deflate, as if air were being squeezed out through a fissure in the wall. I feel sorry for the cod. I look around to see if anyone else does, too.

Bruce and the client are comparing notes on deck renovations, and the studio technician is on the phone, arguing about money.

"Do you believe this?" I ask Bruce and the client, loud enough to interrupt their conversation over a Home Hardware flier. Bruce cranks his head my way.

"What?"

"The cod fishery collapsed. It's on the radio."

"Wow," Bruce says, his lack of interest as thick as cement.

"That's too bad," the client says. He turns to Bruce. "What do you think of deck stain?"

"I prefer varnish. It doesn't hide the grain."

I roll my eyes. A second later, a strange voice speaks to me out of nowhere. *How many times have you ordered cod before becoming a vegetarian?*

My eyes widen. Who said that? As I try to figure it out, the voice says, *Did you ever once think that you were helping deplete the Grand Banks? Did you ever consider the life of a fish beyond her place on a dinner plate? Did you even think she might not want to be eaten?*

The voice sounds like mine, but it's not mine. A wave of briny guilt washes over me. Before becoming a vegetarian, I ate a lot of cod without thought. Cod was low in calories and cheap. I never saw a fish, but only a slab of white flaky ocean-smelling food on my plate.

When the sandwiches arrive, I watch Bruce and the client reach for their overstuffed fish subs. How can I fault them when I, too, helped deplete the cod stocks? Still, I can't stop feeling repulsed.

Don't get on your high horse. You're in a studio, recording sound—for a commercial for a film made from toxic emulsions and PCBs—onto a film made from toxic chemicals and emulsions, the Doppelgänger says.

Yes, that's what she is—a doppelgänger! And worse, she's right. Not only am I marketing a film company, but I'm also using their films to do it. I struggle with my hypocrisy. How do I reconcile my self now with my self then? It dawns on me that no matter who I was before, what I did before, or no matter where I belonged before, I don't belong here now.

9

BLINK

IN 1993, THE European Union becomes a single European market and voting bloc, allowing free movement of citizens and goods between member countries. Protectionist trade barriers severely disadvantage Canada's commercial seal products trade.[1] Nevertheless, 25,175 harp seals, mostly raggedy jackets and beaters, are killed.[2]

"What the fuck!" the newly elected federal Fisheries and Oceans Minister Brian Tobin (November 4, 1993–January 8, 1996) might say as he stares at the piddly number of seals killed and the even piddlier number of seal parts sold during the 1993 hunt. The harp seal population is growing and the cod population is still declining, despite the 1992 moratorium. But Tobin knows just how to fix it. He's determined to revive sealing to its rightful glory. He's not simply rah-rah about killing seals and saving cod. Somewhere in the back of his mind, he's formulating a plan to win Newfoundland's 1996 election for premier. To get there, he needs the fishing and sealing industries behind him. Expanding the seal hunt is the magic carpet to bring them to him.

Yet opposition to sealing continues, at home and abroad. IFAW accuses sealers of skinning baby seals alive and the federal government for failing to bring offenders to justice. To combat the public relations nightmare, Tobin establishes the Marine Mammal Regulations (MMR), a set of rules governing marine mammal hunting in Canada. The MMR tries to balance two conflicting sets of interests: Canada's national economic interests and international cruelty concerns. For the cruelty-concerned, the MMR introduces the blinking reflex test. Each sealer must touch the eyeballs of every seal they kill before they remove the pelt. Should a seal blink, further cranium-crushing is necessary.[3]

* * *

In a blink, my relationship with Dave bleeds into acquaintanceship. When a friend wants to introduce me to Ben Ouellette, I'm receptive. Ben has a quiet stability I find at first plodding, and then comforting. We hike up Rattlesnake Point, part of the Niagara Escarpment; we carry picnic baskets to High Park; and we return again and again to our favourite Chinatown restaurant. Nine months later, Ben asks me to marry him. But before that, he tells me, "I once hit my ex-wife and pinned her against the wall. It was . . . like . . . because she never loved me. I'd never do that to you." A shortage of love would put a strain on any marriage. Without blinking, I say *yes*. Ben and I plan a wedding for the following year and rent the bottom floor of a 1940s Toronto brownstone.

My mother blinks several times. She flies in from Florida, with her new husband Eddie, to meet Ben.

"You don't have to marry him," she says in the ladies room of Toronto's Sheraton Hotel restaurant.

"Why are you saying this?" I ask, washing soapy water off my hands in the sink.

"He's a *truck driver*, for God's sake," she says, reapplying her lipstick in the mirror.

"Mom! I'm going to marry him. I never liked Eddie, but did I ever tell you not to marry him?"

She sighs, blots her lips, and steps back to examine the effect. She is stunning: natural red hair, high cheekbones, eyebrows perfectly arched and penciled. Satisfied with her reflection, she turns to me and sighs again. "I just don't want you to regret it." Glancing once more at the mirror, she smooths the front of her designer sweater and heads back to the table, with me trailing behind.

We barely have a chance to sit before Eddie blurts out, "Shirley, Ben was telling me they're moving to Gulf."

My mother purses her lips and glances from Eddie to me to Ben. "Where the hell is Gulf?"

"Guelph, Mom."

"Gwalf?"

"G-U-E-L-P-H," I spell.

"Gu-elf. When do you plan on moving?"

I shrug. "After we get married. It's near where Ben works."

"I just don't know what to say," my mother shakes her head. "I just don't."

When the waiter comes, she orders a prime rib. I shoot Ben a thin smile, then stick my pinky nail into my thumb and relish the pain.

In August 1994, in a lawn ceremony on the grounds of a charming Toronto coach house, Ben and I pledge our forever-lasting love. When he places the ring on my finger, his touch is so gentle, I know these are the hands I will hold the rest of my life.

On our honeymoon, we hike and camp in Algonquin Park and decide to postpone indefinitely our move to Guelph. All our friends are in Toronto, as is the advertising agency where I work. "It's just not the right time," I tell Ben.

Between being married and working, I have no time for or interest in watching TV. I don't hear about the enraged fishermen screaming "poverty" on Newfoundland fishing docks or fisheries minister Brian Tobin promising the cod will recover and fishermen will soon return to fishing as they always have done. I don't know that 52,913 harp seals have been slaughtered. I'm still under the impression the seal hunt has ended.

10

VACUUMS AND VIAGRA

IN SEPTEMBER 1994, the transport company Ben works for gives him a steady route, hauling stereos and TVs from Aberfoyle, Ontario, to Harlem, New York City. He's gone all week, so when he's home, I try not to talk about my dissatisfaction at work. But dissatisfied I am. In the last few months, my creative director has given me a slew of non-negotiable pharmaceutical assignments—retribution, perhaps, for my earlier pickiness. Each study I read, with its Josef Mengele–style animal trial, makes me want to shoot electricity through my head.

As I pick at a raisin biscuit over breakfast at Tim Hortons one morning, I burst into a spree of jalapeño invectives, using words like "hate," "scourge," "ignoble," "deviant," and "alcoholic."

"Why don't you freelance?" Ben says, taking the last bite of his breakfast sandwich.

Freelance? I've worked for advertising agencies ever since I moved to Canada. Despite the stress, the politics, the cigarette-advertising assignments, and the pharmaceuticals, I've never considered freelancing. It's the feast-or-famine part of advertising. You don't work for one agency, you work for many: none of them provides benefits, a steady income, or loyalty. Each assignment could be your last. When you're out of assignments, you're out of money. Still, freelancing comes with a bonus. You can refuse morally objectionable assignments and you can work from home.

While I'm scurrying around Toronto collecting freelance clients, Brian Tobin is scurrying around his department encouraging DFO scientists to come up with a way to show harp seals are a menace to cod, fishing families, and Canada at large. If he can prove harp seals are vacuuming up all the fish in the North Atlantic, and that an extended seal hunt will pull the cord on the harp seal's fish consumption, then he will likely be voted in as Newfoundland's next premier.

My first freelance project is writing a user manual for a vacuum manufacturer. I leave the TV on for company and settle into writing on the kitchen table, since our apartment is too small for me to have an office. As I try to find a simple way to describe the vacuum's particle-sucking mechanism, my ears attune to the news playing quietly in the background.

"Seals," the male commentator says. My fingers stop mid-air above my keyboard. I turn toward the TV to see CBC News anchor Peter Mansbridge standing in front of an enlarged photograph of a cod.[1] "Fisheries minister Brian Tobin says the explosive growth of the seal population has helped devastate the East Coast cod stocks. And he's unveiled a study to prove it." Mansbridge's face fades out as a gloomy Magdalen Islands' fishing harbour fades in. Empty fishing boats strain against their moorings. Waves knuckle the barren docks.

Cut to the House of Commons. Brian Tobin jabs his index finger in the air: "Whatever the role the seals have played in the collapse of the groundfish stocks, seals are playing a far more significant role in preventing [. . .] a recovery of the cod stocks."

I shift my eyes away from the TV screen and refocus on my computer. My fingers key in *Suctions up dust.* Then I hit BACKSPACE and retype: *Suctions debris and dust particles from carpets and rugs.*

An off-camera voice says: "The seals eat nearly seven million tons of fish . . ."

Into our unique Cyclone System's airtight container.

"Almost five million seals . . ."

A five-year-guaranteed warranty.

"More than twice as many seals as in the early eighties . . ."

Three times as many cyclone rotations as other vacuums.

"The only solution . . . an expanded seal hunt."

The only solution for home and office.

The study Mansbridge references, conducted by DFO scientists, implicates harp seals in the consumption of 6.9 million metric tons of fish, including 142,000 metric tons of Atlantic cod, and thus gives Tobin *carte blanche* to up the 1996 TAC to 250,000 harp seals.[2,3] And there's an added incentive. Although there's little to no market for seal pelts or meat, there are penises. Erect penises. Which male doesn't want an erect penis? There's a huge market to help men achieve them. Dry and crumbled adult harp seal penises steeped in tea may not be a favoured aphrodisiac for Western men, but they are for Asian ones. Although it's illegal for Canadians to kill an animal solely for their organs, that's exactly what sealers do.

"The only thing we have in our favour now is the lucrative market for seal penis and testes. We are aware that to kill an animal for an organ is against the law, but that doesn't seem to stop people. There's still hundreds and even thousands of seals killed along the Northeast Coast [Newfoundland] every winter just for penis and testes. When this reaches the right people, nobody will be allowed to hunt seals," says Mervin Rice, chair of the Green Bay South Fishermen's Committee, in a March 20, 1995 call-in to CBC.

But the "right people" already know. And they are content to turn a blind eye. Going back as early as 1993, briefing notes and working documents confirm that John Crosbie and subsequent federal fisheries ministers, including Ross Reid and Brian Tobin, were well briefed.[4–7] Not all sealers are on board. Newfoundlander Garry Troake, whose family has been sealing for over a century, tells *New Maritimes* magazine, "I don't think Brian Tobin is concerned about sealing being a viable industry. [. . .] Tobin just wants seals out of the system because of pressure from fishing [. . .] communities here."[8]

In an interview for "The Killing Floes," a January 20, 1996 article in the *Toronto Star*, Troake tells reporter Lynda Hurst that he knows it's the older male harp seals that are now sought after, but it's not for their pelts: "I'd be angry if I thought the only reason I'm out shooting these animals is for their penises. It's disgusting and degrading. But I know there's a black market for them, and the government turns a blind eye."

A reason for the blind eye is that seal penises are selling. The meat, pelts, and oil components are the deadbeat dads of the sealing industry, refusing to pay the sealers what they've been accustomed to. To encourage sealers to take the meat, the DFO is willing to give sealers twenty cents a pound to land it. The DFA (Newfoundland's Department of Fisheries and Aquaculture) also steps in with its own subsidies. It's a way to prove that all parts of the seal are used.[9,10]

Where does the meat eventually end up? Likely, a small portion of it ends up as petfood. However, much of it is dumped—an additional cost to taxpayers. If the success of the penis trade is based on the sealers' ability to kill adult harp seals, one may wonder why more adult seals have not been taken. When I review the 1996 landing reports documenting the age classes and numbers of seals killed, which the DFO reveals is 170,714 pups and 55,443 adults, I'm surprised to find that more baby seals (raggedy jackets and beaters) are landed than older seals (bedlamers and adults). There's a good reason. Baby seals are by necessity so weighted down by the reserve of their mother's fatty milk they can barely move. Unlike older seals, who spend most of their time in the water and can dive to unreachable depths, baby seals are like fat, immovable blimps with a target painted on their backs.

In the spring of 1997, the TAC is upped again, this time to 275,000 seal pups. By the end of the hunt, 220,467 pups and 43,782 adults have been killed. In a June 25, 1997 *Ottawa Citizen* article entitled "Trade in Seal Penises," scientists say they're "concerned that seal-kill figures [are] far off mark. Trade in penises could mean half of [the] catch [is] unreported."

With all the illegal slaughter and butchery of harp seals, one may assume the cod are performing headstands and throwing liberation parties. Sadly, they're not. The Grand Banks cod still have not returned and fishing community outrage spirals like a top. Three Canadian university professors publish a scathing critique of the DFO's harp seal management, accusing the department of relying on agenda-pushing bureaucrats and politically tainted science.[11] They also castigate previous federal fisheries ministers for failing to heed scientists' advice to cut cod landings by 50 percent when the first inklings of a cod crisis appeared in 1988. The two federal fisheries and oceans ministers responsible—Tom Siddon (1985–1990) and John Crosbie (1991–1993)—justify their myopic decisions to avoid drastic cuts. Crosbie explains during a 1989 press conference in St. John's that "We couldn't suddenly cut the TAC by more than half. [. . .] [It] would have wiped out the offshore fishery. [. . .] We are dealing with thousands of human beings who live and breathe and eat and need jobs."[12]

In May, John Efford, Newfoundland's minister of fisheries and aquaculture, realizes that to gain support for his sealing agenda, he must tell his constituents that the seal hunt is an economic success. Therefore, he catapults the value of the 1998 Newfoundland portion of the seal hunt to a stratospheric C$25 million. He does so not because the seal hunt is an economic powerhouse for Newfoundland, but because he needs his constituents to believe that it is.

"The seal hunt's value has been grossly exaggerated," IFAW says, claiming that once the government subsidies are subtracted, the hunt is worth little over C$2 million. Clive Southey, economics professor at the University of Guelph, backs IFAW's claim. In his report, "The Newfoundland Commercial Seal Hunt and Economic Analysis of Costs and Benefits," he shows exactly how the catapulting sleight-of-hand works. The federal and provincial fisheries departments, the DFO and the DFA, fail to subtract the meat subsidies that each gave to sealers to encourage them to return to sealing after the whitecoat ban, and the DFO forgets to subtract the costs of dumping the landed meat because no one wished to buy it. Even more confounding, the DFO double-counts areas of profit, either deliberately or incompetently. The sleight of hand is massive. Unfortunately, Canadians are unaware that anything untoward is happening.

But it wouldn't be Canada if seal hatred and political bellicosity didn't prevail over economic facts. Efford rants before the province's House of

Assembly on May 4, 1998: "I would like to see the six million seals, or whatever number is out there, killed and sold, or destroyed or burned. I do not care what happens to them. The more [sealers] kill, the better I will love it." Commercial sealers kill 282,070 harp seals, exceeding the 275,000 TAC. Efford loves it.

* * *

Viagra, a little blue pill designed to improve the blood flow to men's penises and alleviate erectile dysfunction, pops to life in 1998 thanks to Pfizer UK. To prove its safety, Pfizer carries out "essential" experiments involving removing the penis foreskins of anaesthetized beagles, inserting electrodes down their penis shafts, and shocking their genitals. At the end of the experiments, the dogs are killed.[13] With Viagra, there's no need for Asian men to drink dried, crushed seal penis tea; they can just pop a pill. For Canada's fishermen-sealers, however, the news is crushing. Before Viagra, one seal penis could sell for C$650. After it, the market has shriveled.

Canada's Fisheries Resource Conservation Council warns the new federal fisheries minister, David Anderson (June 1997–August 1999), that the cod stocks are continuing to decline and "the outlook [. . .] is even more bleak than at the beginning of the moratorium."[14]

Who's to blame? The government of Canada? The province of Newfoundland? Viagra? Fishermen? Beagles? Ex-DFO harp seal population research expert George Winters has the answer: harp seals. The senior fisheries consultant testifies before the Standing Committee of Fisheries and Oceans. In his expert, scientific response, he says: "Science can't prove the seals are there. Well, everybody else knows the seals are there. Out in Bonavista Bay, where I went [. . .] last Sunday [. . .] everybody, all these people, could tell you, they saw seals eating cod, driving cod up on the rocks."[15]

* * *

Although many Canadians look to the government to protect cod, others suggest they should take matters into their own hands. In "Sealing Our Fate" in the March 1999 edition of *Compass*, Jamie Baker, a journalist from Newfoundland, editorializes:

> Let us arm ourselves to the teeth, jump into anything that floats and head off to the ice floes. [. . .] After looking at the pictures of all those dead fish on the ocean floor at Deer Island Tickle, I've decided it's time to swing into action. It's time to stop getting mad and start getting even. It's time for everybody to head to the basement, shed, bedroom or wherever you keep your weapons, and bring forth water pistols, sling-shots, and pea shooters—it's time to prepare for war. [. . .] Hah! Double the price of an activist pelt as compared to the seal!

Along with such goodwill and science, 244,552 harp seals, mostly raggedy jackets and beaters, are killed. The cod fishery remains closed.

11

Arms, Breasts, and the Man

"HOW ABOUT THIS?" Nora asks me later that year. She's the owner of PROMO MOB, the advertising and marketing contractor I rely on for freelance work. She sifts through her outstanding-jobs folders and slides a photograph of headache tablets across her desk.

"The client needs a new print ad."

I stare at the bottle with the yellow twist top, willing myself to accept the job. "I don't do pharmaceuticals," my mouth says as I push the photo back across her desk. *Are you crazy? You need the money!* my Doppelgänger protests.

Puzzled, Nora scopes my résumé. "You've worked on Bayer and McNeil Consumer and Astra when you were at the agencies. All pharmaceutical companies!"

"I know."

"Well then," she says, shuffling through her folders. "We need a writer for Raytheon. They're doing a lot of recruitment advertising right now and they need someone with your talents." I look at the client sheet. Raytheon, a defense contractor, produces attack aircraft, ballistic missiles, tanks, and unmanned aerial vehicles.

"I can't do that."

"You don't want it?" An edge of annoyance creeps into her voice.

"Sorry, I just don't want to support a weapons manufacturer."

"Well then, I don't know what to give you."

This month's negative bank balance flashes through my mind. We spent too much. A romantic getaway weekend at Blue Mountain Resort in Collingwood: luxury accommodations, gourmet food, a renowned Scandinavian spa in a serene forest; my new winter coat; Ben's survival suit in case his truck got stuck in an ice storm. Then there were books. I must buy books. They are my life blood. I can imagine Ben's distress if I come home without work.

It's money, for God's sake! Doppelgänger telepaths.

Blood money, I telepath back.

"Don't you have a bank or computer company?" I ask.

Nora sighs. "Well, you're not going to like it, but the only other thing I have is this." She reaches into her desk drawer, pulls out a box, and lifts out a contraption.

What the hell is that? I wonder. Then it dawns on me. A breast pump! "I'll take it."

As I head down the hall with the client brief and breast pump clutched to my breast, Nora calls after me. "Either start being less choosy or find another profession."

Back home, I stand in front of our master-washroom mirror, trying to adhere the breast pump to my left breast and work the pumping mechanism so I don't crush my nipple. The brief indicates I should write about comfort without forsaking the product's superior durability and ease of use. But the hard-plastic shield feels like car cables clamping my mammary glands.

"What's that?" Ben stands in the doorway, watching me wrestle with the pump.

"It's my compromise product."

"Your what?"

"It is either this or writing recruitment ads for a weapons manufacturer."

"That's all Nora had?"

"Yeah. Or pharmaceuticals."

I glance at Ben's reflection in the mirror. His face is white.

"What's the matter?" I ask.

Silence.

"What *is* it?"

"I'm starting to have trouble lifting my left arm," he says.

Ben uses his right hand and arm to change gears in the eighteen-wheeler he drives for Schneider National. It takes colossal strength to switch from one rebellious gear to another. Six months prior, Ben had begun having difficulty raising and lowering his gear-shifting arm. We both assumed it was a repetitive strain, something that could be easily fixed by a few sessions of physiotherapy. But after a month of visits, we both realized physio wasn't working. And now his left arm.

Our family doctor has no idea what is going on. He calls a neurologist who agrees to see us.

Ben and I enter Dr. Masskoff's office, a catastrophe of clutter, with scattered papers and half-filled cardboard boxes mazing through the room.

"Don't mind the mess." He waves dismissively at the boxes and then over to some chairs.

I step over a box of medical journals and almost trip. "Are you moving to another office?" I ask, as I remove a pile of folders from a chair and place them on the doctor's fraught desk.

"I've been offered a position with one of the teaching hospitals in Britain. St. George's in London," he says self-importantly. "Do you know it?"

I shake my head absently before his words set in. "Wait! You're leaving?"

"It's unfortunate that you've come now. You're one of my last appointments. I will refer you on, of course."

I go from surprise to glowering. "Did you *at least* read Ben's file?"

He pulls it from a pile on his desk and flips it open, glancing cursorily, and then flips it shut. He looks at Ben from above his black-framed glasses.

"I'd say you've got a motor neuron disease. I'd rule out ALS."

"ALS? You'd rule it out? You're sure?" Just the name is terrifying.

Dr. Masskoff ducks his chin once.

"You haven't even checked him!" I bristle.

Dr. Masskoff flips open Ben's file again and scans it. "You went to your family physician three months ago. At that time, he wrote you had muscle weakness in both your arms." He raises his eyebrows at Ben, turning his statement into a question.

Ben nods.

"If you had ALS, you'd be dead by now. How's your breathing?"

"Good," Ben says.

"Swallowing?"

"Fine."

"Tingling in your arms or legs?"

"Mmm. A little."

"Balance?"

Ben pauses to consider Dr. Masskoff's question, then says, "No problem."

It's Ben's pause that worries me more than the doctor's matter-of-factly tossing out ALS as a possible diagnosis.

"You'll have to hand over your driver's licence."

"I'm a truck driver!" Ben gasps.

"Well, you can't do that anymore," says Dr. Masskoff, oddly sarcastic.

Ben hands over both his driving licence and his Class D truck driver's licence, and we watch, our mouths open, as Dr. Masskoff reaches into his desk for a pair of scissors and cuts Ben's livelihood and freedom in half. He tosses the pieces into his wastebasket.

"I'll have my secretary make an appointment for you at London Health Sciences Centre. There's a top neurologist there who will take on your case."

I step over the box of medical journals, nearly tripping again, as Ben and I head for the door. In the lobby, my head explodes.

12

Roots

WE UPROOT OUR lives in Toronto and finally move to Guelph, a sleepy city with a population of 97,000, mostly pig and chicken farmers, university professors, veterinarians, and insurance agents. It's an hour west of Toronto and close to Schneider National's headquarters; a work friend picks Ben up and brings him home. Instead of driving an eighteen-wheeler, Ben dispatches them from a cubicle at head office.

We purchase a condo with an elevator and a stomach-stabbing mortgage. But we're on a street with old-growth maples, tail-wagging dogs, and trim, if unimaginative, gardens. There's a geese highway that crosses skyward from one side of Guelph to the other, and the Speed River slowly winds through town. The Boathouse, a former storage shed for canoes and kayaks, is now a quaint teashop with four o'clock high tea served in mismatched china cups.

I set up my office in the second bedroom, instructing the Staples deliverymen where to put my new desk, bookshelves, and red swivel chair. In the living room, where boxes of belongings wait patiently for me to unpack them, I find my cartons of books. The boxes once held oranges, toilet paper, and cereal, but now, as I rip off the packaging tape, I pull out advertising annuals and writers' magazines. I rip open another and coax out books with dog-eared covers and pages tumbling out. In another box, I find my Nancy Drew collection: *Nancy's Mysterious Letter*, *The Secret of Shadow Ranch*, *The Clue in the Old Stagecoach*. I've never outgrown its motivational wisdom.

As I fill my office shelves, I keep an eye out for one special book, *Seal Song*. When I have emptied out the boxes of books, I still haven't found it. I can see myself packing it. But where? I search through other boxes, at first methodically, then anxiously, pulling out knickknacks, toiletries, and picture frames. What if I only imagined packing it? What if I left it back in Toronto?

Just when I'm about to give up, I open a box of art supplies and rummage through the tubes of oil paint, the palette knives, and the narrow and fat brushes piled on my painting apron. I scoop out the paraphernalia and pull out the apron. That's when I find it: *Seal Song* with its touching cover photograph of a baby seal. I hug it to my chest. I feel as if I'd found a missing child. Too happy to move, I sit cross-legged on the floor and flip through the pages. There they are: the white zeppelin bodies, the charcoal noses, onyx eyes, puddling hope and earnestness, and the Brian Davies quote I've memorized a lifetime ago. I turn more pages until I find the baby seal resting on her pillow of ice. From the box of art supplies, I extract a stick of graphite and my drawing notebook and begin to sketch.

* * *

It doesn't take long to settle in. By mid-September, Ben and I are already hiking up our favourite, craggy, root-knotted paths at Rattlesnake Point. On one hike, Ben finds a branch he can use for a walking stick. In awe, we look out over the sloping edges of limestone cliffs, the majestic purple hills, and the wizened cedars so close to the edge that some have fallen off.

"Stay back, Ben. You're too close," I say as Ben takes a step closer.

"I just want to, you know, like, I just want to remember it."

The paths are well maintained. Orange flags and trail maps appear regularly, as do the loopy cedars with arms reaching out of the earth to grab the feet of walkers.

"There's a root coming up," I notify Ben. I turn around to watch him dig his stick in front of the root and lift his legs over it.

"There's a rock: go around it," I call. "Go to the right. It's easier."

Ben reaches for a cedar beside the rock and twists himself around it.

With each obstacle, I try to maintain my cool, but in my mind I see Ben tripping over a root and breaking an ankle, and me trying to drag him back to the car.

Feel the fear and do it anyway, the Dop says.

Easy for you to say, I shoot back.

"Aren't you tired? Don't you want to go back to the car?" I ask Ben hopefully.

"Before we go back, I want to do something."

"What?"

"You'll see."

Ben points up ahead. All I see is an upward path that bends to the left.

"Remember, we have to walk all the way back," I remind him, noticing the effort he puts in with each step.

"I know. It's just up ahead," he says, grabbing a trunk for balance.

As we walk slowly, the "up ahead" destination is further up ahead than Ben let on.

"We should turn around," I say.

Ben is insistent.

I continue as Ben's mobile sentinel, sighting rocks, roots, and low-hanging branches. When I turn to check on him, I see he's down on his hands and knees, crawling slowly upward.

"Oh my God, Ben! Did you fall? Are you okay?"

"I'm okay. I didn't fall. It's just easier this way," he tells me.

"Where's your stick?"

He turns his head to look behind him. "I left it down there. I couldn't carry it and climb."

I rush down the slope to retrieve it. This time, carrying his stick, I walk behind him, praying he doesn't lose his grip and slide down the incline.

It takes us ten minutes, with Ben crawling, to reach the top of the slant. When I help him to his feet and hand him back his stick, we're standing on a lookout railed by a wooden fence. In front of us is one of

Ontario's most breathtaking panoramas. Thousand-year-old cedars cling to the pockmarked faces of the limestone cliffs. As we look below, we see a man rappelling down one of the cliffs; a turkey vulture soars overhead. We inhale the beauty of the Niagara Escarpment and reach for each other's hands.

After a few minutes, Ben steps close to the rail and shouts, "Goodbye, Rattlesnake Point."

It takes a second for me to realize what he's doing. But then I get it.

"Goodbye, Rattlesnake Point," I call after him.

"Goodbye, cedar trees," Ben calls.

"Goodbye, turkey vulture," I yell.

"Goodbye, limestone cliffs."

"Goodbye, rappelling man."

"Goodbye, Niagara Escarpment. Thank you," Ben shouts to the escarpment.

"Thank you," I say, with the softness of a prayer.

When we return home, we sit on the sofa, our thighs touching, and drink wine. I bury my head in the cave beneath Ben's arm, grateful and sad at the same time.

The next evening, as we walk from the parking lot to the town's only Chinese restaurant, Ben's feet tangle. He loses his balance and topples onto the pavement.

"My legs are just tired from walking so much yesterday," he says as I help him up. It's something we both want desperately to believe.

The first weekend in October, on our way to a picnic spot, Ben tumbles down a small slant at Riverside Park.

"FUCK!" he bellows so loud that a flock of geese feeding on the grass flies off, honking. His fall is so sudden that for a moment I can't think of what to do. I just watch as he rolls down, then stops, his arms and legs sprawled out like a beached starfish.

"Fucking goddamn shit," he yells, "don't just stand there. Help me!" I race down the hill and bend over him. My goal is to hoist him up by his arms. But I can't do it without his help. His legs are bent and as I struggle to lift him from behind, I see that he can't crabwalk his feet back under himself. In the mid-distance, I see a couple watching us, unsure whether to offer their assistance.

"There are people over there, let me ask them for help." I nudge my head in their direction.

"No. I don't need help." Ben shakes his head adamantly.

The couple watching us calculates our body language and assumes we're okay. They're out of hearing when Ben growls, "You're fucking hurting me, goddamn shit." I ease him into a sitting position in front of an old maple.

"Sling your arm over my shoulder," I suggest, bending my knees and leaning forward, reaching for his closest arm. He pulls his arm away. "Can't you do anything right?" He crawls to the thick, corrugated tree trunk and claws himself up.

In the evening, Ben apologizes. I accept it, but my heart is pulled down at the corners.

A week later, we try a flat path paralleling the Speed River embankment. By avoiding the lumpy grass, we find a spot that's flat and cozy along the river's edge. Hidden among the serviceberry and witch hazel, we're invisible. I shrug off my backpack and pull out a book. We take turns reading aloud from *Anger: Wisdom for Cooling the Flames* by Buddhist monk Thich Nhat Hanh.

"Looking deeply, you may realize that the seed of anger in you is the main cause of your suffering," I read, then pause to contemplate the message. It's not only Ben who is angry, I realize. I, too, have an anger seed. I'm about to relay new insight to Ben when he says, staring at the cloudless sky, "It's so peaceful here. I wish we could stay forever."

"Among the shrubs?" I joke.

"No, in this place." Ben places his right hand over his heart and turns to me. "I feel like right now, we're . . . like . . . you know . . . we're one. We're really *being* with each other." He spreads both hands wide to encompass the river, the embankment, the ducks and the geese gliding and diving into the river, and the squirrels chasing one another from tree to tree. It's like nature TV, but without the commercials. "This is our place," he says.

13

INTO THE BELLY OF THE BEAST

AS I STARE at the black window glass and steel architecture of London Health Sciences Centre, my mind plays tricks on me. For a moment, the black-and-steel high-rise towering in front of us resembles a whale with all her ribs showing.

We meet Dr. Ryan in a third-floor examination room of the neurology clinic. After a few minutes of questions about Ben's muscle weakness, the doctor asks him to undress and put on a hospital gown. Soon, a technician arrives to take us to a diagnostic testing and monitoring lab. As we ride the elevator, it feels as if we were descending into the bowels of the hospital. We are. The underground lab, with multiple testing rooms for CT scans, MRIs, and EEGs, is a radiation hotspot where medicine is waging a nuclear war on cancer and neurological diseases. Here, patients are infused with radioactive substances that light up inside them whenever an abnormality is detected. The lab is deep underground, the technician tells us, so wandering isotopes can't escape into the general population. I don't ask what happens if wandering isotopes escape into a specific population: us.

A second technician replaces the first and I can't help staring to see if any parts of his body light up. He helps Ben onto a stretcher.

"Can you make a fist?" he says, grasping Ben's arm.

Ben curls his fingers and squeezes them into the palm of his hand. The tech ties an elastic tourniquet around Ben's upper arm and injects a mild anaesthetic to ward off any pain. Then he collects Ben's blood and muscle tissue samples. Those tasks completed, he next sticks electrodes on both of Ben's shoulders and hips, and then up and down his arms and legs, to test Ben's muscles and nerves. Once finished, the tech tells me I must wait here, wherever *here* is, while he wheels Ben off to another room for more tests. *Please don't let it be the radiation room*, I plead to God. (I'm an on-and-off-again believer—mostly off—but like they say, there are no atheists in fox holes.) When the tech returns Ben, I ask him about the radiation.

"It's so little, you don't have to worry," he says. "It will give us good images."

Don't worry! I worry about everything: hurting people's feelings, going down in a plane crash, getting fat from vegan curry. With so much to worry about, the last thing I need is for Ben to glow like a reading lamp. Of course, we'd save on hydro. But who wants their husband to glow in the dark?

When we return to the world above, Dr. Ryan asks Ben to lift and lower his arms and legs, bend and unbend his elbows and knees. She has him stand on one foot, then the other. She reaches for the little reflex hammer, the kind with the pink rubber triangle I used to love as a kid, then hammers his knees to see if his legs kick out. She listens to his heart through her stethoscope, pulls out a tongue depressor to peer into the cave of Ben's throat, then holds up a tube attached to a motor, called a spirometer, which Ben has to blow into to test his lung capacity.

Finally, Dr. Ryan asks Ben to lift up his hospital gown so she can see his legs.

"Have they always been this thin?" she asks.

"He was a runner," I interject, hoping to provide a reason that isn't alarming.

"Not when I was young," he replies. "I began noticing it in my twenties. I always assumed it was because of running."

"Running builds up muscles. What you're seeing here is wasting," Dr. Ryan grasps Ben's left leg with her right thumb and forefinger and slides them up and down.

Wasting. What an ugly word. I squeeze my eyes shut and open them again.

Now sitting in a chair, Ben leans forward so his upper arms can rest on his thighs. He hangs his head and stares at his folded hands. Dr. Ryan observes him, sighs—a sound more like a gasp—and gnaws at her upper lip. Perhaps because he is alarmed by the distinct audibility of her breath, or perhaps because he has nowhere else to look for answers, Ben looks up at her and furrows his brows. That's when I imagine I am seeing Ben as he looked when he was a little boy, afraid and surrendering fear at the same time. "What do you think I have?" he asks.

"I need to wait for the lab results, but I agree with Dr. Masskoff that based on your muscle weakness, you do have a motor neuron disease. The lab tests will provide us with a more specific diagnosis."

"But if you had to guess?" I ask.

"I suspect it's either muscular dystrophy or spinal muscular atrophy."

"Oh God," I say, dropping my head into my hands. "What about chronic fatigue? What about fibromyalgia?" At least those diseases aren't deadly. My voice sounds whiny and pleading. The word *no* harpoons out of Dr. Ryan's mouth. She explains with infinite patience why Ben doesn't have either of those syndromes.

All I know about muscular dystrophy is from playing with a boy who lived on my street in Framingham. He was confined to a manual wheelchair and when my mother visited his mother, I used to give him a ride, speeding him back and forth in his living room. But spinal muscular atrophy? Even without me knowing its specifics, it sounds ominous.

But wait! "Muscular dystrophy is a children's disease!" I spurt out, remembering the Jerry Lewis telethons I used to watch on TV as a child.

"You're right. It's rare in adults. We find it mostly in men. Women tend to be carriers."

"How could this just happen? Why didn't anyone find this out before? How could they not know he was sick? How is that even possible?"

Dr. Ryan folds her top lip over her bottom one and nods. "Likely, the disease progresses slowly, so you could have had it in your twenties without knowing it," she says to Ben. "You say that's when you first noticed your legs getting thin. Most people who acquire motor neuron diseases like muscular dystrophy or spinal muscular atrophy don't notice it right away. Muscle weakening would be minimal at first. And as some of the muscles are wasting, others are taking over or helping the weakened muscles along. You'd still have most of your muscle capacity. None of your relatives have been diagnosed with a motor neuron disease, have they?"

Ben shakes his head.

"Do any of your relatives have difficulty with their mobility?"

"My relatives are drunks. They all have difficulty with their mobility."

"There's a cure, right?" I butt in.

The doctor shakes her head. "We know so little about these diseases."

I shake my head from side to side. "This is just incredible. We can send a man to the moon, but you can't correctly diagnose one here at home."

"Karen, it's not Dr. Ryan's fault," Ben says, unusually sympathetic.

"I get angry, too, at how we know so little about these adult-onset diseases. It doesn't seem fair," Dr. Ryan says to both of us.

I jump in. "But there's a cure, right? Just tell us what we need to do, and we'll do it."

She looks from Ben to me and then says, "I know this is hard to process." She reaches for my hand and squeezes it. "Why don't you both go home now and take it easy? Let's wait for the lab results. We shouldn't be speculating." She looks at her watch. "I have to see my next patient. You can call me at any time, just leave word for the receptionist and she'll know how to reach me."

She stands and offers her hand for Ben and me to shake. "If it gets any worse, you should use a cane," she tells Ben, then shuts the door gently behind her. We look at each other in disbelief.

"Maybe it still could be fibromyalgia," I suggest to Ben, as he slowly gets dressed.

* * *

Driving home, I miss exits and take wrong turns. Ordinarily, Ben, who is an adept and focused driver, would blow his top. But he doesn't. He just looks silently out the window. How ironic it is that Ben, who has been driving professionally most of his adult life, loses his driver's licence, and I, who am admittedly not the best driver, am the one who drives us home.

A few weeks later, the phone rings. Ben picks it up.

"Dr. Ryan, hi. We've been waiting for your call," he says buoyantly, as if he were expecting to hear good news.

My hand clutches the beveled edge of the bedroom dresser, which we've moved into the living room to house our videos. There's a coffee mug ring on its surface. I stare at it, afraid to look at Ben, afraid of what his face might convey.

When I raise my gaze, I see Ben's cheeks sagging, his head moving in barely perceptible nods. I sidle closer, trying to listen in, but Ben's pinned the receiver to his ear. I can't hear a thing.

"Okay," Ben says into the phone.

"What?" I whisper loudly, nudging his sneaker with my toe.

"Shush!" he hisses.

A few minutes later, he places the receiver into its cradle and stares at some invisible point on the wall.

"What?" I ask.

Ben's eyes meet mine. "She says I should get my affairs in order."

"You're kidding!"

A moment passes, and then another.

"Ben?"

He opens his lips, but no sound comes out.

"BEN?"

"Dr. Ryan thinks I have amyotrophic lateral sclerosis."

"ALS!" I gasp. Lou Gehrig, the New York Yankees' baseball player, and Morrie Schwartz, a sociology professor at Brandeis, both had ALS. And they both died, but not before they lost their ability to move, to swallow, to breathe. "What else did she say?"

"Most people die within three to six months of diagnosis."

Tears begin to shower my cheeks. I choke. Ben's face whitens. We reach for each other. All we can do is cling together and blink in disbelief.

* * *

We watch for signs. Ben can still walk freely throughout the condo. When I dance to music in the living room, letting myself go free and wild, he can do it too, by raising and lowering his feet like a marionette and swinging his arms mechanically. Outside, however, his confidence wanes. He no longer wants to go out without his cane. He has given up even going out on short walks around the block. But he can still bend his wrists and elbows. He can move his hands and ten fingers easily. He can make a fist and grip hold of any object, including my hand. While I always could beat him in arm wrestling, now I do it more quickly and with less effort.

In my office, between freelance assignments, I comb the Internet for cures. There are none. I turn to vitamin therapies, crystal healing, copper bracelets. If we can find the right therapy—herbalism, homeopathy, acupuncture—I'm confident we can furlough the disease. Other times, I light candles and fall on my knees to pray. ALS is no longer just a disease. It's an unwanted roommate who refuses to leave. To take my mind off Ben's disease, I search the Internet randomly for high-velocity distractions: wars, floods, murders. I read about the Kosovo War and refugees coming to Canada; I read about Dr. Jack Kevorkian, convicted for lethally injecting a terminally ill man. I read about the seal hunt. . . .

Wait a minute! What? The seal hunt! It ended, didn't it? My eyes are the size of hockey pucks. They turn into basketballs as they latch onto a number: 244,552. That's how many seals were killed that spring, according to the article. I stand up so violently my swivel chair rolls back and crashes into my bookcase. My temple is a knot of disbelief. I pull off my glasses. I wipe their murky lenses, lean over my desk, and read again. The number 244,552 stands stubbornly on the page. Dumbfounded, I type "Canada's commercial seal hunt 1999" into the search bar. When I press ENTER, articles line up on my screen like guests arriving at a lawn party. There are interviews with government bureaucrats who intimate the harp seal population is expanding. There are news reports of DFO scientists helicoptering to the ice. There's even an article about Paul

Watson debating Newfoundland fisheries minister John Efford in front of the cameras. Watson likens Efford to Joseph Goebbels and likens his suggestion that two million harp seals should be killed and fed to the Kosovo refugees as resembling the Nazis' "Final Solution." To my horror, the seal hunt is alive and well on the ice floes of Newfoundland. It may no longer be legal to hunt whitecoats, but it is *carte blanche* to go after pups only a few days older.

* * *

Ben and I mourn each new twinge or throb in his arms or legs. We have learned that they are the signs that ALS is progressing. Unless you have been through it, ALS is just three letters of the alphabet stuck together. But if you or your loved one has it, you soon discover it is a penitentiary with a warden who won't let you out. It is in these most dreadful times that Ben and I are closest. But it's a perverse kind of closeness. We are both prisoners of the disease. It makes us insular. I try to encourage normalcy. I still speak to friends on the phone, but if I speak too long, Ben sees it as a betrayal. The one or two visits I manage to squeeze in with friends at their homes causes Ben to summon a list of accusations when I return.

"You don't understand what I'm going through," he says, as if I *could* understand how his body betrays him. His urgency, his demands are exhausting. The messages on my answering machine pile up. I resent Nora, who calls asking me to promote her clients' dystopian products and services. *Could you write a brochure for the casino opening, the breakthrough industrial chemical that poisons the environment one percent less than the others now on the market, the "organic" produce* (that turns out not to be organic).

The only person I stay in contact with is my best friend Catarina. Catarina is a sixty-seven-year-old hippie with silver rings on all her fingers, a helmet of thick blond hair, and ropes of handmade necklaces slung around her neck. One afternoon, when I'm thinking of buying a Kevorkian-style hypodermic needle and filling Ben's veins with bubble soap, I rush to see her. Sitting in her farm's kitchen on her plush red

Victorian couch, I let the tears flow. She pulls a tissue from a box and hands it to me. I swipe under my eyes and down my cheeks. The streaks of my mascara are a calligraphy written on the tissue. But I'm not just wiping away cruelty-free cosmetics, I'm wiping away all the years I have spent hating my career and all the hope my marriage would become something other than cement blocks tied around my feet.

"Why don't you get a job working with animals?" Cat asks.

"There aren't any jobs working with animals unless I become a zookeeper or a veterinarian. I write ads. That's what I do. I'm not trained to do anything else. The closest I'm going to get to a job with animals is advertising Canadian pork."

Catarina wraps me in her arms and I cuddle into her. "Breathe," she tells me. "You look so tired. You've lost weight. Are you eating? Do you want me to make you something?"

But I can't eat. Food lodges in my throat and won't go down.

That evening, before going home, I stop at a bookstore and glance through the magazine section, hoping to have a eureka moment of how to change my life. I buy a *National Geographic* with a baby seal on the cover. Heart-melting occurs, but no eureka moments. That year, 92,005 seals are killed.

14

WHAT'S YOUR EMERGENCY?

AS THE CLOCK ticks into the first seconds of the new year, the world is holding its breath. A computer glitch could stop everything, computer scientists have told us months before. Planes would crash; banks wouldn't open; tap water wouldn't flow; retail and industry would shut down; the world as we know it would no longer exist. No global incident occurs in the first seconds, minutes, hours, days of the new millennium. However, there is a domestic one. Ben hits me for the first time, smacking away all hope of a happy new year. Rage has been brewing on his face all day. Trenches have formed in the skin between his eyebrows. His brain was working on something I did (or didn't) do.

Driving to my painting class, I'm a nervous wreck from trying to keep Ben's anger at bay. But I need to paint. It's my medicine. For two hours, I work on a 4 x 6 in. canvas-board painting of the baby seal in my *Seal Song* book. When our class is over, I don't want to leave. I chat with some of the other students in the parking lot after our teacher locks up. When they drive away, I sit in the van, trying to breathe through my fear.

As I step through the door of our condo, I can see Ben in the living room waiting for me.

"I could kill you," he bellows, sending Bella, our calico cat, scrambling into the bedroom; Levi, our tabby, is one leap behind her.

"Where were you?"

"At painting."

"You're half an hour late!"

"Big deal!"

"It *is* a big deal. You're supposed to be home. What if I needed you?"

"You have a cellphone. Use it," I shout.

"You goddamn good-for-nothing bitch."

"Go to hell."

Ben swings his free arm out in awkward, muscle-weakened movements. His fist clenched perfectly, he hits me obliquely on my left side, above my hip.

It doesn't take me long to reach the washroom and lock the door.

"Open the fucking door!" he says.

Breathe, I tell myself.

"All I ask is that you come home when you say you will. You've been at your goddamn painting class all night."

Images of Inky huddling in my arms on the washroom counter of my parent's house flash through my head. Unlike my childhood home, the condo has no long counter to climb on, so I sit on the toilet lid, cradling Inky's invisible body in my lap. I sob for him; I sob for me. *Who hits dogs? Who hits women?* I ask myself.

Ben's fist bashes the door once, twice, before he huffs out of the bedroom. When my rubber legs can stand, I open the door a crack, then tiptoe across the bedroom floor to peek outside. Ben sits in front of the TV. I can hear the *Law & Order* opening—the sound of jail doors closing. I quietly shut the bedroom door behind me, tiptoe to the night table, pick up the telephone, and punch 911.

"What's your emergency?" a voice asks.

Ben spends the night in jail. And the next night, and the next. On my first day without him, I scroll down the addresses of lawyers in the phone book, dial their numbers, then hang up. Do I need a lawyer? What can a lawyer do? Can she protect me from Ben? Can she keep him from coming home? I decide to wait until Ben's court date in a few days to figure it out.

I sit beside one of the policemen who arrested Ben. He tells me to press charges.

"If you don't, the judge will consider you wasting the court's time. It'll be harder to bring a case against your husband in the future."

When the judge asks me if I want to press charges, I say *yes*. The judge tells Ben he will not be able to come within ten kilometres of me. He wipes a hand over his balding head, then wags a thick finger at Ben.

"You should be ashamed of yourself. You're going to have a police record."

Back home, I throw Ben's food in the garbage: the hotdogs, hamburgers, carton of milk. I have nowhere to bury these products from once-living animals. It feels sacrilegious.

While I'm being angry, tossing food into our waste bin, angry out-of-work Newfoundland cod fishermen toss 226,493 harp seal pelts, called sculps, into rustic fishing boats. The seal hunt will at least provide them with a month of work, but only a month. They can't live off the seal hunt, and if the government thinks they can, they'll march down to the local offices of their members of Parliament and make sure they know it in the future.

To mitigate the wrath of the devastated fishing communities, the federal and Newfoundland governments help fishermen transition from the cod fishery to the lucrative shrimp and snow crab fisheries. By the end of the season, the fishermen have seen their profits rise. Maybe losing the cod wasn't a bad thing after all.

* * *

With Ben gone, the condo has a new energy. I'm no longer afraid to open the front door. I no longer need to wonder which Ben—the loving or hating one—will greet me. Ben is court-ordered to transition from the condo to wherever he now will live. His mother comes to help him pack.

Throwing out whatever Ben left behind—ratty sneakers, natty socks, his do-nothing-to-cure-you supplements, an old sweatshirt—gives me hope for a new start. I fill up one bag after another and lug them down to the condo garbage room. As I'm about to leave, I glance at the communal shelf used as the condo library, a place where we get rid of the old books we no longer want and find new books we never thought we needed to read. The book *Over the Side, Mickey: A Sealer's First Hand* [sic] *Account of the Newfoundland Seal Hunt* by Michael Dwyer catches my eye. My first thought is: *Oh no, a sealer's living in our building, tossing his blood-and-guts propaganda!* My next thought is: *What the fuck? Who reads books like that!?* I'm about to toss it in with the food waste when I stop to leaf through it. The words *head hockey* catch my eye. I scan down the page, curious to find out if it's what I think it is: the numbskull who plays hockey without a helmet. Dwyer corrects me:

> It was like hockey but, instead of using sticks, we used our hakapiks to try to shoot the head between two twitching carcasses we used as goal posts. We all took turns in the net. By the time the game was over, eyeballs, teeth, fragments of skull bone and lower jawbones were scattered all over the rink. [. . .] We all had a great bit of fun.[1]

I slam the book shut. Dwyer is talking about using a decapitated seal head as a hockey puck! Instead of tossing the book in the food waste with all the rotten vegetables and kitty litter, which seems a perfect place for it, I stick it under my sweater and head upstairs. Better I have it than anyone who may get ideas.

15

BY ANY MEANS NECESSARY

IN 2001, NECROPSIES of seventy-six harp seal carcasses show that up to 42 percent of the seals were likely conscious when they were skinned. A report conducted by five independent veterinarians documents the type of abuse the seals endured: being shot and left to suffer, possibly being skinned and hooked alive, possibly being bled alive, being clubbed with a boat hook and left to suffer, possibly being struck and then lost. The report concludes that the hunt causes "considerable and unacceptable suffering."[1]

When the public learns of the report's findings, it is outraged. To counter the furor, federal fisheries minister Herb Dhaliwal creates an eminent panel of economists and fisheries scientists to prove killing harp seals by any means necessary is justified because they eat all the cod.

I'm too focused on how to pay the next month's mortgage to read a veterinary report. When the University of Guelph's Research Communications Office advertises a job in the *Guelph Mercury*, I jump at it. I'm offered a six-month contract to copyedit the university's monthly research magazine. Sitting at a dented metal desk on a non-rotatable swivel chair in the research communications building, I close my window overlooking the lawn, which smells of pesticides, and feel sorry for the squirrels who'll likely die of cancer. Nevertheless, I'm thrilled to be at a veterinary college. They love animals; I love animals. What could be better?

My first editing project is on genetically modified pigs! I force myself to read the article and scribble copyediting symbols onto the draft copy. Next, there's an article on the artificial insemination of goats using silkworms. I begin wondering if they really do love animals. Didn't I promise myself I would never work to promote animal research? Well, here I am.

I need the money, I justify to myself.

Hypocrite, my Doppelgänger unjustifies.

Days later, I'm editing text on asthma inhalants given to beagles when I read that students and faculty can walk them. I add a final comma then head out on my lunch break. The animal care facility has locked doors and a pre-entrance voice box, through which I must identify myself. I explain my interest in walking the beagles. Seconds later, a middle-aged administrator peers through the small rectangle of the door's window. I wait while she summons someone higher up. Ten minutes later, the door creeps open. A petite woman in a white lab coat appears. She leads me to an empty lunchroom and grills me.

"Why would you want to walk the dogs?" Her penetrating eyes study me, looking for any ill intent.

"I love dogs. But I don't have one now."

"You can only walk the beagles during university hours," White Lab Coat says. Her stiff, purposeful posture makes me think of wharf pilings bracing for a storm. "Don't discuss the beagles with anyone outside of the university," she warns.

"Of course not."

White Lab Coat walks me down a cinderblock hall, past rooms with photocopy machines, desks stacked with veterinary journals, and a marker board with names scribbled in black marker, dates and times beside them.

We stitch right, then left. I can hear dogs whining behind grey doors. White Lab Coat opens one and ushers me inside. The tiny room reeks of ammonia. On each side are four floor-to-ceiling wire cages. A beagle sticks her nose through the bars of one of them. I move my hand toward her, letting her sniff my fingers.

White Lab Coat points to the card above her cage. "Mocha," she says.

I read the other cards above the cages: *Anneka, Peanuts, Snickers, Daiquiri, Noodles, Margarita, Georgie,* and *Winnie*.

"It's great they all have names," I say.

"The researchers know them by their numbers," White Lab Coat replies. She opens the door of Mocha's cage and a tubby beagle happily steps out. White Lab Coat flips back her ear, showing me the numbers tattooed on the inside flap.

Immediately, I think of the numbers tattooed on the wrists of the children I've seen in photographs of the Holocaust.

"It's the vet techs who name them. They're the ones looking after them," she says, pushing Mocha back into her cage.

I move to the next cage. "Hello, Anneka." Anneka's teats hang down around her elbows. White Lab Coat tells me all the dogs in the study are females, four to five years old, and bred in an animal supply facility. "We get them after their fourth litter."

I pause in front of Anneka's cage.

"Go ahead and open it," White Lab Coat suggests. She shows me how to unhook the lock. Without waiting for the door to fully open, Anneka shoves her way out. White Lab Coat gives her a pat on the head. Across from Anneka's cage is Noodles, a long-legged beagle who is spinning like a rotating handheld cake mixer.

"Why's she spinning?" I ask.

"Some do that. It's nervous energy. Noodles is high-strung. You can see she's slightly bigger than the other beagles. So is Daiquiri. They're Walker hounds."

"They look like large beagles," I observe.

"We use beagles and Walker hounds because they're easy to handle. They don't give the researchers any problems."

Two cages down, Margarita gnaws on the bars of her cage.

"Now that's boredom," White Lab Coat says. "They all go a little stir-crazy. There's no money set aside for dog walkers. We rely on staff and students. There can be weeks when they don't go out."

"Can I bring them some chewy toys?"

White Lab Coat shakes her head. "We can't have them choking or swallowing something when no one's looking."

White Lab Coat pushes Anneka back inside her cage and we walk out of the room.

Back in the lunchroom, White Lab Coat tells me the dogs are in the asthma study's second year. Each morning and evening, a vet tech sprays inhalant into their mouths. "We have over fifty dogs in the study," she says proudly.

"What happens at the end of the study?"

White Lab Coat's eyes lower and she sighs and stands. "Why don't you get familiar with some of the dogs in the other rooms? They're all in the same study. They all need walking."

The next day, I kneel in front of Mocha's cage, fitting my fingers through the bars, letting her sniff me. I open her cage and sit on the floor in front of it. When she tries to lick my face, the stench of halitosis makes me jerk back my head. Mocha's fur feels greasy and she smells like a rotting grapefruit. The ammonia cuts the smell's intensity. Although the dogs' hygiene leaves something to be desired, the room and its cages are immaculate, with no poo or pee in sight. There are eight cages in each of the closed-door rooms. How will I walk all the dogs? I decide to choose a room and stick with it. I choose their room. Every day at lunch hour, I'll take two for a walk. By the end of each week, eight tail-wagging, greasy dogs will have inhaled fresh air and felt grass under their paws.

At the end of my lunch hour, I walk out the same way I came in. On the marker board in the hall, the names of several dogs from one of the other rooms are listed. Above the list, the word *leaving* has been scribbled. I pull over a vet tech and tilt my head toward the board.

"Does this mean they've found homes?"

"The only way a dog on the board leaves is they're headed for a terminal surgery," he says.

Each day, I glance at the marker board, afraid I'll see the name of one of my beagles. When I see another dog's name on the board, I sigh with relief. My beagles are safe; yet this one isn't. Relief turns to anguish. I walk the beagles in their small exercise yard, often fantasizing about stealing them. I picture myself running from the animal facility, beagles bracketing my torso. Outside the perimeter of the veterinary college, a getaway vehicle is waiting. All I have to do is hop in and drive to the nearest safe house. But which dogs will I take and how can I leave the others behind?

There is no escape vehicle or safe house, my Doppelgänger says. *You'll be arrested, labeled crazy . . . criminal.* Doppelgänger is right. My rescued beagles will be wrenched from my arms, sent back to their cages, or worse, to a terminal surgery. The irony doesn't escape me. In a facility where dogs are forced to undergo invasive, painful experiments and death, I'd be the one labeled *dangerous*.

For weeks, I walk my dogs under the cloud of knowing that it's only a matter of time before their names will be on the marker board. On rainy days, when my beagles refuse to go outside, I squeeze myself inside their cages, feeling like a priest at the bedside of a death-row inmate, and massage their greasy white bellies and caress their waxy ears. When I learn the asthma study is ending, I sit in Mocha's cage, stroking her head on my lap.

"I will get you out, and Anneka too, by any means possible," I tell them. "I just don't know yet what those means will be."

What about Noodles and Daiquiri and Margarita . . . and all the other dogs in all the other rooms? Doppelgänger asks.

She's right. How could I take only two when all of them need my help? But it would be hard enough to get two out. And if I did manage to get all eight out, where would I keep them? Certainly not in my condo. The super would have a fit! I push the thought from my mind.

My first inkling of opportunity comes when White Lab Coat tells me as I pass her office that the lead asthma researcher has decided to put the beagles up for adoption.

"That's wonderful! Are you going to put a notice in the *Mercury* so people will know?"

"No. We'll do it from inside here. We'll put an adoption board by the front door. Anyone who wants to adopt them can see what dogs are available."

"How are people going to know about them if they don't come to the animal care facility? There's lots more opportunity if we spread the word."

"We only adopt to people working or studying at the university. Or their close family and friends."

"But . . ."

"No one else."

"But what happens if they don't get adopted?" They aren't the most well-behaved dogs. They don't know how to sit or come or heel. What if they pee in someone's house? My thoughts flit back to Inky and the *Boston Globe* my father used in order to train him. I already know the answer; I just want White Lab Coat to say it.

White Lab Coat looks down at her hands and takes a deep breath. "They'll go into another study or our advanced surgery program."

"And then what?"

White Lab Coat gives me a fifteen-second stare, cocks her head, and half-smiles. "Why don't you take one? You'd have to fill out an application, be vetted like everyone else. But if you care about the dogs. . . ."

"What about a rescue group?" I don't know of any, but I'm sure I can find one.

"Absolutely not. We're not opening our doors to the Animal Liberation Front."

Who said anything about the Animal Liberation Front? Does she think that's what rescue groups are? Never mind, I have work to do and beagles to get adopted.

I find a dog trainer, who teaches me the training basics. Norma-Jeanne, the owner of Puppy Power, is adamant about no-touch training—treats instead of newspapers. She freeze-dries her own liver treats and sends me home with a stash. I practice the doggy commands with my beagles. They love the treats but refuse to sit or stay. Heeling is impossible. And still, there's the issue of peeing. Whatever happens, I'm going to adopt Anneka and Mocha. As they are the smallest beagles in the room, I know I can fit them in my condo. But what if they bark or howl, as they notoriously did inside their cages? I envision the condo supervisor pounding on my door, threatening eviction. I need another solution. But what?

Suddenly, it comes to me. I'll ask some of my friends to adopt the dogs. Since I'm connected to the university, they are too . . . sort of.

"Sorry, Karen, I have Sky. I can't take another dog," says one.

"We're not allowed to have dogs in my building," says another.

I hear of a newly formed animal rescue group in Guelph. Surely they can take a few beagles. The founder of the rescue group declines, afraid of repercussions from the university. I call an international animal protection group with a fierce campaign against animal research. "If we took those dogs, we'd have to take everyone's research dogs," the director explains.

I call more groups.

"No."

"Sorry."

"Wish we could."

"Good luck."

Then the director of a rescue group tells me about Animal Alliance of Canada and Project Jessie, its rescue farm for research dogs. I phone right away and leave my telephone number. Several nights later, I finally speak to Shelly.

"How many dogs are there?" she asks.

"Eight in my room."

"How many rooms are there?"

"About seven."

"How many dogs can you get out?"

"Fifty . . . maybe more."

"We'll take them."

Did I hear right? "All of them?"

"As many as you can bring us."

That night, I call my friends who couldn't adopt and ask them if they'd just fill out an adoption application. "I'll take the dogs from you. I have a place to bring them."

I get a copy of the adoption application and coach my pseudo-adopters on how to fill out the application and what to say if questioned. They connect me to their relatives and friends, who connect me to theirs.

With my applications for Mocha and Anneka approved, I head for their room. I open their cages and buckle the collars and clip on the new leashes I've bought them. Daiquiri and Noodles bark urgently. Margarita jumps frantically against the bars of her cage. Somehow, they know Mocha and Anneka are being rescued. "Don't worry, I'm coming back for you," I tell them as I lead Mocha and Anneka out of the room and out the front door of the animal care facility. I load them into the back of my van equipped with blankets and pillows, and drive to Project Jessie. It takes three months to get all fifty-two research beagles and mixed-breed pound dogs out of the veterinary school. When it's over and all the dogs are adopted, I hand in my notice to the research communications director. I can't work there any longer, nor can I go back to advertising. I'm suddenly adrift. What will I do now?

You got fifty-two dogs out of a research lab; you'll think of something, my Doppelgänger reassures me.

* * *

On September 11, 2001, two planes hit the Twin Towers in New York City, and 9/11 enters the world's vocabulary. Riveted to the TV, I watch people trapped inside the crumbling towers jump to their deaths. In all, 2,977 victims die, their bodies never found, and 6,000 others are wounded. Three months earlier, the DFO has announced the final tally of the seal hunt—226,493 harp seals died. How many had been struck but managed to escape under the ice, their bodies never found?

Ground Zero's toxic fumes have not yet settled when my resentments and grievances with Ben crumble.

I turn off CNN and call Ben. "We can work things out. Come home."

"You've got to be kidding!" my mother says on the phone through gusts of exasperation. "Don't tell me you're going to take him back. It's only been three months!"

I leaf through my mental filing cabinet of possible responses, but before I can find one, she says, "Don't tell me you already have!"

"Mom."

"After everything!"

"Mom!"

"My very smart daughter is being stupid."

"Stop!"

"What can I say?"

"Say you want me to be happy."

"Always."

"Say you believe in us, that we can work things out."

"It's going to take a lot more than my saying it to make it true."

"Mom!"

"You don't think I should tell you how I feel? I'm your mother. I can see things you can't."

"Can't you just say it? Can't you just say, 'Yes, Karen, you and Ben can work things out'?"

"I can't stay on the phone. I've got to make Eddie's dinner." She lets out a robust sigh, then hangs up.

16

NOODLES

NEWBORN OR ADULT, the harp seal has four flippers. On land, she is cumbersome, like a caterpillar inching forward, her two back flippers dragging behind her. But once she gets the hang of swimming, her back flippers like an outboard engine propel her through the sea, and her lower body shimmies to a beat only she can hear. With her front flippers as rudders, she moves forward and backward, left and right. Each flipper has five digits attached by webbing. Each front digit has a claw, longer than a geisha's nail and twice as sharp. The harp seal's jaw is a formidable weapon, with up to thirty-six pointed teeth, not for chewing but for ripping and breaking. These are much needed if the harp seal is to survive her predators: polar bears in the northern part of her range and sharks making their way back to the Northwest Atlantic.

* * *

In 2002, 312,367 seal pups are killed for their pelts. The hunters exceed their Total Allowable Catch (TAC) of 275,000. It's not the first time that quotas have been clobbered. The years 1975, 1976, 1977, 1981, and 1998 all saw sealers unlawfully going over quota.

The anti-seal hunt movement is growing. Activists are keeping tally of the infractions. I keep my own tally of infractions in my marriage, but in the wake of 9/11 I'm willing to wipe the slate clean. If we can learn anything from the Twin Tower collapse, it's that we must love, not hate. Letting go of past recriminations is work enough; I know nothing about the TAC overrun.

* * *

Three months after Ben moves back in, the shouting and swearing begin. "Cunt," "bitch," "good-for-nothing." I let the words roll off me like seawater.

A handful of stiff spaghetti noodles falls through my fingers into a pot full of boiling water. I meditatively watch the water relax the stiff muscles of the noodles. As they slink down into the pot, Ben comes into the kitchen and stands behind me. He peers at the pot.

"What are you doing?"

"Making dinner. What does it look like?"

"You're doing it wrong! You can't let the noodles slide in." At six foot one, Ben is a head and a half taller than me. I turn around in a wedge of space between Ben and the stove.

"What are you talking about?"

"You can't let them slide in. You have to break them up."

"They're fine the way they are."

"They're not fine." Ben heaves a breath and jabs his index finger at the pot. "The tops of the noodles are above water."

"So?"

"They won't cook. I can't believe you don't know that!"

"Give it a rest." I turn back to the pot and give the half-stiff noodles a prod with my fork.

His tongue clicks off the roof of his mouth. His nostrils flare. Ben is no longer my husband but a raging bull of emotions ready to trample.

"Calm down. It's no big deal."

"Don't tell me it's no big deal."

"It's not."

Pushing me out of the way, Ben stares into the pot with the intensity of someone trying to find a drowned mosquito in their soup.

"Can I get in here?" I squeeze between him and the stove and impatiently nudge him with my shoulder. He shoves me aside and, grabbing the plastic handle, he wrenches the pot from the burner, water volcanizing over the rim, and tosses the noodles into the sink, scalding his arm.

"Son of a bitch! Look at what you did." Red speckles sear white flesh. He grabs a towel, presses it to his burn, and glares at me.

"I didn't do that. You did."

"You good-for-nothing fucking bitch," Ben roars.

My legs are as rubbery as soggy noodles. Yet all my thoughts focus on getting to the front door. If I could just open it, I could . . .

Ben grabs my arm and pushes me against the wall. "Can't you do anything?" he roars. I feel like a butterfly stuck on the head of a pin. My mind flashes back to a self-defense course I have taken, compliments of a former employer. I thread my hands up like a needle through the hole made between his outstretched arms. I stiffen my arms, then plunge my forearms down as hard as I can against his elbows. His fingers unfasten their grip. I try to run, but just as I gain traction on the waterlogged floor, Ben grabs me by the waist.

"Let go, you *fucking goddamned shit.*" I wrench my upper body, hurling it right, then left, then right. He is easily put off balance and as he totters, I burst from his arms. His body folds and hits the floor. I grab my jacket and purse and turn to look back at Ben sprawled out like an overturned beetle. I run out the front door, jump into the car, and head down the street.

At first, I don't know where I'm going. Maybe I'll go to Florida to visit my mother. Maybe I'll drive to the airport and take the first plane to Paris or Rome. But I pass the airport exit. City becomes towns and farmland. When I pull my car into a hidden drive, my tires grind up bits of worn gravel, and the car bounces and jolts up the rutted path between rows of hundred-year-old maple trees. I park in front of the eighteenth-century farmhouse.

A squirrel darts up the trunk of one of those large maples in front the stone building and chatters annoyance as I get out of the car. Behind the house, a threadbare brown barn sits at the head of a hill. A dirt path descends from its open doors and down a carriage run, past a pregnancy of irises.

I can see Catarina peeking through the screen of the kitchen door. I step out of the car. She runs to me.

"I thought I heard someone coming up our noisy drive. Usually, it's someone looking for directions. I wasn't expecting you." She wraps me in her arms and leads me into the kitchen. Within seconds, I transmute into a six-year-old, tears streaming down my cheeks and words bubbling out of my mouth. When I stop to catch my breath, I find myself sitting beside her on her red velvet farm-kitchen couch. She hands me a tissue.

"Phew!" she says, waving her hand in front of her face as if to ward off emotion. "I need a cup of coffee," she says, standing. "You?" She wipes a tear from her own eye with the tip of a finger.

I watch as she puts water into the coffeemaker and measures out six scoops of dark roast. "Have you thought what you want to do?" she calls over her shoulder.

"No."

"You can stay here."

"Forever?"

"Until things settle."

She brings two cups—white, with Swedish blue flowers—full of steaming black coffee. I reach for mine and smell the coffee's comforting breath. Could I shrink myself enough to fit inside? Living in a cup seems preferable to returning home.

"Do you love him?" she asks.

I stare down at my lap, not wanting to meet Catarina's eyes. I can hear the clock on the kitchen wall—*tick, tick, tick*. In the distance, a lawnmower *mheeerrrs*, chewing up grass. The house groans under the weight of its hundred-year-old self. The silence between us is aging, too.

"I don't know."

She gives a skeptical "hmm," stirs a small silver spoon methodically around in her coffee, then places her cup and the spoon on the saucer in front of her. "I didn't want to believe my first marriage was ending," she says. "I was in *such* denial for years. I look at photographs of myself at the time. It's all in my eyes."

"What?"

"The same thing I see in your eyes."

"What?"

"Despair."

"Yes, but you could leave. I can't leave Ben. He's dying."

"It wasn't so easy for me either. I had two children under five. All my family were in Sweden."

"So what made you . . . how did you . . . ?"

"Leave?"

I nod.

"I knew if I didn't get out, Garry could grind me down to a place where I might never get up, where I could never be the mother I wanted to be for my children."

"I don't have children."

"But you have an inner child. And she's dying."

"Ben's my child. He's like a temper-tantruming, trash-talking, fifty-year-old child."

"It probably would have been better if you two had not gotten back together."

"All I could think about when the towers came down was: What if an attack happened here? Who would help him down the stairs? What if he fell and got trampled? How can I leave him? His health's getting worse. He has no place to go. I can't just kick him out."

Soggy tissues pile up on my lap. Cat fills and refills our coffee cups and brings plates of warm cornbread. I break off a large section with my teeth and chew, as if getting inside the rhythm of my jaws could take me away from my life. The light dappling the stone walls slowly greys as darkness fills in the crevices and crags. I lift the last crumb on my plate with the tip of my forefinger and lick it off. The clock's arms are rotating, its ticking insistent. What should I do next? Should I stay here with Catarina? Should I go home? Would I find Ben still on the floor? What if I never went back? But my cats are alone with Ben. And he's alone.

"What do you want to do?" Cat asks.

The country roads turn menacing as I drive home. My hands shake as I park the car beside our apartment and pull the key from the ignition.

The kitchen is immaculate. No water on the floor, no noodles in the sink. When I turn on the light in the bedroom, Ben is lying on his side facing me. His eyes look red. Not wanting to acknowledge him, I pull a blanket out of the closet and turn off the light.

In the front room, I pull out the sofa bed, cover the mattress with my blanket, and climb inside, my dress still on.

"Aren't you coming to bed?" Ben shouts from the bedroom.

"I need some sleep. I'll talk to you in the morning." I pull the blanket over my head.

At dawn, I tiptoe into the washroom. Staring at the mirror, I wet my fingers and run them through my hair, and smooth the creases in my dress. Grabbing my purse and house keys, I hurry to the bus stop. In the filmy grey of a sunless morning, I climb aboard the first bus, though I'm not sure where it's going. The bus motors down Edinburgh and stops at the Stone Road Mall, where a half-dozen workers coming off their shift get on. It continues until I pull the stop cord and slows at Tim Hortons.

As I'm waiting in line for coffee, my cellphone rings.

"Where are you?" Ben asks, his voice alarmed. "I woke up and you were gone."

"Nowhere."

"What do you mean 'nowhere'? I can hear noise in the background."

"I can't talk to you right now."

"I'm sorry," Ben's voice says. "I know it was wrong . . . like . . . it's just been, I've just been . . . you know, like. . . ."

The person in front of me is ordering. It will be my turn next, but I don't want to order while Ben is on the phone. I don't want him to know where I am. I step out of line, allowing the person behind me to move up.

"I just wanted you to . . . I got afraid. . . . My mother always told me, like, the right way to do noodles is like. . . . It doesn't matter. . . . I should have just let you. . . . Are you there?"

"I gotta go."

"Wait." The word sounds more pleading than demanding. "You know, like, I just want you to know you are the love of my life."

Like . . . you know—these bridging words always appear when Ben's nervous, uncertain. But never when he's angry. Then, the free flow of speech rages unimpeded. The words *cunt* and *bitch* need no *like* or *you know* to cushion them.

"I gotta go." I click off my cellphone. I walk to the back of the coffee line.

There must be a hair's width between love and hate, I think, as I wait for the guy in front of me to order. I hate Ben most days now. But there are a few when I. . . . It's a strange kind of love. Not one that Harville Hendrix's book *Getting the Love You Want* ever mentions. Ben's not the kind of man who can read about changing behaviours to make one's marriage better and then follow through with it. He wants to, but something in his brain turns off that "want" quickly, especially if he feels I've slighted him. Still, there are those times when my heart cries for him, and that's a kind of love. And sometimes, I can tell myself things aren't that bad, or I have to cut him some slack because he didn't have it so easy as a kid.

I remember Ben telling me that when he was sixteen, his father Ralph had taken his uncle George to the pub to get wasted, a not-unusual event. Ben loved his uncle. George was just ten years older, more like his brother than his uncle. Together, they read poetry, walked along the gorge, and talked about girls and what they both wanted to do in the future. And they talked about his father.

"Your grandma hated Ralph," George had told Ben.

"Hated! Why?"

"She was as mean as a rattlesnake to everybody, but your father more than most."

"How come?"

"I'm no doctor, but I think she was a bit not right in the head. Can't put it any other way than that. If it weren't for your grandpa, I don't know where Ralph would be."

Past midnight that night, Ben's father kicked in the front door and tottered across the living room until he veered to the couch and collapsed.

Ben's mother Madeleine was crocheting in her rocking chair. "Where's George?" she asked.

"In the car."

"It's freezing out there, Ralph. Why didn't you help him in?"

"Ben, go bring him in."

"No! It's not my responsibility," Ben said.

"I'll give you responsibility." Ralph lurched himself upright, curled his fist, and swung, missing Ben by miles.

"Ben, please go get your uncle," Madeleine said.

Ben would do anything for his mother, so he got up, put on a parka, and headed out to the car. He saw his uncle in the driver's seat, his head tilted back against the headrest.

Ben knuckled the window. "Uncle George, wake up." He knuckled again, then tried the door handle. The door opened. Uncle George toppled sideways, the stench of vomit strong enough to blow out Ben's nostrils.

"Fuck. Goddamn it. Fuck, Uncle George!" Ben bent down and lifted George by the shoulders. "Wake up, for fuck's sake." He shook George, slapped his cheek, yelled. "Wake the fuck up!" Vomit expectorated out of George's mouth. "Fuuuuuuuuuck!!!!!" Ben pulled his hands away and watched George flop back on the ground.

Ben tried to wipe the vomit off George's face and clear his nostrils, but it was frozen and all Ben got was stink. He backed away, turned, and ran to the broken-hinged front door.

I don't know what's making me think of this now. I brush my cheek with my hand, shake my head briskly to snap out of it, then step up to the cash register to place my order.

17

THE FIRST ASSASSIN

IN THE FRENZY of the hunt, as a sealer adjusts his balance against the agitation of the sea by leaning against the vessel's handrail, he aims, shoots, and hopes he's hit his mark. The Marine Mammal Regulations command sealers to palpitate their victims' skulls as soon as possible to ensure the seals are unconscious or dead. Herein lies the problem: it can take sealers up to ten minutes to reach wounded seals. Their distance from the victims, the disequilibrium of the waters, and their unwillingness to empty two bullets into a pelt—thus degrading its value—cause sealers to leave the pups wounded but not dead. Minutes are like hours for a baby seal unable to breathe through the blood filling her lungs. Sometimes, the sealer will lose sight of her altogether. It may take hours for her to die.

"You can't build a national economy on the back of cruelty to animals," says the senior vice president of the Humane Society of the United States (HSUS). "Clubbing seals is not a livelihood for the twenty-first century."

But in 2003, it's global warming, not a sealer, who is the first assassin on the ice. Even before hakapiks swing, the grim ocean reaper slays an estimated 260,000 baby harps with ice so fragile it will not hold a newborn harp seal's weight.

That doesn't stop the DFO from allowing sealers a three-year helter-skelter killing spree of 975,000 harp seals in total—289,512 of whom are taken the first year of the 2003–2005 plan.

* * *

"Mom, can you come up?" I ask. I balance the phone between my head and right shoulder as I browse through the colour photographs of a coffee-table book on harp seals that I've just bought at Chapters, after my afternoon gynecology appointment.

"Why? Are you and Ben fighting again?"

"I have a polyp on my ovary. The gynecologist wants it removed. She's scheduled me for surgery." I turn to a page of two whitecoat seal pups lying side by side in the snow.

"When?"

"June." I give her the exact date.

"So far away! Couldn't you get an earlier date?" Without even waiting for an answer, she launches in: "I don't know about your healthcare system."

"It's the only one we have, Mom. It's just three months."

"What about Ben? He's your husband. He should be the one taking care of you."

"Mom, please; I need you."

To get to Guelph General, one must cross the bridge on Eramosa and take a left onto Delhi. A quarter of the way down is the 165-bed redbrick hospital. On the fifth floor, I'm just waking up from surgery. A morphine drip that I can control myself is to the left of my bed, and Mom and Ben are in visitors' chairs to the right.

"Are you in pain?" Mom asks.

I pump another dose of morphine. It works in no time. "No, I'm good."

"Thank God they didn't kill you. Have you heard what's going on in Florida now? A man went in for a kidney operation, and the doctor misread his chart and took out the wrong kidney!"

"What happened?"

"The family sued."

Ben sighs and rolls his eyes and says he's going to the cafeteria for coffee. When she's sure Ben is out of hearing, my mother slides her chair closer.

"You know, I couldn't get him out of the house. He told me last night to be ready at nine in the morning. And I was. I kept saying, 'Ben, I'm ready. Ben, where are you? Bennnnn?'" She throws up her hands. "I don't know what's wrong with your husband."

"Thanks for coming, Mom."

"You're welcome, sweetie."

When Ben returns, my mother leaves to go to the washroom. He moves his chair closer, and when he's sure she's out of hearing distance, he says, "Your mother took forever to get dressed." He lifts the lid of his coffee and tries to blow the heat away. "Who needs fucking makeup to go to the hospital? The only way I got her out of the house is I threatened to go without her."

"Ben, be nice."

"I am nice."

In front of our condo building, my mother helps me out of the car, and Ben parks it. I lean against her, her arm tight around me, as we walk from the car to the condo elevator, and then down the hall to our unit. The two extra-strength Tylenols she gives me with water barely take a notch out of the pain.

18

LOW-HANGING FRUIT

IN EARLY AUGUST, my cellphone rings as I walk into the condo. I kick off my shoes, drop my bag by the door, and head into the bedroom. I flick up the phone lid, press the green button, and flop onto the bed.

"Hello?"

"Hello?" says a female voice. "I'm looking for Karen."

"I'm Karen."

"You got the beagles out of the university?"

"Yes."

"I'm calling from Animal Alliance of Canada. I'm Liz White. I'd like to meet you and tell you a little bit about what we're doing."

Mid-August in Guelph is so hot that all life curls brown from lack of water. The marigolds in my neighbour's planters are flagging. The leaves of the maple trees have the crispy edges of burnt human flesh. The day I'm to meet Liz White, however, a shower threatens to crack the heavens open like an egg.

Poised inside the Williams coffee shop door, grasping my black advertising portfolio, and dripping like an overturned teacup, I try to remember how Liz described herself during our morning confirmation. *Green rain slicker* is all that comes to mind. The only woman wearing one is sitting beside a man in a Tilley adventure hat. Her hair is styled in a 1920s flapper's bob. Underneath her slicker is a blue-jeans shift, the kind

I wore in the 1970s. Both are staring my way. I take a few uncertain steps toward them.

"Karen?" the woman asks.

When I nod, she rises to greet me.

"I'm Liz White." She holds out her hand. Her grasp is of just-right firmness, her smile as warm as freshly baked bread. We sit and Liz introduces the man as Stephen Best, the founder of Environment Voters, an offshoot of Animal Alliance of Canada (AAC). He leans across the table and we shake hands.

I had never heard of AAC before the beagles, so Liz gives me a brief introduction. It began in 1990 with a group of activists who had sharpened their teeth at larger organizations like the Toronto Humane Society and IFAW. Animal agriculture, trapping and hunting, animal transport, and animals in research are just a few of its campaigns.

"Our work is mostly legislative," Liz explains. "We focus on changing the laws. Canada has some of the worst animal legislation among first-world nations. But now I want to hear about you."

I slide my résumé toward her and she and Stephen glance at it. When they lift their heads from the paper, I hoist my portfolio onto the table and slowly flip through my award-winning advertisements for Nikon, CTV, Foodland Canada, and a literacy nonprofit in Africa, having made sure to remove any pharmaceutical advertisements. Surprisingly, Liz and Stephen seem only mildly interested.

"I know you can write and I know you can organize," Liz says. "You got fifty dogs out of the Ontario Veterinary College. But I need to know why you want to work in animal protection. The money is awful, the work demoralizing, the hours long."

"Animals are my life. I want to change the world for them. It's my life's purpose." The words fly out of my mouth, sounding corny.

Liz and Stephen glance at each other, acknowledging something between them.

"We've been searching for a way to make the environment and animal issues relevant to politicians," Liz begins. "Not by pulling heartstrings, but by offering a political benefit to those who protect animals and the environment and by extracting a political price from those who don't." At that point, Liz rises and takes our coffee orders before heading for the food counter to place them.

"Almost every animal and environmental problem in Canada can be solved by our elected officials," Stephen says. "They have the power to change existing laws and to pass new ones. Yet Canada has one of the worst animal and environmental protection records in the developed world. Politicians are focused on getting re-elected. Winning votes overwhelms almost every other consideration. Animals and the environment have little, if any, currency. Politicians can get elected no matter how bad their animal and environmental protection records are."

I sit with my legs curled under the seat and try to absorb it all. Nothing is what I expected: all this talk of politics, the Zelda Fitzgerald hairstyle, the safari getup. I expected a discourse on protests, undercover investigations, and rescue operations, like the one I had pulled off at the University of Guelph. My brain tries to reorient itself.

"The future strategy of Animal Alliance is to use electoral politics to achieve victories for animals. By campaigning in 'swing ridings,' [constituencies] we'll be able to shift votes toward politicians who oppose factory farming, wildlife culls, and animal research."

My eyes glaze over with a patina of boredom. I don't follow Canadian politics. What's the point? When friends chide me about my ignorance, I tell them politics has nothing to do with me. Nothing ever changes. Politicians only look out for themselves. But then Stephen says the word *seal*. My eyes jolt to attention.

"We believe that the seal hunt is the low-hanging fruit of animal protection. It's the most reviled hunt for animals in the world and activists around the globe are demanding its end. Yet they give millions of dollars every year to animal organizations that can't end it because their campaigns don't target the people involved with the seal hunt. A maple syrup boycott won't end the seal hunt. Maple syrup producers have no stake in it. Why penalize those who have no vested interest in keeping the seal hunt going?

We need to target those who are directly responsible for killing the seals: Canada's fishermen, seafood companies, and the politicians across the country who support it. These are the people who can make a difference."

"How?" I ask, and then mentally kick myself. Maybe it should be obvious.

"Sealers are fishermen. In season, they fish snow crab and lobster and shrimp. But once those fisheries close, they go sealing. But that's not the only connection between the seal hunt and fishing industry."

Liz returns with our drinks.

"I was just telling Karen how the seafood industry and the seal hunt are connected," Stephen says, and then turns back to me. "Most of the seafood companies support the seal hunt. Some process both fish and seals. Politicians go along with it because doing so wins them votes. No politician in Canada could get elected without supporting it." Stephen attends to his coffee while Liz takes over.

"With a boycott of Canadian seafood, we can hold the people who hunt the seals, the companies that buy the pelts, and the politicians who support the hunt—through legislation and government subsidies— accountable. We're building a campaign, and we want you to run it."

"I'd. . . . Oh, my gosh, I'd love to."

"Great," Liz says, pulling something from her satchel and sliding it toward me. It's a twenty-page, double-spaced brief, *Understanding the Political Reality Behind Canada's Commercial Seal Hunt*. "If you are to understand anything about Canada's sealing policy, you must understand this." She pokes the document with her index finger. "This is the political reality in Canada. To understand this is to understand the seal hunt."

I flip over the cover page and begin reading:

> The Canadian seal hunt persists after more than 30 years of protest because anti-seal hunt advocates have failed to undermine the fundamental political rationale that sustains it. The authority for deciding seal hunt policy in Canada is vested solely in federal Members of Parliament (MPs). For support of sealing, MPs from all political parties have been taught by

the sealing community that there is a political benefit to be had and have been taught by anti-seal hunt advocates that no political cost is to be paid.[1]

As I scan further, the idea of the strategy begins to take shape: take away the political benefits of the seal hunt and turn them into disadvantages. I can't help but smile. I'm finally here! The days of wondering how I'd ever get to the seal hunt are over. Today, I have found my way. Abruptly, my mind turns to Ben. My excitement deflates. Have I forgotten I've a sick husband at home? *How can I work in Toronto while caring for Ben in Guelph?* I ask myself.

"There's just one thing," I hesitate. I explain about Ben's neuromuscular condition, the falls, his eventual need for a walker. "We don't know how quickly things will progress. One day, he won't even be able to feed himself. I want this job so much. But I need to work from home."

"There's no reason you can't," Liz shrugs. "Just come into the office when you need to."

Back home, I can barely contain my excitement. When I tell Ben about the interview and the job, his forehead creases.

"You can't forget about me. I'm going to need your help."

"I won't."

Soon, business cards and campaign materials arrive by FedEx. I begin setting up the second bedroom as an office.

Ben goes from needing a cane to a walker to a wheelchair. When the chair arrives, it barely fits through the front door. Ben gives it a test drive down the hall, with no room on either side for me to pass. The condo shrinks.

Some Saturdays, a mobility van takes Ben to the senior centre. This Saturday, as the late September morning melts into afternoon, I sprawl on my still-unmade bed, luxuriating in my alone time, and thumb through *Seal Song.* I find my special seal pup on her snow pillow and caress her. "I'm going to end the hunt. You'll never have to worry," I tell her. But I know she's likely dead, consumed by the seal hunt years ago. I slide my middle finger over the top of her page and as I turn it, the edge slices my finger. Blood drips from the slivered skin onto the page. I rush to the washroom for a bandage and a toilet paper roll. I'm wrapping the Band-Aid around my finger when the phone rings.

I click the ON button with my elbow and negotiate the phone under my chin.

"Karen, it's Mom!" she says in her loud Boston accent.

"Hi, Mom. Hold on. I've just cut my finger."

"What happened? Are you all right? Do you need a doctor?"

Blood seeps from under my bandage. I pull off a length of toilet paper and wrap it around my finger.

"No. It's nothing." I stare at the dribble of blood defacing my beautiful baby seal.

"You sound upset."

"Oh, it's just. . . . I've got blood on my book."

"What book?"

"Just some book I bought."

"That should be the least of your problems. So, have you found a job yet?"

I press my thumb against my bandaged, still-bleeding finger and pull my knees up to my chest.

"I've got a job campaigning against the seal hunt!"

"How much are they paying you?"

"Thirty thousand."

"How much?" she says, aghast.

"It doesn't matter, Mom. I love seals."

"You can still love seals and do something that pays better."

"Mom! Calm down. It's not just about money."

"I know: you love seals. I don't know how you can love seals when you've never even met one."

"Mom!"

"I see how you can love dogs or cats. But seals? Don't you have to know something to love it?"

"How can people love Jesus? Or God? Most people have never met either of them, and yet they still love them. At least there's definitive proof seals exist."

"What about people?"

"What about them?"

"Don't you love people?"

"You love interior decorating. Does that mean you can't love people?"

"If you say so," my mother sighs. "You still need a better-paying job. Ben isn't working. How are both of you going to survive on thirty thousand dollars a year? You used to make so much in advertising."

"I hated it."

"You used to love it."

"Mom!"

She sighs again. "I can't talk anymore. Eddie just came in and told me *Psycho* is on TV. I love Alfred Hitchcock!"

After I hang up the phone, I spit on a piece of toilet paper and try to lift off the stain. When it doesn't work, I raise the open page to my mouth and kiss the baby seal streaked with blood.

* * *

For year two of the three-year management plan, the Department of Fisheries and Oceans increases the Total Allowable Catch to 350,000.[2] By the hunt's end, the DFO reports that 365,971 harp seals, mostly babies, have been slaughtered, almost 16,000 over quota.[3]

"Unsustainable!" marine biologists cry. But the federal government isn't listening. It's too busy negotiating new seal pelt markets in Russia and Poland.

19

GOOD KARMA

HEMLOCK IS EASY to come by. It grows on the banks of rivers and streams, near fences, on the side of roads, in ditches, and on construction sites. It's also known as devil's bread or devil's porridge, as well as poison parsley or spotted corobane. It's a death-inducing toxin that creates a neuromuscular blockage that paralyzes respiratory muscles. Death occurs by respiratory failure. It's December, two months into my new job, and Ben is threatening to use it.

"But things aren't bad enough yet," I say. "You don't need it now."

"I need to do it before I can't move or breathe," he says.

The Hemlock Society is an online group that supports the terminally ill who don't want to wait for death. I can't imagine how they'd assist Ben. Would they send someone like Dr. Kevorkian? Would they mail the hemlock or expect me to root around construction sites to find it? What then? Do I dry and crush it, sprinkle it into his coffee?

Ben and I are in a good place now. He doesn't swear at me. I'm more attentive. It's like we've turned a corner and there'll be smooth marital sailing—until his epiglottis and lungs give out.

"Even if they find a cure tomorrow, it'll be too late for me. It'll take years before it's available. I'll still have to eat through a feeding tube. I'll still have to breathe through a machine. I'll never get my muscles back."

I'm sitting on the edge of Ben's newly purchased hospital cot, my hand covering his. Tears that he can't wipe run down his face.

"I'm not afraid of dying," he tells me. "I just don't want to be in pain."

Shortly after my Animal Alliance job began, Norma-Jeanne calls. I haven't spoken to her in years, not since she helped me train the research beagles. She tells me about a group of puppies born in the wild outside an Inuit village called Wapekeka, in Northern Ontario.

"They're at risk of being shot," she tells me.

"Shot! What on earth for?"

"It's called Dog Days."

"Dog Days?" It sounds like a late August retail sale.

"It's when locals drive around and shoot all the dogs not chained in people's yards. I don't know if they're asked by the municipality—it's their way of thinning the population."

"Who do the dogs belong to?"

"No one. There's not much spaying and neutering. So, there are lots of stray dogs. Starving puppies. Dogs that are skin and bones. They're looking for food in people's garbage. They're trying to stay warm under trailers."

"And they just shoot them? Are the dogs dangerous?"

"Look," says Norma-Jeanne. "I was contacted by a teacher who works up there. Nothing she told me says those dogs are dangerous. From what I can tell, it's the dogs who are getting abused. Kids are going up to puppies and kicking them or throwing them like basketballs. Adults are stealing the food she puts down for them." She pauses. "So, do you want one?"

The puppies are only three weeks old. They'll be flown down from Wapekeka in a Bearskin Airlines metroliner with their mother, a silver-and-black husky. They'll land at the Thunder Bay International Airport, and from there they'll be driven in a transport truck to Norma-Jeanne's house.

When I enter Norma-Jeanne's living room a few days later, one of the puppies barks a hello. He has a black circle around one eye, a white double coat of fur with long and short strands, and black-and-toffee patches. It's as if he knew me. I name him Karma.

Our new puppy keeps Ben occupied. Karma teaches him how to hand out doggie treats after saying the words *sit* and *stay*. Ben is getting pretty good at it. Karma is Harvard material. With Karma watching Ben, I can shut myself in my office and familiarize myself with the seal hunt—not only of today but of past years. I read about Brian Davies's IFAW 1980s boycott, which Stephen and other Animal Alliance board members participated in. The effectiveness of that boycott forced Canada to ban what I'd thought was the entire seal hunt but learned was only the hunting of whitecoat seal pups.

In October, I drive from Guelph to Toronto to attend my first meeting with activists outside of AAC. In less than two hours, I'll glimpse firsthand the inner workings of a new anti-sealing campaign, right from its inception, and I'll meet some of the most influential anti-sealing activists of my generation. The agenda for this meeting has been set weeks earlier. We'll be discussing Stephen's strategy to end the commercial seal hunt with a boycott targeting Canadian seafood in the United States.

If our meeting is successful and the invited groups form a coalition, we may be able to end the hunt in little more than two years. We'll also be inaugurating something incredibly rare in the animal protection movement: organizations laying aside their differences. Animal protection organizations can be fiercely independent and proprietary. People who defend the status quo tend to live in worlds of certainty, but reformers and visionaries are forever questioning themselves—their views, their goals, their values, their motives, their strategies, and anything else there is to question. Even small "philosophical" differences can loom large. Forming a coalition means that each group would have to give up some of their autonomy and perhaps even compromise some of their beliefs. Would they?

As I drive east along Highway 401, "Revolution" by the Beatles plays on the radio and I belt it out, tapping my fingers on the steering wheel. I follow the signs past the Lake Shore, heading toward the hideous, slapdash towers slandering the skyline and the warm, friendly CN Tower, its spire pointing at heaven.

Half an hour later, I drive into the Sutton Place Hotel's parking lot. I look at my watch. Yikes—10:15! I'm fifteen minutes late. I hurry across the lobby's Persian carpets and marble tiles and throw myself between the closing doors of the elevator. Once inside, I comb my fingers through my hair, tug the tail of my shirt under the waistband of my skirt, and reapply lipstick. Before the door fully opens, I'm racing down the hallway.

Liz stands in the conference room doorway. She flashes me a warm smile and leads me toward a cluster of people. A man with a jubilee of silver hair holds out his hand. Liz introduces him as the vice president of wildlife at the HSUS.

"I understand you're going to help us put this hunt to rest once and for all," he drawls.

"I hope so," I say enthusiastically. "I've wanted to help the seals for years."

"Good. Everyone in this room feels the same way. It's going to take a lot of passion to end this hunt."

"The vice president thinks there's a chance of ending it quickly," says a woman standing beside him. "But I'm not so sure. Whatever we decide today, I believe it's going to be a long haul." The woman introduces herself as the director of the HSUS's Protect Seals campaign.

"She is the pragmatist among us," the vice president says.

We're about to fall into silence when a woman with waist-length brown hair enters our circle and extends her hand.

"Hi. I'm Rebecca."

I freeze. It's her! The one I've seen in the videos of the seal hunt. A picture of her standing on a thick pan of sea ice in an orange survival suit flashes across my mind. I'm standing with Rebecca Aldworth, the face of the twenty-first-century anti-sealing movement. Wow! I'm about to gush when the Dop catches me.

Will you please just shake her damn hand!

I do so. "I've read all about you. You're in almost every article about the seal hunt. It's an honour to meet you."

Out of the corner of my eye, I see the vice president and the director recede into the background like some special movie-camera trick. Rebecca and I are alone.

"Is this your first time working on the seal hunt?" she asks, backhanding a lock of hair off her shoulders.

"It's my first time on any campaign. I used to work in advertising." I throw out the names of some high-profile advertising agencies I've worked for, hoping to impress her. I see they mean nothing. "I used to dream of spraying green paint all over the baby seals when I was younger."

"The seal hunt has been a big part of my life too. I'm originally from Newfoundland, where 90 percent of the sealers live."

I want to let her know that I know. But the fact is I didn't know until three seconds ago. I feel undeserving, speaking with her. What can I offer? Nikon advertisements? Breast pump directions? I'm trying so hard to hide my ignorance that it takes me a few seconds to realize I'm not listening to her. I refocus.

"And I grew up in a small fishing community, and my family knew sealers. I even ate seal meat when I was very young."

"How did you get into it?"

"One day, I saw a TV broadcast of the seal hunt. It was the first time I had ever seen a live seal, let alone one being killed. Back then, it was a hunt for whitecoat baby seals, and the images were horrific. It changed me forever. Next March, it will be my eighth year bearing witness."

Just then, Liz calls the meeting to order. I find a seat beside a dark-haired woman representing the Fur Free Alliance, an umbrella organization for groups that oppose killing animals for fur. There's also a representative from People for the Ethical Treatment of Animals (PETA) and one from Born Free. I glance around the table and wonder if this is how activists normally look. These people could be attending a marketing convention rather than a meeting of animal rights activists.

The only group missing from the table is IFAW. Stephen has spoken to a colleague there, Dr. David Lavigne, a zoologist and science advisor for the organization, and gotten the lowdown. "They're focusing on getting a European Union—wide ban on the import of seal products," Stephen tells us. "They think they can get politicians there on board. We, however, must change the political realities in Canada so they favour seals rather than sealers. To do that, we must go beyond lobbying the government.

"The Canadian Seafood Boycott is a consumer, retailer, and industry-wide boycott of Canadian seafood products to end the commercial seal hunt in totality. The beauty of it is that every consumer can participate. We're not asking them to give up all seafood, just Canadian seafood. But a boycott won't be effective if we just launch in Canada. The Canadian domestic market is not large enough, even if chefs and grocery stores buy into the boycott—and we don't know how many will. We will not have the political clout, because seafood companies can still sell into the United States and Europe. The United States is Canada's largest trading partner."

Stephen looks down at the page of notes in front of him. "Last year, Canada exported two-thirds of its total fish and seafood exports to the US at a value of 3.3 billion Canadian dollars. And Canada's fish and seafood exports to the European Union recorded the highest growth rate among the major markets, increasing by 21 percent to 440 million dollars in 2003.[1] For the boycott to be successful, it must also launch in the United States and Europe. Animal Alliance is a small organization. We don't have the resources to be as effective in the United States and Europe as some of the larger US and European groups." Stephen leans back in his chair. I haven't seen him take a breath through his entire speech. I expect any minute he will burst.

"What about those who'll say a boycott is too radical, too extremist?" the HSUS vice president of wildlife asks.

"That's what they said when Brian Davies launched the first Canadian Seafood Boycott in the United Kingdom," says Liz.

"We tell them we've tried for over thirty years, ever since the ban on whitecoats, to negotiate an end to the seal hunt," Stephen replies. "If those critical of a boycott have a better idea, let's hear it. Until then, our strategy is a consumer and food industry Canadian Seafood Boycott."

"Keep in mind—we may not need the boycott," Liz adds. "We may only need its threat. If the government wants to avert the boycott, let them end the seal hunt."

"That would be the wise thing to do," the HSUS vice president says.

"How likely is that?" the director of the Protect Seals campaign asks.

Liz and Stephen look at each other. "Not likely. But there's always hope," Liz says.

"But it's a threat we must be prepared to carry through," says Stephen. "So we hope that the HSUS and their international partners will join us. But before you decide," he says, turning his head toward the HSUS vice president, "I see Liz giving me the 'look.' So I suggest we hold off any decisions for the moment, and let's get something to eat."

When we've returned to our seats after lunch, the vice president of wildlife pushes back his chair, stands, and addresses the entire room. "On behalf of the Humane Society of the United States, it will be our pleasure to spearhead the boycott campaign in the US. Of course, I'll need to get approval from the top, but I don't anticipate there being a problem."

A collective sigh releases from around the table. It's agreed Liz and Stephen will write to Geoff Regan, the minister of fisheries and oceans, asking for a meeting to avert the boycott. Should their efforts fail, Animal Alliance, the HSUS, and any other partners we can muster will spring into action. The Canadian Seafood Boycott will start on the day that the first seal is killed, sometime in late March or early April of 2005.

The HSUS will utilize their staff and resources. They'll reach out to their members to organize protests in front of major seafood-buying establishments—such as Red Lobster, the largest purchaser of Canadian snow crab—and Publix and Safeway supermarkets. Stephen will design a form that volunteers can hand out to restaurant owners and chefs to sign, pledging not to buy Canadian seafood. I will run the boycott campaign in Canada while coordinating my efforts with the HSUS's Protect Seals campaign. I'll also be the point person for all contact with the public; I'll be training volunteers, reaching out to animal protection groups globally to get them to sign on to our campaign, and maintaining the Canadian Seafood Boycott website. I'll write articles, respond to emails, and—most importantly—sign on chefs.

Half an hour later, the meeting ends. As I put on my coat, I take a last glance at Rebecca. We exchange smiles. I wonder if she knows how Silly Putty-ish I feel next to her. I wonder if she knows my dream is coming true. I'm now part of an anti-sealing campaign that will change the world forever, at least for seals and, of course, sealers. I've finally found my purpose. *Bon voyage, old life.*

As I drive back to Guelph, I play a Joan Baez CD of her promising we'll prevail. I sing along, confident that one day we will overcome the seal hunt. But as I turn off the major highway into a four-laner a few miles from home, my stomach collides with my lower intestine. The closer I get to Guelph and Ben, the less confident I am about overcoming anything.

The next day, as promised, Stephen and Liz draft a letter to the Honourable Minister of Fisheries Geoff Regan, requesting a meeting to discuss calling off the commercial seal hunt to avoid a Canadian Seafood Boycott. I await word with the same electric anticipation I had as a child waiting for my birthday.

At AAC, we're all hopeful the minister's office will respond quickly. But as days go by, my teeth tear my nails to nubs. Each morning, I rush to my computer to check my emails. Each night, I sit in bed, whittling my cuticles.

20

WE WILL NOT GO AWAY

"OF COURSE THEY ought to meet with us," Liz says during an evening conference call with Animal Alliance board members.

"But what if they don't?" a board member, formerly with IFAW, asks.

"It's been two weeks," another says.

I sit with my elbows on my desk, windmilling a pen, my right knee thrumming uncontrollably. The commercial seal hunt is just five months away. If we're going to meet with the minister, it must be done quickly.

"The minister might not want to be seen bending to our demands," says the first board member.

"Maybe he hopes we'll tire of waiting and go away," says another.

"We will *not* go away," says Liz. "If I haven't heard from the minister by end of day tomorrow, I'll call him."

* * *

Catarina looks after Ben, Karma, and the kitties while I commute to the Animal Alliance office to listen in on Liz's conversation with the fisheries minister.

The Animal Alliance office is about as visually appealing as uncooked tofu. A small room with black metal shelves contains videos and books. A larger room has floor-to-ceiling shelves with boxes of sign-on letters, direct-mail appeals, buttons, tote bags, and thank-you cards. A troop of metal desks guards the perimeter. On the walls are posters of the spring bear hunt, the cormorant culls on Pelee Island, and a seal pup adrift on a thin raft of ice.

Every so often, I glance over to Liz, who is working on a white paper for the Canadian Food Inspection Agency outlining inadequate animal transport regulations. Occasionally, I catch her leaning back in her chair, staring at the phone, and pinching her lips. The small office staff and I wait for her to pick up the phone. A few minutes after ten o'clock, she does.

"It's now or never," she says before dialing the minister's office and turning on the speakerphone so we can listen. "Geoff Regan's office, please."

After a few minutes, a woman claiming to be his assistant comes on. I lean closer, wanting to capture every word.

"I'm Liz White from Animal Alliance of Canada. I'm calling to see if the minister's received the letter we sent him over two weeks ago." Her voice is as steely as the girders supporting the CN Tower.

"I passed it on to him."

"Has he read it?"

"I don't know."

"Does he know we want to set up a meeting?"

"I'm not sure what his intentions are. You'll have to speak to him."

Liz clenches her jaw. I hope she doesn't break teeth; our dental plan doesn't cover cosmetic surgery. "Okay, let me speak to him."

"He's in a meeting."

Liz looks like she could spit. "Have him call me when he gets out of his meeting."

A few days later, there's still no word from the fisheries and oceans minister. Liz calls again.

"I'm not sure the minister understands," Liz says to the assistant. "Ignoring us will not make the boycott go away."

"I'll tell the minister your concerns. That's all I can do."

"These are not just my concerns, or Animal Alliance's concerns. These are the minister's concerns, or at least they should be," Liz says.

"All I can do is tell him."

"You tell him this: the boycott will begin on the day that the first seal is killed. The minister can meet with us in the quiet of his office or he can meet with thousands of angry fishermen on the docks. Ultimately, it's his decision." Liz slams the phone onto its cradle.

"How did it go?" Catarina asks after I toss my backpack on the floor and my body onto the sofa.

"Liz was amazing."

"What did the minister say?"

"She couldn't get the minister on the phone, just his assistant."

"That's disappointing. Here it's been quiet. I've just been reading. Karma's been walked. I helped Ben into bed."

I throw my arms around her. "Thank you so much for doing this." I suggest she sleep over—it's too late to drive home. She, unlike me, has a husband she wants to get home to.

In the morning, I turn on my computer and see an email from Liz. She received an early morning call from the office of David Bevan, the assistant deputy fisheries and aquaculture minister, saying he would meet with us. My first thought: *Damn! I wish I had been there.*

When I call into the office, Liz tells me, "I'd like you to come to Ottawa. It'll be a good experience. You'll get to see Canadian politics in action."

I run squealing into the living room, where Ben is watching TV.

"Jesus Christ!" Ben scowls. "I can't hear the TV."

I jump up and down, unable to contain myself. "The deputy minister's going to meet with us. Liz wants me to go to Ottawa with her and Stephen. Rebecca Aldworth will also be there!"

"Can't Liz and Stephen do without you?"

"I want to go."

"But you don't need to go."

"I'm going."

"Catarina is away! Who's going to look after me? I can't even get a goddamn cup of coffee for myself. And who's going to take care of Karma and the kitties? I sure as hell can't."

"Hospice sends volunteers. And there's a companion animal–sitting service I can call."

"I don't need hospice."

"You have a terminal illness. We need all the help we can get."

Selfish, selfish, selfish, the Dop says out of nowhere as I walk down the hall to the phone. *How can you think of yourself when your husband needs you?*

I didn't sign up for this. I don't want to be somebody's caretaker. I'm not even good at it, I reply.

Poor you, Doppelgänger says.

Yes, poor me. What about my life?

The Dop doesn't respond. Her silence speaks volumes.

"Screw it," I say aloud. I grab the phonebook. "It's only going to be for one night."

21

GETTING TO "NO"

CANADA'S COMMERCIAL SEAL hunt is not orchestrated from
near a cozy harbour tucked into a quaintly named cove among towering
cliffs and rainbow-coloured houses. Its centre is in Ottawa, a city that
speaks of urgency and politics and slick propaganda. Steel-and-glass office
buildings dominate the skyline and tower over narrow sidewalks. Bleary-
eyed pedestrians carrying their takeout drinks rush into the buildings
while homeless men smoke in front of coffee shops and minimarts. The
Department of Fisheries and Oceans at 200 Kent Street's Centennial
Towers is where the government determines all things sealing: the dates
when the seal hunt opens and closes, the regions where it takes place, and
the Total Allowable Catch of seals.

In the lobby, a middle-aged woman in a tired business suit ushers Liz,
Stephen, Rebecca, and me past small partitioned offices, with file folders
stacked on unkempt desks, photos of smiling children, and plaques of
inspirational quotes such as *Every day may not be a good day, but there's good in
every day* leaning against pencil holders.

As we wait for the deputy minister in the conference room, Liz pulls
out a bundle of handouts from her knapsack and creates two stacks. One
contains the photocopied advertisements Stephen has mocked up to
announce the start of the boycott, ready to be published in newspapers
should the seal hunt commence. The other contains thick stapled copies
of Stephen's Canadian Seafood Boycott strategy. Is it my imagination or

does the air tingle with the possibility of being a defining moment in the long and tangled history of the anti-seal hunt movement?

At last, the assistant deputy minister (ADM) arrives. David Bevan's tennis-star looks surprise me, as does the lock of blond hair (so nongovernmental) sweeping his forehead. His pressed navy suit (so Brooks Brothers) is what someone would have on if they wanted their boss's job, as is the leather-bound binder tucked under his arm. He is followed by three bureaucrats: the first in a grey, finely pinstriped suit; the next in plain grey; and the next a good ol' boy I might have a drink with if I enjoyed sitting at a bar and talking about baseball. The ADM positions himself at the head of the long conference table, opposite Stephen. Alpha vs. Alpha.

"What can we do for you?" he asks.

Stephen leans forward, his arms braced against the table. "I hope the minister didn't ask you to sit in on this meeting without briefing you on why we're here."

The ADM looks with distaste at Stephen. "We know why you're here. You're planning to launch a seafood boycott aimed at Canadian fishermen."

"Unless the minister calls off the commercial seal hunt," Liz says.

Pinstripe snorts.

Stephen takes aim. "After years of attempting to end the commercial seal hunt with rational, well-constructed, scientifically supported arguments, and after three decades of lobbying not only your party but every political party in Parliament, and after using every method of activism in our possession, we have come to the conclusion that there is nothing we can do that hasn't already been tried, short of implementing a seafood boycott that will target those responsible for killing seals: the minister of fisheries and oceans, and his party most especially."

Liz passes around copies of Stephen's boycott strategy, flashing her disarmingly warm smile. "I mailed copies of these. But in case you didn't see them."

The ADM eyes the copy, then pushes it aside. "We've each seen a copy."

"We feel it's only prudent and fair to inform you, should the seal hunt begin this year, that we *will* launch a boycott of Canadian seafood in the United States with our American and Canadian animal protection partners," Liz says.

The ADM slides his copy in front of him again and scans the first page. His bureaucrats follow his lead, flipping through their copies.

"We've come here as a courtesy call, out of respect for your minister," Liz says. "Whatever happens here and however you feel about the seal hunt personally, we believe the minister ought to be concerned what a boycott will do to his party and his own political future."

"So how can we help you?" the ADM asks again.

"It's really how we can help you," Stephen counters. "The boycott will affect the people who are most financially vulnerable—fishermen in some of the most economically deficient regions of the East Coast. But it will also have an electoral impact on this ministry, and on your boss and his party."

Grey Suit rolls his eyes. Good Ol' Boy and Pinstripe whisper. Watching them, I get a momentary flashback to high school. I shake my head to clear the depressing memories and focus on Stephen. His face is turning a flag of colours. Liz takes over.

"What will it take to end the seal hunt?" she asks.

"The minister has no intention of ending the seal hunt," the ADM says, casually reclining and hanging his arm off the back of his chair. "The seal hunt is vital to the economy of some of the poorest regions in Canada. The minister has no intention of taking it away from those who need it."

I look around the room. All forty-two muscles on Stephen's face clench. Grey Suit and Pinstripe smirk as Rebecca and Liz watch.

"The seal hunt is an economic boondoggle," Stephen says. "There's no economic or political advantage in maintaining the seal hunt once the boycott begins."

"You'll be hurting people who are already living hand-to-mouth. They'll not be able to withstand a boycott," says Rebecca. "I'm from there and I know what it's like. You're putting these people in jeopardy. We hoped for more from our government. We hoped the minister would protect our fishermen. Telling them they must rely on a seal hunt that brings them only a few hundred dollars each is irresponsible."

"It's not going to happen," the ADM says, folding his arms across his chest.

Rebecca shakes her head. "So you're prepared to put the people who can least afford it through a boycott to justify your political position?"

"This is not about politics. It's about economics." The ADM turns to Good Ol' Boy. "How many licenced sealers do we have?"

"Sixteen thousand," Good Ol' Boy says.

"Ask our sixteen thousand sealers," the ADM suggests. "See what they have to say about ending the seal hunt."

"How many of those sixteen thousand licence holders go sealing? They may hold sealing licences, but they don't use them. I'm out there every year and you can't tell me there are sixteen thousand fishermen out there sealing," Rebecca says.

"We don't count how many use their licences," Good Ol' Boy says.

"In the thirty-five years I've been fighting to end the hunt," Stephen says, "never has the hunt ended poverty. One could argue it's what's keeping East Coast fishermen *in* poverty. Yet every year, your department tells sealers the only thing standing between them and poverty is the commercial seal hunt."

"The seals are eating all the fish. You don't think that cuts into their income?" Grey Suit says.

"You know as well as I do that you have absolutely no evidence to prove that," Rebecca says.

"We have fishermen who are telling us this all the time. They're the ones out there. They see it with their own eyes. Seals are ripping the stomachs out of cod. All our ground fisheries are in trouble," Pinstripe says. "There are six million seals out there. Each one of them eats a ton of fish."

"Our groundfish are never going to recover if we don't cull the seals." Good Ol' Boy shakes his head at the uphill battle he faces.

"The DFO's own scientists don't even believe that," Rebecca counters.

I have been reading about cod and seals. Cod represents only about three percent of a harp seal's diet. Harp seals are opportunistic feeders, which means they eat a wide variety of sea life depending upon the season, including herring, capelin, sculpin, shrimp, prawn, and even krill. They also eat squid, the predator of cod, which would help the cod recover if the fishermen didn't trawl up everything in the ocean.

"Canada has one of the worst records of fisheries management in the Western world," Stephen says. "You know as well as we do that it's fisheries mismanagement and overfishing that caused the cod crash. There's no evidence seals are responsible for any of it." I know that the DFO's own scientists also back up Stephen's claim, having just read an article by them on this very issue.[1-3]

Stephen pushes back his chair and stands. "We are done talking. The day that the first seal pup is slaughtered, the Canadian Seafood Boycott will begin."

Liz slides Stephen's advertisements to the middle of the table, then turns toward the ADM. "You ought to think about the consequences to those poor fishermen and their families. You ought to consider whether holding on to a twelve-million-dollar sealing industry is worth losing a part of a three-billion-dollar seafood industry."

The bureaucrats push back their chairs, reach into their pockets for business cards, and scatter them around the conference table.

"We'll be in touch," the ADM says.

Outside, Liz throws up her hands. "How do you work with a government you can't talk to in a rational way, with no rational basis for their decisions?"

"You can't," Stephen says. "We're dealing with people who are incapable of listening and incapable of making rational decisions."

22

GIRL DETECTIVE

Ned said: "Nancy Drew is the best girl detective in the whole world!"

"Don't you believe him," Nancy said quickly. "I have solved some mysteries, I'll admit, and I enjoy it, but I'm sure there are many other girls who could do the same."—**Carolyn Keene**, *Nancy's Mysterious Letter*

THE NEXT MORNING, as I sit in my office sipping coffee, I reflect on the fact that the seal hunt is getting more complex, the more I learn. How can I make sense of it all? Each time I think I know something, more questions arise. I learned yesterday there were sixteen thousand sealers. But Rebecca challenged that number. She said there *might* be sixteen thousand fishermen who held sealing licences, but not all of them sealed. "How many licence holders *do* seal each year?" she asked. Good Ol' Boy responded he didn't know; they didn't count them.

Odd, I thought. If the seal hunt is such an important part of the economy, wouldn't everyone who held a licence use it? And if not, why? And wouldn't the DFO know about it? What would Nancy Drew do with this amalgam of contradictory and incomplete information? After a few more sips of coffee and a washroom break, the answer comes to me: she would make a list of her questions and figure out how to answer them.

I open my new spiral notebook and begin writing: *First question: Who are the men and women of the seal hunt?* I want to think of them as real human beings with good and bad qualities, like Ben and me, and not the barbarians some people make them out to be. Who are they off the ice? I tap my pen on my bottom lip in reflection. Do they love dogs? Do they teach their children how to ride bikes and fish, like my dad taught me? How can I know anything about them?

Liz sends me books. One of them is *Animal Rights, Human Rights: Ecology, Economy, and Ideology in the Canadian Arctic*, written in 1991 by George Wenzel.[1] Wenzel spent time with the Inuit in Clyde River researching his book. That alone makes it worth reading. In it, I learn that the Inuit primarily hunt adult ringed seals, bearded seals, and harbour seals, not harp seals, unless they swim into the area. Harp seal babies are not taken at all because they are born in ice caves and are harder to reach. The Inuit hunt throughout the year, unlike commercial seal hunters, who begin hunting in late March or early April and end mid-June. When I'm not reading, I force myself to watch videos.

"What's it like to visit the nursery?" I ask Stephen days later on the phone.

"The experience is humbling," he says.

"Why were you there?"

"In '73, I shot a documentary about baby harp seals and the harp seal hunt."

"Where?"

"On an ice floe in the Gulf of St. Lawrence."

"Wow! It must have been awesome to see the babies."

"It was. Imagine this: a moonless night, darkness all around, not another human in sight. Millions of anxious whitecoats, invisible in the dark, calling for their mothers: *Maa? Maa?* A mother seal can pick out her baby just from the sound of his voice or his scent. You can hear them hauling themselves out of the leads. Then you hear silence, as they begin to nurse their babies."[2]

"Spectacular. What I wouldn't give to see that."

"At first light, on the horizon, I could see the *Lady Johnson* and the ship's men skiffing out to the floe, scrambling over the pressure ridges, and jumping over the leads as they rushed from pup to pup, clubbing and skinning them in front of their mothers."

"Ugh!" I gasp.

"That's the job. The key shot for a baby-seal hunt documentary is the close-up of a sealer clubbing a baby to death and skinning it, preferably while the pup continues to writhe. It's the close-up that evokes emotion: the viewer feels inside the scene, involved in the action. To get the shot, the cameraman must be inside it too, involved in the action."

"How inside? How involved?"

"If you can't reach out and lay hands on your subject, you're too far away."

"You were that close?"

"I laid my hand on the baby seal and then filmed her slaughter. The shot earned me a best director award for a public service commercial."

23

POWER MUST BE TAKEN

IN 2005, THE government sets a sealing quota of 335,000 to accommodate the high demand for seal pelts.

"Too high," scientists warn. "Not sustainable."

But the real threat to seals is climate change. According to DFO marine biologist Garry Stenson, ocean temperatures off Newfoundland are rising, and in March the ice is already starting to melt. Without solid sea ice, which must be 30–70 cm thick and covering 60–90 percent of the water, newborns will drown or be crushed by chunks of pack ice. Such conditions can eliminate an entire cohort of seal pups.[1]

* * *

On February 19, 2005, Animal Alliance of Canada receives a letter from Geoff Regan, the minister of fisheries and oceans. "The Canadian Seafood Boycott will do nothing to end the seal hunt and will only serve to add to the level of unemployment in an area already suffering enormously from economic hardship," he writes. Despite his acknowledgment of the hardships a boycott will bring, his message is clear. The government will not negotiate an end to the seal hunt.

Liz dashes off emails to the HSUS vice president of wildlife and the director of the HSUS's Protect Seals, Ingrid Newkirk of PETA, Barry Kent MacKay of Born Free, and Paul Watson of the Sea Shepherd

Conservation Society. I send emails to my list of global groups to update them. Several of us remain hopeful that Regan is bluffing, thinking he'll call the hunt off at the last minute. We wait and wait for him to say uncle. February turns to March; March 1 turns to March 15, and then to March 28. Acid eats the lining of my stomach. Could this be the beginning of an ulcer? Still, I hope the hunt will be cancelled.

Early morning March 29, 2005, an armada of snow crab, shrimp, and lobster boats leaves the docks of the Magdalen Islands in Québec and the harbours of Nova Scotia and Prince Edward Island. The boats head off to the nursery in the Gulf of St. Lawrence.

I wake before dawn and rush to my computer. The Animal News Canada List Serv has dropped an item in my inbox. I open it. And crumble.

As I prepare Ben's breakfast, I wonder who the one was to raise his hakapik and crash it down on the slightly moulting head of the season's first baby seal, triggering the most aggressive boycott of Canadian seafood since the 1980s.

Breathe, I tell myself as I pour oatmeal from a package into a bowl and stick it under the kitchen faucet, covering the flakes with water.

"I don't want too much water. You always make it too liquid-y," Ben calls from the eating table.

I turn off the faucet and pull the bowl from the sink. As I do so, I hit the edge on the faucet head. The bowl cracks, like a ship hitting an iceberg, into the sink. Wet oatmeal spills out, clogging the drain.

"See what happens when you don't pay attention!"

I lift a new bowl from the cupboard, tear open a new package of oat flakes, and carefully turn on the faucet. When there's just enough water covering the flakes, I set the microwave for two minutes. I lean against the counter, imagining the first hakapik spiking down on the first baby's head. When the timer buzzes, I jump.

Ben scowls when I put the bowl and spoon on the table in front of him. Just as I'm about to sit, the phone rings. I jump up and sprint into my office.

"Goddamn it, Karen!" Ben shouts after me.

I grab the phone.

"It's begun," Stephen tells me. "You know what to do."

When I return, Ben raises his eyebrows, "Who was that?"

"Stephen."

"Stephen! I can't even get breakfast around here without Stephen. . . ."

"Shut it, Ben."

"You shut it."

I grab the bowl from the table and slam it down on the counter, where he can't reach it. "When you want to be nice, I'll be nice."

"You fuckin' no-good bitch." Ben's eyes narrow, but through their slits I can see revenge peeking out. I get the bowl and put it back on the table.

"Eat and be quiet."

Five strides to my office and I plop into my swivel chair, anxious to make my first call. Then I stand. Nobody's going to listen. Nothing I can say will matter. I pace the short length of the office, back and forth. I'm not a salesperson. I don't even like talking on the phone. I sit back in my swivel chair and rub my arms. I can hear Ben swearing at me in the background. Ignoring it, I think about the kitschy plaque on the wall of my doctor's office. *Sometimes you find your wings on the way down.* It seems like good medicine now.

I dial the first number at the top of my list and wing it.

"*Hello. My name is Karen Levenson I'm with Animal Alliance of Canada. We have a campaign to end Canada's commercial seal hunt. Please support our boycott of Canadian seafood.*"

"Support what?" the voice asks.

"Our boycott. We are trying to end the seal hunt with a boycott of Canadian seafood."

"What's that got to do with me?"

I remember my sessions at the seafood case in Zehrs, where I mentally practiced my spiel to the fishmonger in the blood-smeared apron. "Canadian fishermen are the ones who are killing all the seals."

"So?"

"So we need you to stop buying seafood from Canadian fishermen."

"Can't do it."

"Why not?"

"I'm not the chef."

"Then who are you?"

"The day manager."

"The day manager! Well, can I speak to the chef?"

"Not here."

"When will he be . . . ?"

Click.

To my relief, my next call goes better. For starters, I make sure before starting that I'm speaking to the chef.

"Your what?" he asks when I mention the boycott.

"Our Canadian Seafood Boycott to help end the seal hunt."

"How does boycotting Canadian seafood help end the seal hunt?"

"Well. . . ." My palms become sweaty. I begin chewing on my cuticle. Dense fog fills the space behind my eyes where my brain should be.

You can do it, the Dop says.

I can't think!

You know what to say.

I don't.

And then I do. I tell him about the fishermen who seal, about the fishing boats they use for sealing, and about the seafood companies that also process seal pelts. I'm as polished as a tour guide at a maritime museum. But then . . . silence! I've given my best and now all I get back is silence, the loudest silence I've ever heard. Silence that needs to be broken.

"Helloooooo?"

"Yeah, I'm listening."

"Well, would you boycott Canadian seafood?"

"I only buy snow crabs."

"You can buy snow crabs from Chile or Russia or even Alaska."

"I'll need to tell my suppliers."

"All the chefs who've joined have done the same thing!" I fib. (It's only my second call, after all. I'm sure by my fifth, it'll be true.)

"Mmmph," he grunts.

"By doing this one small action, you can help save the lives of hundreds of thousands of baby seals. Think how great you'll feel knowing you've helped save two-week-old baby seals from Canadian fishermen who want to bash in their skulls. By pledging to not buy Canadian seafood, you can do something to stop it. All it takes is . . ."

"Okay, okay. Send me the pledge. I'll sign it."

Hallelujah!

"Why boycott the entire fishing industry?" my mother asks that night when I phone her. "What about all those fishermen who don't seal? Why hurt them?" I can hear her TV playing in the background.

"I'm not sure, Mom."

"How can you not be sure? It's your job!"

"Mom, I'll have to get back to you," I beg off the phone. The weight of all I don't know makes my shoulders stoop. If I can't even answer my mother's simple questions, how will I answer the chefs' more complex ones?

Rebecca would know. Should I call her? It's late Friday evening. No, I'd better not. She told me I could. But I'd be intruding. I should know the answer myself, but don't.

"What do you think, Karma?"

Karma, who has been lying at my feet the entire time, woofs.

"I think you're right. I should wait."

When I call mid-morning on Monday, Rebecca zips through her explanation. "The federal government has said that when the seafood industry asks it to end the seal hunt, they will." I scribble into a notebook, determined not to miss a word as Rebecca explains how the fishing and sealing industries are intertwined. "Although not all fishermen in Canada participate in the seal hunt, no part of Canada's fishing industry—not even the sustainable fisheries and aquaculture sectors—has taken a stand against it. In fact, Canada's seafood industry has remained solid in its support of the commercial seal hunt. Even in British Columbia, where sealing is banned, fishermen hate seals so much they'd love to bring it back. They're not going to sell out East Coast fishermen."

When I hang up the phone, I look at my scribbled notes. There are so many layers to the seal hunt, no wonder so few Canadians understand it.

24

SEEING RED

BACK IN EARLY March 2005, Stephen suggested our first target should be Red Lobster, America's number one seafood chain and the largest purchaser of Canadian seafood, especially Newfoundland snow crab.

"If Red Lobster stops buying Canadian seafood, the seal hunt will end," Stephen says.[1,2]

The vice president of wildlife from HSUS writes a letter to the president of Red Lobster, urging the chain to join the boycott. "Red Lobster can no longer support fishermen who kill seals," he says.

Several weeks later, the president responds: "We have no intention of joining the boycott."[3]

Another letter comes shortly thereafter from the CEO of Red Lobster's parent company, Darden: "We feel it is much better to negotiate with officials rather than [to] pursue some purchasing boycott that only ends up hurting tens of thousands of innocent people."

The vice president of wildlife writes back, asking for the specifics of Red Lobster's negotiations with Canadian officials, but his request goes unanswered.

On the weekend after I read an email about the latest Darden response, I sit in my chair, too depressed to swivel. Ben has been picked up by the mobility van to visit the mall. Alone, I can mope in peace. Shuffling to the living room, I turn on the TV and flop onto the sofa just as a Red Lobster commercial appears, offering all-you-can-eat shrimp.[4]

Suddenly, gastric content rises to the base of my throat, my glottis shuts tight, and my stomach spasms. I race to the washroom, kneel in front of the toilet, and dry-heave.

* * *

Ben no longer can transfer from his wheelchair to the toilet. He needs his toenails clipped, his beard trimmed, and his hair washed. What he truly needs is a chronic care facility. But when a health evaluator comes to assess him, she says Ben is too self-sufficient.

The next time Ben has an outburst, I'm sitting cross-legged on the sofa, working on my drawing of a seal pup and her mother from the book *Seal Song.* I've propped the book open on one knee, my sketchbook on the other.

"You can't even sit with me and watch the goddamn TV."

"I'm not your mother, Ben. Just because she didn't pay enough attention to you doesn't mean you have to take it out on me."

"Stop talking about my mother."

I lean my head back on the sofa and close my eyes. *We're going to find a way to get out of here,* I tell myself.

Did I hear you correctly? the Dop interrupts. *Did you say you're planning to leave Ben? Who will take care of him?*

That's his problem. I put my number-two pencil into the gully of my sketchbook and fold my arms across my chest, sulking.

People won't understand. They'll think you're terrible.

I don't care what people think!

Yes, you do.

Karma, lying beside me on the floor, licks my bare feet. He knows about the Dop. The kitties, cuddled on either side of me, know too.

"You're always doing something," Ben says.

"I'm spending time with you, watching TV, for God's sake."

"Then put the fucking drawing down and watch."

I shut my sketchpad, drop the pencil in its case, and head down the hall.

"Where're you going?"

"The bedroom."

"That's what you really want, isn't it? To get away."

I ignore him and keep walking down the hall. Ben follows, his electric wheelchair growling behind me.

I've had enough. I turn, guns blazing, when . . .

"Bloody hell!" I scream. Ben's footrests bang into my shins. Have Ben's lips turned up at the edges? I step back and pull up the legs of my sweatpants. Red welts but no broken skin. I step toward him. "Do that again and you'll be out of this house so fast it'll make your head spin." I limp down the hall and slam the bedroom door.

25

HAKAPIKS AND HEROES

April 2005

ON THE HORIZON, a snowmobile hurtles across the ice—so far away that it's as small as the pupil of a seal pup's eye. Sheryl Fink, a seasoned seal hunt observer, keeps an eye out for the snowmobile, while watching over her IFAW team of eyewitnesses and the photographers and television cameramen accompanying them. What interests the photographers and cameramen now is a sealer who is raising his hakapik over an inert seal pup ten metres away. Creeping forward as silently as their thermal boots will let them in ice-covered snow, the photographers and cameramen hope to capture another slaughter on film. They plant their tripods' spindly legs, mount their cameras, twist their super-telephoto lenses onto their cameras, and begin to shoot.

"Hey!" Sheryl shouts, hailing them back. When they return, she reminds them of the rule, outlined in the MMR, that states that observers must not come within ten metres of a sealer. It's a rule IFAW never breaks. She also reminds them of the danger of not remaining together with the team. Snow-covered breathing holes and cracks riddle the ice.

The distant snowmobile is less distant now. It rockets toward the observers, closer and closer, until it's the size of a seal pup's nose. Now it's only 150 metres away, and then 100. The hakapiking sealer steps over the now bloody and pulpy seal pup, and out of the corner of his eye he sees the photographers in front of IFAW's helicopter. He charges toward them. He raises his hakapik above his head and then swipes it like a machete.

The alarmed team have nowhere to run. It's too dangerous to disperse helter-skelter over the ice. All they can do is back up, trying to maintain the ten metres between them and the sealer. Aware of his advantage, the sealer deliberately lunges at, and deliberately misses, one of the activists by less than a metre.[1,2]

This is not the first time that sealers have assaulted activists. Sealers have punched, kicked, and struck witnesses with clubs. They have destroyed cameras and damaged helicopters. Sealing vessels have rammed inflatable dinghies and crippled propellers; fishermen have pelted activists with seal entrails and discarded carcasses. Sealing families have mobbed and threatened observers, holding them hostage in their hotels, and doing so all under the watchful gaze of the Royal Canadian Mounted Police.[3]

The snowmobile now speeds toward the witnesses like a motorized torpedo. In their bright orange survival suits, the observers are clear targets. At the last minute, the snowmobile veers sharply, nearly hitting the observers with the trailer swinging behind it, and careens past.

"It was scary," a photographer later recounts, for a moment happy that no one was killed. But his happiness evaporates like breath in the frosty air as he realizes that no one was killed except for the seals.

I'm not a witness to the assault. I read about it.[4] My fight is not on the ice. It's on the phone and in the streets—leading AAC's boycott, gathering support, and analyzing government documents. In my own way, I will bear witness.

Days after the IFAW attack, I sign for a thick mailing tube delivered by the postman. I slice the cellophane securing the tube's red plastic top with a box cutter, work off the lid, and tilt the tube. The tightly wound red banners and protest posters slide onto the living room floor.

"You're not going to leave those around the house, are you?" Ben asks. He's watching a Canadian TV talk show, though he seems more interested in what I'm doing.

"Don't worry." I pick up the posters and banners, rewind them back into the tube, and head to my office. Once there, I store the tube in a corner and then check my emails to see if anyone has responded to my

Protest Red Lobster action alerts. Hallelujah! Activists from Minnesota, Florida, California, Massachusetts, New York, Colorado, and Ohio want to host Red Lobster protests.

In Ontario, I help organize one in London, St. Catherine's, Ottawa, and Kitchener. In Toronto, Paul Watson attends my biggest protest yet at the downtown Red Lobster, looking just as he looks in all the photographs in all the books I've read: grey-haired, formidable, eyes as kind as the sun caressing a newborn seal. Next to him is a video monitor broadcasting footage of the last seal hunt, looping the video around and around for passersby to see what the hunt really looks like. Someone has brought a Sammy the Seal costume and I shimmy it over my clothes. But the front zipper catches and won't pull up. As the television cameras roll, I stand beside my hero, Paul Watson—the world-renowned cofounder of Greenpeace and founder of the Sea Shepherd Conservation Society— me tugging at the zipper as he speaks through a megaphone. In my unzipped Sammy the Seal costume, I nod at his every word. But all I keep thinking about is that if Paul ever wants to use this video, I've just ruined it.

You look like a plush seal who ate an animal activist, the Dop says. *Can't you do better than that?*

Shut up, I answer, tilting my head over at Paul. *Don't embarrass me.*

Once the cameramen are gone, I climb out of the suit and hand it over to a volunteer, who manages to climb into it and zip it up lickety-split. I hate her. And me. The one chance I have to be in a photo with Paul Watson, I make it look like Sammy's guts are spilling out as I stand beside him.

I need to do something to shake the thought out of my noggin, so I grab a megaphone and blast "Don't buy while seals die," and begin parading along Dundas Street.

After I've walked up and down the sidewalk and built up a sweat, two women weaving through the sign-wielding protesters stop at Red Lobster's front entrance.

"What's going on here?" one asks.

"Red Lobster buys Canadian seafood!" I pant, unobtrusively wiping sweat off my forehead and smelling under my armpits.

"So?"

"We're boycotting restaurants that sell Canadian seafood."

"Why?"

"Because Canadian fishermen kill seals just two weeks to three months old."

The women hesitate in the doorway, looking at each other and communicating silently. For a moment, I believe my words will guide them away from the restaurant like a gentle hand on the shoulder. But one of them pushes the door open and my heart sinks.

Well, that was successful, the Dop says. *Good on you!*

Never mind. I walk a short distance up College Street, close to the Eaton Centre, and begin to hand out flyers, offering one to each person who passes by. A young Mary Tyler Moore look-alike plants herself in front of me and grabs a flier.

"What's wrong with Red Lobster?"

"Red Lobster buys seafood from sealers," I explain.

"I care more about people than I do about *animals,*" she says, thrusting the flier back at me.

"I care about people, too," I say, trying to engage her, but she flounces off to the Eaton Centre and my words ("I just don't want them killing baby seals") trail off as she quicksteps away.

"I'll take one," says a guy in a red hoodie reaching for a flier. As I start to explain our campaign, he says, "I know. No Canadian seafood!" And just like that, he walks off toward Yonge Street.

Next, a middle-aged woman with an armful of shopping bags heads my way. Her tussled hair and red cheeks make her look like she's just run a marathon.

"Thank you so much for what you're doing. I had no idea Red Lobster killed seals," she says, out of breath.

"Red Lobster doesn't kill seals, but they do buy seafood from fishermen who do," I explain.

"I ate there last week. I wish I'd known," she sighs. "It's just awful what those fishermen do." She drops one of her shopping bags and reaches for my hand. "Thank you," she says. "I appreciate what you're doing. Believe me, I'll never eat there again!" She glares at the Red Lobster, and I glare, too. A moment later, she picks up her shopping bag and heads for the subway.

As dusk settles in, activists, tired of promenading in front of Red Lobster, begin to wane. When the streetlights turn on, I sit on the concrete planters in front of the restaurant and chat with the volunteers. Across the street is a convenience store, and I race for much-needed drinks of pop for those remaining. When I return, a reporter asks me for a statement. As I'm formulating my words, I see out of the corner of my eye, illuminated in the streetlight, Emily Hunter, the daughter of Greenpeace cofounder Bob Hunter, the other man on the ice with Paul Watson in the Greenpeace poster I saw outside my math professor's office in university.

I turn to her. "You should be the one speaking. Your father and Paul are the reasons I'm out here." I turn to ask the reporter if he'll interview Emily, but when I turn back, she's gone.

* * *

On Friday, April 8, 2005, the *Chronicle Herald* writes, "More than 100,000 people have already pledged to boycott Canadian seafood." A photograph of a sealer dragging a bloody seal pup to his snowmobile runs alongside a photograph of nude PETA volunteers demonstrating outside the Canadian Embassy in DC.

26

DIDN'T THE SEAL HUNT END?

WHO WOULD HAVE thought that on the hottest day in June, our air conditioner would be on the fritz and our heater would be huffing out hot air like a fire-breathing dragon? Karma is sprawled out on the laminate, melting under his felted fur like a bowl of Jell-O in the oven. Sweat is dripping into my eyes and gathering in the creases of my neck. Sitting on the sofa, I watch balls of husky-malamute fur dance across our floor.

Ben is at his anger management class, enjoying air conditioning, group meditation, and coffee on demand. If he were sweating it out with us, all hell would have broken loose hours ago. Heat is one of the ingredients in his stewpot of rage. I'm the other. Given that Ben is not home, Karma and I head outside to sit on the grass near the parking lot. Both of us try to capture an infinitesimal current of air. I can't tell the time by the position of the sun, but I can by the position of my neighbour's car. Wendy's parking spot is empty, but we can hear the tires of her Toyota gnashing up parking lot grit as she sloppily backs it up between the yellow lines. Karma, his ears like radio antennae, opens his eyes halfway and with great effort raises his head. When he sees it's only Wendy and not someone who's likely to bring him treats, he drops his head back perfectly into position between his paws.

Karma and I watch Wendy pull two shopping bags of groceries out from the back of her car. Karma's nose is like a radar measuring Wendy's echo time as she walks toward us. Wendy works in telemarketing in Kitchener, half an hour away. She and her husband Albert live several doors down from us. They're friendly and talkative, though we hardly ever see them.

Wendy plops down on the grass beside us, not minding that one of her grocery bags is spilling its contents. She pulls out a grocery flyer and fans herself.

"How's work?" she asks. "Are you still doing that stuff with animals?"

I tell her I'm working on a campaign to end the seal hunt.

"Really! Didn't the seal hunt end already?"

"You mean for this year?"

"No. I thought they weren't doing *it* anymore."

"If you mean Canadian fishermen, they're still doing *it*."

I find it odd she doesn't know. Americans I can forgive. Me being a former one, the amount of information about other countries I learned in school could fit into the puncture wound of a mosquito bite. But Wendy is Canadian. She should know. And then I wonder how many other Canadians don't know the seal hunt is still going on. Many? Most? If they don't know, how can we stop it?

"Hmmm!" she says thoughtfully. "I thought I heard something about it. . . ."

"The only thing that has stopped is the killing of whitecoats."

Just then, I notice Karma's nose sniffing the air in the direction of Wendy's grocery bags, and particularly the bag with a package of fish poking out.

"Is that fish from Canada?" I ask, pointing to the offender. She pulls it out and looks at the sticker on the cellophane front, then turns it over.

"I don't know. Probably," she replies. "Why?"

"Canadian fishermen from the East Coast are the ones who kill the seal pups for their fur. Most likely they're the ones who caught that fish."

"That's horrible," she says.

I nod in agreement.

"That is *so* horrible!" she says, punctuating her tone with exclamation marks.

I nod again. "If you want to end the seal hunt, don't buy Canadian seafood."

"How can you tell if it's Canadian?"

"Ask the fishmonger behind the seafood counter," I suggest. "If they don't know where it comes from, don't buy it."

"Albert and I love seafood," she says, closing her eyes and smacking her lips. "It tastes soooo good."

My eyes bulge. What are the words I can use to convince her that saving seals is more important than savouring seafood? How much can I push before I cross the line, before she becomes defensive and tunes me out? These are the things I'm wondering as Wendy gets up from the grass, reassembles the fish package in its grocery bag, and reports that she has to get dinner started. Karma and I watch her carry her groceries inside, each of us for different reasons.

By June, out of a TAC of 319,500 individuals, 329,829 have been killed.

The heat continues into August. While Guelph evaporates, Florida and Louisiana are deluged with Category 5 destruction. Hurricane Katrina fills the news; links to the catastrophe fill my inbox. Millions of Americans evacuate.

I call my mother, frantic. "Are you guys okay?"

"Don't worry. The storm's missed us," my mother reassures me.

Relief is a dish gobbled quickly, but I can't get the storm out of my mind. People are not allowed to flee with their animals, and because there are no evacuation plans for nonhuman animals or laws to protect them, over 600,000 animals are killed or stranded. I hug Karma and my kitties close.

27

A Tale of Two Polls

"HAVE YOU READ about the government poll?" a colleague asks over the phone in late September.

"About Katrina?"

"No! The seal hunt! I'll send it to you."

I click on the link she sends me.

"What the hell?" My eyeballs spring out of their sockets. There's no way Canadians support the seal hunt! Not most, at least. Activists have been claiming for years that only a small minority of Canadians favoured it and as many as two-thirds opposed it. Have they been wrong?

In less than a minute, I find "Public Views on Commercial Hunting and Current Federal Seal Hunting Policy," the Ipsos Reid polling report on the DFO's website. I quickly print it out, staple it together, then sit back in my chair and begin to read.

"Hmm!" I say, allowing my eyes to travel down the highway of each sentence. "Hmmm!" I say again. I take out a yellow highlighter and tap it on the report, scanning the first page.

"Love, can I get more coffee?"

Dammit! I lay the report on my desk and place the highlighter against it. "Not now, Ben," I reply under my breath. Just as I'm about to vent my annoyance, I remember that our marriage is momentarily sailing on a calm sea. One ill-spoken word from me could bring a storm crashing down.

"Thanks, love," Ben says, pulling his wheelchair up to the table. He watches me fill a new mug of coffee on the table in front of him. I pull up a chair and together we wait in awkward silence for the Arabica to cool.

"How's your work coming?" he asks tentatively.

"Okay."

"What are you working on?"

"It's okay. You don't have to pretend you're interested."

"No, I am."

"Well, if you really want to know, a new government poll just came out showing 60 percent of Canadians approve of the seal hunt."

"What? That's crazy!"

"I know, right? But the big question is how the government got 60 percent of the respondents to say they support it. It just doesn't make sense. There must be some trick!"

Ben looks anxiously over at the coffee mug.

I stick a finger into the liquid. Sure that it's cool enough, I insert a plastic straw. Ben takes a hearty suck.

"It has to be with the way the questions were written, right? It's the only thing I can think of. I mean most Canadians don't even know that the seal hunt happens every year," I say, remembering my conversation with Wendy.

Ben fastens his eyes above the rim of the mug as he takes another suck and then another, until a stuttering slurp rises through his straw, announcing he has reached the end. When his lips let go of the straw, I stand.

"Don't go," he says.

"What?" I look from Ben to his mug. "You want more?"

"No. I just wish you didn't have to go back to work."

"I'll sit with you later."

"You promise?"

"I promise," I say, though even I can hear that the words sound forced. When I look at Ben, I see he does, too. "Do you need anything else?"

"No, I'm good for now. Can you just pull up my blanket?"

It's a thin blue fleece that's fallen down from his shoulders. I tuck it in between the headrest and the back of his neck.

Back in my office, I find there are just two polling questions and, as I read them, I understand how the government could claim Canadians approve of the hunt. The questions suggest hunting seals is the same as hunting bear, or deer, or caribou (which it's not), and that it can be conducted humanely (which it can't, according to years of witness testimony and video evidence). The people answering the questions don't know the realities of the seal hunt. How could they, unless they watched hours of video evidence, read decades of articles, and studied scientific documents issued by teams of veterinarians and marine scientists? Still, their answers are reported as well-considered public position statements on the seal hunt.

I call Stephen.

"If people don't understand how the seal hunt works, the poll is meaningless," I complain.

"Not meaningless," Stephen says. "Polls measure perception. The seal hunt is appalling no matter how you look at it. But most people have never seen it. So, by asking a misleading question—'If the seal hunt has kindly sealers, gentle killing methods, and happy seals eager to die sustainably for the economy, would you approve of it?'—the government gets the answer it wants."

"If only people knew it's not a hunt but a competition, with everyone racing to get the most seals in the least amount of time," I say, repeating something I read in the Independent Veterinarians' Working Group report.[1-4] "Or that government patrol officers are nowhere in sight."

"You know something?" Stephen says. "If the media did a fair and impartial investigation of the sealing industry, the public's understanding of it might be very different. Why hasn't the media investigated activists' claims about violations? Why haven't they looked into how economically valuable the seal hunt is for East Coast sealers? 'Most of the things we hear from animal rights groups are false,' the government says. So why doesn't the media investigate?"

Before I hang up, Stephen adds: "You want to see a real poll? Look at the IFAW poll. It was done around the same time as the government's. But Hurricane Katrina hit and drowned out the news. It didn't get much coverage. But I think you'll find it interesting."

After hanging up, I quickly find the September 2005 IFAW poll, "Survey on Canadians' Attitudes towards the Seal Hunt," by Environics Analytics. Like the government poll, it's designed to measure Canadians' positions on the seal hunt. But unlike the former, it finds that "69 percent of respondents stating an opinion" oppose commercial sealing. IFAW's questions are direct and simple, asking only about the seal hunt (not hunting in general) and how sealing is really conducted (not how the government would like people to think it's conducted).

"Talk to me," Ben demands, wheeling into my office. "You never talk to me anymore."

"I'm working."

"You promised you'd stop and sit with me."

"I know, but I can't do it now. You need other people in your life."

"I don't want other people. You are the love of my life."

"Well, you need some interests other than me."

"You are my interest. You always will be."

"Okay, I'll be there in a minute."

When Ben leaves, I pick up a shiny new paper clip from my desk and wrestle its tiny wire arms apart. I elongate the wire and curl up one of the ends into a hook to gouge into my bottom lip.

28

Painting at Trafalgar

GLITTERY HAPPY NEW YEAR letters dangle over Woolwich Street. I struggle against the January gale as I try to open the front door of the Trafalgar building, gripping my paint box in one hand and my canvas in the other. The Trafalgar is one of several Victorian buildings in downtown Guelph. Across the street is the Wellington Hotel, iron-shaped with cupolas and awnings, dating back to 1877. The Trafalgar, with its weather-beaten redbrick curvilinear arches and zigzagging black fire escapes, is Depression-era Boho.

I climb the stairs. The studio I share is on the third floor, down a paint-splattered hallway that's all creaking floorboards and scary shadows. I pass the rope-and-pulley elevator and the scent of turpentine becomes heavy in my nose. I tread across the chipped yellow linoleum, curve around a centuries-old staircase, and see the first of the three wooden doors, one in front of the other, that we must unlock should a fire break out. The last, the one with the tricky latch, leads to the fire escape. I've nicknamed it Heaven's Door, after the Bob Dylan song.

As I step inside the studio, I notice that my studio mates have all arrived before me. They each are standing behind their easels situated around a long table. Do they raise their heads to notice me? Their attention is so fiercely focused on their canvases that I could be an axe murderer and they wouldn't catch wind. I'm late. By the time I drop my paint box on the table beside my friend Cal Kirkland, it's ten past seven. The noise startles him. When he turns to see me, he—Mr. Drama—places his paint-smeared hand over his heart, as if he were about to have a heart attack. Cal is a Toronto fire chief. If the building ever bursts into flames, I'm hoping he can get me out.

"Well, well, well, look who's made it!"

"Pshaw!" I say, swiping my hand. "I'm only ten minutes late! Don't get your knickers in a knot!"

"Well, excuuuuuse me!" he Rodney Dangerfields.

Cal is larger than life, and between he and Murray, who paints across the table from me, it's like having Abbott and Costello as studio mates.

I drag an easel across the floor and set it up. Music plays softly in the background. Brynn mixes paint on her palette. April dips her filbert into cadmium yellow and dabs it onto a field of green leaves and sunflowers waving in front of a ready-to-tumble-down red barn. Cal tints a blank canvas with burnt sienna, and Murray's eyes seesaw between a photograph of old fishing boats and his canvas. I secure my canvas between the easel brackets, tighten the screws, and tape my sketchbook drawing of the baby seal and her mother to the upper frame along with the source photo. After squeezing out my palette colours, I begin to sketch the lines of the seal pup in a mix of alizarin crimson and ultramarine blue.

"Not another animal!" Murray's eyes twinkle as he peers above the wire rims of his glasses at my canvas. "Why not people, or at least boats? I have a million photographs of boats you could use."

"When you paint something other than boats, I'll consider painting something other than animals."

"Someone's in a bad mood!" Cal says without taking his eye from his canvas.

Oddly enough, beneath the harsh ceiling light, I allow myself to float above the teasing, the orchestra of sounds lulling me into a deep, almost godly concentration. When the wall clock strikes nine, a petite ice floe cuts the centre of the painting amid rippling layers of blue and lavender brushstrokes.

"Beautiful," Brynn says, already packed up and stopping to examine my canvas before heading out.

"Thanks."

"How are you going to make the baby seal stand out from the ice? Wouldn't it be better if she were in the water? Then you'd get the contrast of dark and light," Brynn suggests.

"I can't," I say. "Baby seals can't swim."

April comes up behind her. "Then why is it on such a small piece of ice?"

"Global warming," I say. "The ice is melting."

April studies the photograph taped to my easel. "What's going to happen to it!?"

I turn to her, "Personal pronouns, please," I say. "Animals are not widgets." Then I incline my head toward my painting. "*She* . . . will drown."

"So sad," April says, *tsking* at the unfairness.

Sitting with Ben in our living room after my painting class, I say, "I forgot to tell you. Paul McCartney is coming to Canada." I wave the article I had printed off earlier in the day telling of the rock star's visit. "He'll be accompanying Rebecca and her team to the harp seal nursery."

Ben turns away from watching the CBC News. "Yeah," Ben says, barely glancing at the article.

"You used to love Paul McCartney."

He narrows his eyes. I can see his teeth gritting as he shakes his head at me. Then I remember: it is I who once loved Paul McCartney, not him. He is a John Lennon fan. When I was a little girl, I collected stacks of Beatles' cards, and pledged to marry Paul. By the time he married Linda, I had long moved on to playing with boys who put caterpillars in my hair and pretended to give me cooties, all in preparation for the time when I could start dating men who, like Ben, made my life miserable. Linda was good for him—she turned him vegan.

"Just because you're a John Lennon fan . . . doesn't mean it's not exciting that Paul McCartney is coming to help the seals. He's still a Beatle."

"It's not about Paul McCartney; it's about your work. It's about the seal hunt, so don't make it sound like this is something I should be happy about. Maybe you should care more that a Taliban suicide bomber outside

Kandahar just drove into an armoured car and wounded five of our soldiers. Maybe if you cared about something other than the seal hunt. . . ."

I put my hands on my hips. "Like what?"

"Like me." Ben glares.

"What do you think I'm doing sitting here with you? No matter what I do, it's never enough." I spin round, square my shoulders, and stride back to my office, where I slump into my swivel chair, start my computer, and discover the CBC.ca is agog with other good news: Not only is Paul McCartney coming to Canada, but so is Brigitte Bardot! I read one article after another. Then I read about another Paul I admire: Paul Watson. But, just like Ben, he is indifferent to the celebrities. He says: "The Canadian media is having conniptions and hissy fits over the fact that celebrities are protesting the Canadian slaughter of seals." I have a different take on celebrity activism, however. Criticize them or not, news outlets still send reporters and cameras out in droves to photograph them and report on every word. No activist, not even Paul Watson, could get that kind of coverage.

* * *

As Paul and Heather Mills McCartney prepare to helicopter to the nursery with HSUS, Respect for Animals, and a dozen journalists tagging along, a sealer corners the former Beatle.

"The hunt has kept our communities afloat for centuries," the sealer tells Paul McCartney.

"That doesn't make it justifiable," McCartney says. "Plenty of things have been going on for a long time, like slavery. It doesn't make it right."

On March 2, 2006, I watch a video of Paul and Heather Mills McCartney visiting the harp seal nursery.

Paul tells the reporters, "You'll hear that the reason why the seal hunt has to go on is that the seals eat the cod and therefore deplete the supplies of cod in the area, ruining the fishermen's living, but [. . .] that isn't true. It is overfishing that has led to the demise of the cod, and these harp seals actually eat some of the predators of cod, so they're part of the very delicate eco-balance."

DFO spokesperson Phil Jenkins, high on his horse, claims that Mr. and Mrs. McCartney are "misleading the public, since white-coated seals have not been hunted since 1987." He's right—in a way. A law was passed banning the hunt of whitecoats. Nevertheless, once the whitecoats start moulting and become raggedy jackets in twelve to fourteen days, they're fair game, even though some still have most of their white fur.

29

WHAT ABOUT PEOPLE?

I STAY UP late to watch Newfoundland premier Danny Williams debate Paul and Heather Mills McCartney on CNN's *Larry King Live*.

"Do we have to watch this?" Ben scowls as an annoyed Williams tells Paul, "I find it [. . .] offensive that an individual with such international influence would come to our province and pass judgment on individuals who are participating in an industry that sustains their lives."

"You love the Beatles," I coax.

"This isn't the Beatles. It's your work. Again!"

The next evening, in the painting studio, I ask if anyone saw the debate.

"*Awww!* I love the Beatles," April laments.

"Was he in concert?" Brynn asks.

"I saw them at Maple Leaf Gardens, 1966," says Murray. "They changed the course of music history. Interestingly enough, my son's name is Paul, and he's also a talented musician. I'll make sure he doesn't eat any seal products. But don't ask him to go out on the ice."

"Ha, ha!" I say, narrowing my eyes and smirking at him.

Not one to be left out of the shtick, Cal drops his jaw and bugs out his eyes. "You've got a son named Paul! You're kidding! Does Paul McCartney know?"

"I haven't told him yet," says Murray.

"This is the difference between you and Karen," Cal booms. "She's trying to save the world, and you're naming your son Paul! I think that says it all."

"Karen doesn't care about saving the world. Just animals. God forbid *we* needed rescuing. She'd be out on an ice floe beating up sealers." Murray gestures toward my painting of the seals on my easel.

"Very funny." I grimace.

Murray swings around to face me. "What about people?"

I look to the heavens. "Most people never do anything for anyone. If they do, nine times out of ten, it's for humans."

"Sheesh Murray! You're so hard to get along with!" Cal winks.

Mixing a dab of cobalt blue and a fingernail of ultramarine on my palette, I say, "I don't know how I wound up in the same room with you two."

Two hours later, as I cross the studio parking lot, clutching my paint box handle in one hand and my canvas, still wet with oil paint, in the other, I feel a headache coming on. I think, *Is it really so hard for people to comprehend that killing animals is not only cruel but insane?*

Behind me, I hear steps.

"Here, let me help," Murray says, running up beside me and reaching for my paint box.

"I can do it myself." I lift my chin in the air and hold my paint box out of his reach as I walk swiftly to the van.

"You know, I'm not as shallow as you think."

I remote-click open the trunk of the van and settle in my wet painting.

"Let me." Murray takes the paint box out of my hand and gently lays it inside, far from the wet canvas, then closes the trunk. "You know, I'm at least ankle-deep."

"I didn't say you're shallow."

"Look, I've spent half my money on gambling, alcohol, and wild women. The other half I've wasted," he says in that damn W. C. Fields, cigar-in-the-mouth voice.

"Good for you," I say, opening the driver's door.

"Why do you have to be so serious all the time?"

"I've got to go," I say, climbing in.

"What do you do for fun?" he asks, right before I shut the door. "You've got to have some fun!" he yells through the window.

"Go away." I turn the key in the ignition.

Murray knocks on the window. I roll it down.

"What?"

"You didn't answer," he grins.

"And you didn't go away." I roll my eyes skyward. "Okay, if you want to know, I work. That's my fun."

Murray gags.

"So what do *you* do for fun then?"

"'I cook with wine, sometimes I even add it to the food,'" he jokes.

"Do you always quote W. C. Fields?"

"If you can't dazzle them with brilliance, baffle them with bull, I always say."

"Goodbye." I roll up my window and step on the gas.

What an annoying ignoramus. I'm not always serious, I reassure myself as I steer down the road.

By mid-March, Loyola Hearn has authorized the slaughter of 325,000 baby harp seals, one of the highest TACs ever. It will be the third successive year in which more than 300,000 pups have been clubbed and shot.

Brigitte Bardot asks for a meeting with PM Harper and Hearn to encourage them to end the seal hunt; they refuse. Québec Senator Céline Hervieux-Payette scoffs at Bardot in a possible attempt to add insult to injury: "[For] the people of Newfoundland, of the Magdalen Islands and of the North, this is part of their livelihood and this is a tradition that has been there for hundreds of years."

"So was slavery, women's disfranchisement, child labour," I say under my breath. What hole has this woman crawled out of? Why have I never heard of her before?

* * *

It's March 25, 2006, the first day of the hunt. I sit in my office and stare at my blank computer screen. A drop of sweat drips from my crown.

145

"Gee, it's hot in here," I say to Karma, who is sprawled out on the office floor, tongue lolling. I reach for the temperature control and turn off the heat. At least this year's unseasonably warm temperatures—around 15°C—will cut down on my hydro bill. They'll also cut down the number of this year's surviving Southern Gulf baby harp seal cohort, many of whom will perish amid the vanishing ice.

"We should be seeing literally tens of thousands of seal pups out here, and at best we've seen maybe a couple of hundred," Rebecca tells the Canadian Press.

But DFO spokesperson Roger Simon disputes her claim. "The ice was actually fairly good for the critical period of pupping and nursing," he tells reporters. "There will always be some mortality and some drowning. There doesn't seem to be any concern this year because we haven't found dead pups floating and beached. That doesn't mean we won't in coming weeks, but there doesn't seem to be anything to be concerned about at this time."

All weekend, my mind replays images of newborn seal pups crashing through the fracturing and dissolving ice while their mothers helplessly watch them drown.

On Sunday, the DFO alleges that Rebecca and her team rammed sealers with their zodiac. In retribution, some sealers hurled seal guts at them. I search for articles that might clarify or update the early reporting, but I find nothing. On Monday, my computer vibrates with a trove of urgent new emails that include links to articles that reveal the latest occurrences in the evolving situation. Many articles repeat the same information: two Canadians and five Americans were arrested Sunday for coming too close to sealers off the Maggies. While Roger Simon withholds the names of those arrested from the press, I wonder if Rebecca is among them. Thankfully, everyone is soon released, and no one is charged. The drama only deepens, however. On March 31, Loyola Hearn's churlish remarks about the observers are published for all to read. He tells a reporter: "If you step over that line and try to interfere in any way with the hunt, then you can be arrested and charged, as people were last week."

The HSUS accuses Hearn of making false and defamatory claims calculated to injure the reputation of the plaintiffs Rebecca Aldworth, Andrew Plumbly, and Mark Glover, by exposing them to hatred, contempt, and/or ridicule. It demands Hearn issue a public apology, or he'd get sued for libel.

None of the HSUS members were charged, and not all participants were arrested. Rebecca tells the CBC: "I, for example, was not arrested. [. . .] He [Loyola Hearn] said that we all had been charged with an offence, and none of us to this day [have] been charged with any offence."

Two weeks later, Hearn apologizes in a statement issued to CBC.ca.

30

EXCUSE ME WHILE I KILL A PILLOW

BEN AND I settle back into stiff-necked, lip-pursed domesticity.

"Would you turn on the TV, love?" Ben asks.

I press the ON button. "Here we go," I say, trying to remain cordial.

"Could you pull my blanket up, love?"

I tug the edge of the fleece up his shoulders and tuck the extra folds between his shoulders and the chair back.

"Would you mind getting me a coffee, love?"

"Sure." I fill the coffeemaker with water, dump the fresh grounds into the basket, and wait for it to brew.

This is what our marriage has become. Domestic pleasantries, which hide our true feelings. Ben is mortally afraid that I will refuse to help him, and I am mortally afraid that I will be helping him for the rest of my life, while receiving little love in return.

Once a week, Ben leaves our condo and for two hours he visits patients and staff at St. Mark's Healthcare Centre, a chronic-care home nearby. And once a week, I watch his wheelchair *gwwrrrrrring* down the common hallway and wait for the latch of our front door to click into place. Then I lean my head against the door's oak solidness and breathe a sigh of relief. Sometimes I scream out my frustrations, even if nothing contentious has happened. Because it's all contentious. Marriage shouldn't be a wart one wants to cut off.

Throw a tantrum, why don't you? the Dop sneers on cue.

148

I need to get on with my life!

How do you plan on doing that? All you do is complain and get depressed.

I DON'T KNOW!

In a huff, I march into my bedroom and do the first thing I can think of: I grab my pillow, pitch it up to the ceiling, and slam it down on my bed. I pitch and slam, pitch and slam until I'm worn out, by which time, I flop on my back. When I close my eyes, I see Ben crashing his footrests into my shins; I see him pinning me against the kitchen wall near a pot of boiling water and noodles; and I see the first time he yelled at me. We were walking home from the grocery store.

"You're going to drop everything!" he roared, and then explained the mechanics of bag holding as if he were a grocery engineer.

At first, I thought he was joking, and I said something funny back. But then he said, "You're good for nothing!" and I knew I was in trouble. Somehow, I knew that this would not be the last time I heard those words. Hell. How did I get here? I wonder, looking up at the ceiling. I'm a women's studies graduate, for Christ's sake!

"Hellooooo," Ben hollers. Initially, I think that the sound of Ben's voice is nothing more than a part of my inner conversation. But then I hear his chair battering the front door as it struggles into the condo. "Where are you, love?"

It *is* Ben! Why is he home so early? I check my watch. Nearly two hours have passed. That can't be right. I tap my watch to see if it short-circuited. Ben's wheelchair *whirrrs* down the hall.

"Are you there, love?"

I open my mouth to silently wail, but quickly stuff in my fists in case I emit a sound. My eyes search for a place to hide. They land on the closed sliding doors of the closet. There, I tell myself. I quickstep to the closet, glide the door along its rungs, and climb between the hangers of folded pants into the small, dusty space.

How's that going to help? You'll have to come out sometime? What do you think he's going to say then?

Good God—the Dop. All I need is her yakking now. What if Ben can hear her? I purposefully hit my head against the wall twice before crawling out.

"I'll be right there," I shout, loud enough for Ben to hear.

At dinner, he tells me, "I want to live at St. Mark's when the time comes. It's close by; you can visit every day."

Is that what he expects? Daily visits? When I don't respond, he says, "Are you okay?"

"Yes. I'm just thinking. . . ."

"About what? You look depressed."

"Nothing," I say, shaking my head and forcing a smile.

"Don't be sad. They'll take good care of me. It's not for a while."

How long? I wonder.

* * *

One day, before the snow melts, Catarina and I stand looking out of her farm kitchen window at the white corn fields descending to Crawford Lake. The tree branches sag with heavy sleeves of new snow and the empty corn husks bend inside their white crystalline sheaths.

Ben and I fought that morning, and barely able to see the road through my tears, I drove to Cat's farm.

"I don't want to live like this," I say, stomping the snow from my boots on her welcome mat. I climb out of my boots and hang my coat in the entryway. Cat puts an arm around me and draws me through the big farm kitchen where I can smell the scent of lemon dishwashing soap and old, distressed wood beams. She leads me to the living room and to the red Victorian sofa I have sat on so many times while I sniffled my way through boxes of tissues. We talk for a while about the difficulties of too much closeness and dependence in a marriage, and how joining together should enhance the lives of a couple and not stifle them. How can it be any different when Ben needs me to do everything for him? I wonder to myself.

"You feel no hope for your future?" Cat asks.

"None," I say.

"Come." She walks back into the kitchen and to the large window overlooking the snow-covered fields, and a thin muster of trees, and the lake beyond. "What do you see?" she asks me as we stand at the window together. I lean my forehead against the glass and greet a thin layer of cold.

"Snow," I say.

She puts her hand on my shoulder. "But do you see what's under the snow?"

I shake my head.

"Even though we can't see it, there's new life under that snow. There are seeds germinating. Soon the snow will melt, and little shoots will poke their heads out of the thawing ground and turn toward the sun. The rain will come to nourish them; and they will blossom, even though all we can see right now is the snow. New life is all around us; it's just out of sight."

The thought that comes to me is of Ben and the nerve cells in his brain and spinal cord that are dying, unable to reach the muscles they are supposed to control. There is no rain that can mend his body or sun that can mend his life. But Cat is right. One day the snow will melt, and I will poke my head out of the thawing ground and feel the warmth of the sun.

31

Don't Mess with Ladies Who Lunch

THE HUNT ENDS early. Newfoundland sealers have found an abundance of seal pups in the colder waters of the Front. Once again, the annual quota is exceeded, this time by 20,000 seals. Only 800 are adult seals; the rest are babies.

Rebecca, Liz, and I meet at a vegetarian restaurant downtown, close to Animal Alliance's office. Initially, our intention was to discuss the Canadian Seafood Boycott. Yet what's on top of our minds as we scan the stained lunch menus is not the boycott but the recent news that Norway has paid its sealers first to hunt its own seals and then to burn 10,000 of stockpiled pelts from the previous year.[1] As we talk, I imagine a sprawling warehouse, with industrial shelving sagging under the weight of unsold seal pelts and forklifts hauling them out and dumping them into a fire pit.

The floor-to-ceiling glass window next to our table is filtering cold-yellow light through a jungle of watermarks and handprints. The only fire comes from the oil being sloshed onto the grill, and then it's like one big fiery hand reaching its fingers up from beneath the grate. Would the fire at the dumping site—one evil, blazing hand—pierce through the discarded skins? We order quickly, barely skipping a beat of conversation.

"And if that isn't bad enough," Rebecca says, "Norway just purchased 10,000 sealskins from Canada."

"Canada and Norway are going to kill seals whether anyone wants to buy their pelts or not." Liz purses her lips like she does when the hot coals of anger inside her begin to flame.

"It makes it look like there's a demand,"[2] says Rebecca, angrily whipping a lock of hair over her shoulder.

I look from Rebecca to Liz. "Is that even ethical?"

"It may not be ethical, but it's legal," says Liz. "Both countries want to make it look like there's a huge demand."

"No shame, no sorrow," I say, disgusted.

"The seal hunt is a way for sealers to qualify for Employment Insurance," Rebecca says.

"How?" I ask.

"Fishermen need to work nine months to qualify for EI benefits. But their fishing season may only give them eight months of work, so they are out one month. But if they go out sealing, they get an extra month of work, so they can qualify for EI."

My mind begins to sizzle as I try to figure out how the hunt helps sealers qualify for EI. In the past, fishermen may have worked for an entire month during the hunt, but sealers today can reach their vessel's quota in a few days. Did the DFO count those few days of sealing as an entire month to help sealers qualify for benefits? That would be a benefit in itself. I snort at the realization, just as the waitress brings our coffees.

"So, the Canadian government subsidizes the hunt with tax dollars so that sealers can work enough hours to qualify for the twenty-six-week EI benefit program?"

"A tax-funded, make-work project is what it is," Rebecca says. "The government should fund infrastructure and twenty-first-century job creation."

I scan the room, as if taking my eyes off Rebecca and Liz would stop my mind from reeling. White stuffing explodes out of the red vinyl upholstery behind cheap Formica tables from the 1950s.

"Anything happening with the European Union?" Liz asks.

"We've been lobbying the EU to ban seal products," Rebecca says, leaning in. "We've gotten a lot of support from parliamentarians there. I'm going over again in the next few weeks. Germany and Belgium look like they might implement their own embargoes even without an EU-wide ban. Without a European market, sealing licences will be worthless, and sealers will have no clout to negotiate buyout terms with the government."

"Buyout?"

Rebecca explains that a buyout is when the federal government pays sealers to turn in their licences and not hunt. If sealers do it now, when the market for seal products is still worth something, they can sell their licences back to the government for a reasonable amount. If they wait, once the ban kicks in, their licences may be worth nothing.

Liz takes a sip of coffee, then glances at Rebecca. "You seem sure the EU will ban seal products."

"I think there's a good chance."

"What'll sealers do instead?" I ask.

"There's not much they can do. Many have only high school educations," Liz says.

"The idea behind the buyout is that the government will invest in retraining programs and infrastructure to bring in new industries— twenty-first-century ones."

Just then, our meals arrive. I pick up my chickpea wrap and am about to take my first bite when an avalanche of tomatoes, onions, and green peppers tumbles out of both ends. I stuff them back with the side of my fork, looking up in embarrassment. Rebecca and Liz seem too busy eating to notice.

"We haven't discussed the boycott," Rebecca says, twisting pad thai rice noodles around the tines of her fork.

"We have about a thousand chefs and restaurants, most in the US," I say, holding my hand over my mouth as I try to chew and swallow my food. I rattle off the names of the James Beard chefs, top chefs, and Michelin chefs we've added to our campaign.

Rebecca reaches for the pepper. "How many do you think you can get by the end of the year?"

"It's hard to tell. There're five of us working. Each of us gets one or two pledges every two weeks."

"How many chefs do you contact in a week?" Liz asks, dabbing a napkin at a spot of tomato sauce to the right of her mouth.

"Thirty to fifty, not counting callbacks," I say, eyeing Liz's bowl. I should have gotten the chickpea stew.

"We've promised to end the hunt this year," Rebecca tells me. "We need thousands more chefs so Canada's seafood industry feels the pressure and in turn puts the pressure on Ottawa."

I self-consciously glide my tongue over my teeth in hot pursuit of telltale bits of chickpea between my teeth.

"I'll do whatever it takes," I say, knowing that in the seafood-boycott business it's not always the quantity of phone calls that matters, but the quality. Speaking two or three times a week with an animal-friendly chef who owns twenty restaurants is more productive than cold-calling ten chefs, five of whom may have no pledging authority, and two of whom are hunters. It's all about relationships.

32

A PUBLIX FORUM

ON SEPTEMBER 26, 2006, the Council of Europe passes a resolution urging its member states to prohibit the seal products trade within the EU.

I print several articles about the resolution and stick them in my red binder. I'm about to add more paper to the printer when Ben shouts from the living room.

"I need more coffee." I look at the time. Nine o'clock. An hour since breakfast and his last coffee. "And get me a blanket. It's cold in this house."

I pull a blanket from the hall closet and check the temperature reading on the heating unit. It's 20°C! Warm enough for a healthy person, but not for someone with a motor neuron disease. I bring him the blanket and wrap it around his shoulders, tucking the ends beneath him.

In the kitchen, I pour the remaining breakfast coffee into a mug and stick it in the microwave. That's when the phone rings.

"It's probably Liz. I'll be back in a minute." I race into my office.

"Don't forget I'm out here," Ben shouts.

I pick up the phone, surprised it's not Liz but a colleague from another organization assisting with the boycott.

"You've got to be kidding! Publix!? They've pledged to boycott Newfoundland snow crab! When?"

She begins to tell me when Ben shouts from the living room.

"I'm still waiting!"

"Just a minute," I tell my colleague, hoping she hasn't heard Ben. I lay down the receiver and rush into the living room.

"I'm on the phone. It's work."

"It's always work!"

Giving him a pointed stare, I say, "Ben, I'll be a minute."

I rush back to my office. "Sorry about that," I say into the phone. "I had to check on something. You were saying?"

When we hang up, I open my mouth wide and scream like a 1960s Beatles fanatic and race down the hall to Ben.

"We just got Publix to sign on to the boycott!"

"So?"

"So! This is huge!" Publix has 900 stores in five states. It's one of the biggest supermarket chains in the United States.

"Now that that's over, are you ready to pay attention to me?"

"Do you know what this means for the campaign? For seals?"

"I don't care."

"Well, I do." I huff into the kitchen, re-microwave the mug of coffee, drop in a plastic straw, and plunk it down hard on the table. I glare at him and he glares back. I bend the straw and thrust it toward his lips. He opens his mouth, takes a sip, and abruptly sputters.

"It's too cold. I can't drink it."

I can still feel the warmth through the walls of the mug.

"It's not."

He abruptly turns his head away.

"So you don't want it?"

"I want a fresh pot, not one that's gone stale while you talked on the phone."

"Fine." I grab the mug and head into the kitchen. At the sink, I pour the coffee out, put the empty mug into the dishwasher, and with a swift turn stride back to my office.

"Where's my coffee?" he hollers after me, right before I slam my office door shut.

With the Publix win, it'll be easier to get other chains on board. Feeling motivated, I look for my restaurant call lists. I lift up papers and books and search the document piles on my desk. Where is it?

Time to clean my desk, I decide. I start gathering up the articles I've printed, sort them by date, stick each one into a plastic sleeve, and then insert them into my red binder.

"I need a coffee!" Ben yells from the living room.

"I'm working." I shout from behind my office door.

"I need a coffee *now!*"

My teeth clench. I put down the article I've been trying to insert into a protective sleeve. "*Fuck!*"

I'm about to get up when I see Ben filling the doorway, his face hot-tamale red.

"How many times do I have to ask you? My blanket's falling off and I need a coffee!"

His blanket has slipped off one shoulder and a corner is dangling dangerously close to a blanket-catching wheel rim. I grab the edge and pull it up over Ben's shoulders, tucking both corners under the neck of his sweatshirt.

"Go watch television. I'll be right in," I tell him.

"I need you."

"I'll be right there."

"NOW!" he shouts, the brown of his eyes darkening. He glances around the room as if seeing it for the first time. "Look at all this junk. How can anybody work in a place like this?"

I follow his gaze, taking in the full effect: the helter-skelter articles and towers of fisheries Standing Committee documents and seal management plans threatening to collapse; a plate with peanut butter smears and rice cake kernels on the ledge of my bookshelf; a ceramic mug with the words SAVE THE MALES on the outside and mould growing on the inside.

"In a minute, dammit. I just need to put this article away." I begin to stuff it into its sleeve and thread the holes into the red binder resting open on my desk when Ben wheels his chair into the room and turns off its motor. My office is small even without Ben confiscating space. But now it's claustrophobic. "Please, Ben, go back into the living room. I'll be right behind you."

For a moment, it looks like that is exactly what he's going to do, but then his mouth sets and the vein in his temple pulses as his tremulous index finger hooks around and juggles the wheelchair's motor control lever. His chair thrusts forward, and with a warrior cry Ben charges the corner of my desk. I hear the plywood crack.

"Fuck! What the hell are you doing?" I shriek, jumping out of the way. I gape at the indentation his chair has made as Ben backs his chair up with his insistent shaking index finger and I watch, dumbfounded, as he thrusts his chair forward again and bashes the side of the desk.

"GET OUUUUUUT!" my inner banshee yells. Ben three-point-turns his chair so it parallels my desk and plows my swivel chair out of the way. With his left arm swinging like a baseball bat with Parkinson's disease, he swipes the three-ring binder and books off my desk. They tumble and crash onto the floor. The rings of the binder shoot open and all my carefully organized articles in their plastic sleeves spill out. Swinging his arm back for momentum, he is about to push my computer off my desk when I grab it. His chair backs up and moves forward as he attempts a three-point turn. But the metal footrests slam into my shins.

"You fucking aaasshole! Get out of my fucking office."

Ben toggles the joystick, turns his chair around, and motors down the hall. I slam the door behind him. I can hear the whir of his wheelchair. I press my back against the door and moments later hear the TV blaring in the living room. My throat is raw. My life breath is somewhere in my stomach. *Breathe, Karen. Breathe.*

When I'm sure he's not coming back, I slide onto the floor and pull my knees to my chest, wrapping my arms around my throbbing shins. On the floor in front of me, a hardcover book tents on its edges; another has as an accordion corner. My red binder splays open on the floor as if for a gynecological exam, the jumbled pages any which way. I can no longer hold my tears back.

"God, help me! I can't do this anymore."

When I raise my head off the floor, I see the sun setting outside my office window, filling the room with an eerie blue-purple haze. I can't remember why I'm on the floor or how long I've been there. Suddenly, I feel the throbbing in my shins. I straighten my legs out and see the blossoming purple-and-yellow bruises. I look up to see the bashed-in corner of my desk and the articles in their plastic protector sleeves scattered across the floor. Out the window, the sky is a panoply of colours: shades of blue-grey, ultramarine, a dab of alizarin crimson, a thick smear of titanium white. Identifying the colours helps me steady my mind. Then I remember Ben in a rage, barreling his wheelchair through my office. My thoughts race. I can't stay here, not just in this room but in the condo. I search for my new cellphone, first patting the pockets of my jeans and then scanning the floor, the top of my desk, the shelves of the bookcase. I can't find it.

It doesn't matter. Just stand up, open the door, and go into the bedroom. There's a phone there, the Dop says. Thank God she's here. I'm surprised she's being helpful.

I open the door a crack and peek down the hall. Ben is parked in front of the TV. I sneak into my bedroom, quietly shut the door, and reach for the phone on the night table. My fingers punch a familiar number. Within moments, I hear my mother's voice.

"Karen?"

"Can I come for a visit?"

"What's wrong?"

"Nothing."

"Your voice sounds funny."

"Please, Mom. Can I come or not?"

"Of course you can come. Who's going to take care of Ben?"

"I'll figure it out."

"Someone has to stay with him. Are there any services in Gulf for that kind of thing?"

"Guelph, Mom. Guelph."

"Well, are there?"

"I said I'll figure it out."

"Are you sure you're alright?"

"Yes."

"You sound . . ."

I cut in. "I'll let you know what flight I'm on."

Next, I call hospice and explain my situation, without the unpleasant details. They have a volunteer, Robert, who will do overnights. I arrange for him to come for a week. My next call is to Liz.

"Meeting chefs face-to-face in West Palm Beach will be more effective than calling them from Canada," I tell her, trying to keep the desperation out of my voice. "I'll just be a week."

"Go ahead, honey bunny," she tells me. "Bring home those pledges."

The last thing I do is sneak back into my office, shut the door quietly, and book my ticket online. I'll leave tomorrow morning. My swivel chair is across the room; I wheel it back to my desk. That's when I see my cellphone underneath. I pick it up, sigh with relief, and kiss it.

* * *

I step off the plane into a slab of Florida heat. I wiggle out of my winter jacket and head for the baggage claim. My bag, noticeable by its lime-green nametag, is circling on the conveyer belt. I pull it off and look around for my mother. She's easy to find with her pouf of red hair. I throw my arms around her.

"It's so good to see you," she says, squeezing me tight. With another squeeze, she steps back, studying me with her critical-mother eyes. "Have you been crying? Your eyes are all puffy."

"No," I lie. "Allergies."

"I hope you don't get allergies here. There's flowers everywhere."

Before long, we are heading down the highway. My mother weaves her Lexus between lanes freely, oblivious to the BMW fast approaching in the right lane. She veers in front of it, missing the car by a millimetre. The driver *hoooooooonks*.

"Mom! Signal!"

"I am signaling."

I groan. "You didn't signal. You never signal."

"All my friends tell me I'm a very good driver."

"They're probably too frightened to speak."

"Don't be ridiculous."

By the time we drive through the community gate, circle around a crescent of pale-pink-and-orange bungalows, and pull into my mother's driveway, I'm ready to kiss the ground in gratitude that we've made it to Mom's alive.

"Be quiet. Eddie's probably asleep," my mother says *sotto voce*.

I check my cellphone. "It's only six o'clock," I whisper back.

"He goes to bed early. Are you hungry?"

After mouthing *yes*, I wheel my case into the spare bedroom and plop onto the bed. A knock on the door wakes me. A plate of apple slices and cheese in her hands, my mother stands in the doorway.

"I didn't know if I should wake you." Outside the window, the light has turned from lemon to a bluey pink.

I sit up against the headboard. She holds out the plate. I take an apple slice, and then another, and then the plate itself, balancing it on my stretched-out thighs. She taps my legs with the back of her hand, and I slide over so she can sit.

"I know something is going on." She gives me her all-knowing, head-tilting, eyebrow-raising, forehead-crinkling look.

I chew on an apple slice, pretending not to notice.

"Aren't you going to eat the cheese?"

"I'm a vegan, Mom."

"Can't you eat cheese?"

I shake my head, eyes rolling.

"Never mind." She looks at me pointedly. "Did you and Ben have a fight?"

I slide the plate onto the night table, turn on the light, and nod.

My mother sighs and rubs her ear, a gesture I know means "If only you had listened to me."

"How long do you want to stay?"

"The hospice volunteer can stay a week."

"Shirrleeeey," Eddie calls from down the hall. I stiffen.

"We're in here," Mom shouts back.

"Who's *we*?" When he rounds the doorway, his eyes shift from my mother to me. "I forgot you were coming," he says in a gruff voice. My lips curl inward.

"Eddie, I told you," my mother *tsks*.

"Flight okay?" he asks.

I nod.

"How's things in Gelf?"

"Guelph," I correct. "Good."

"Good," he nods, then turns to my mother, "Shirley, what are you making for dinner?"

"I hadn't planned on making anything. I thought you were asleep. Didn't you make yourself something while I was gone?"

"I was waiting for you," he says.

She turns to me, side-glancing the plate's uneaten cheese. "Can I make you something else?"

"Chicken," Eddie says.

"She can't eat chicken. She's a vegan," Mom tells him.

"Well, I can eat chicken," he says.

"I wish at least you'd eat cheese. It would make things so much easier," Mom tells me.

I swipe my hand dismissively. "I'm not hungry."

"You just told me you were."

"I'm the one who's hungry," Eddie croaks.

"You go feed Eddie," I say. "I'm just going to bed. I want to get up early to meet with chefs."

"Chefs? Why are you meeting with chefs?" Eddie asks.

My mother stands up, leans over, and gives me a kiss on the forehead. "It's good to have you here, baby." Then she turns and leads Eddie from the room.

"Why is she meeting with chefs? Aren't there any chefs in Gelf?"

"Gulf, Eddie, Gulf. I'll tell you later."

Several minutes later, I can hear the water from the kitchen faucet, the clink of a pot cover, and then my mother calling out to me. "Take my car. Just not on the weekends."

At breakfast, I map out my route, circling the restaurants I want to visit in my Florida tourist guide. Each town appears to have a couple of blocks of restaurants. I can park my car centrally and pop into one after another. Armed with a white binder of seal photographs, information pamphlets, and pledge forms, I drive to Delray and pull into a public parking lot next to a fine-dining restaurant.

I enter the restaurant and ask a waitress to see the menu. Under entrées, I see snow crab, lobster, and PEI (Prince Edward Island) mussels.

"Can I speak to the chef?"

Several minutes later, a chef comes out in his culinary whites.

I hold out my hand and the chef shakes it, bewildered. As I deliver my spiel, I can see the questions percolating.

"We don't kill Canada's seals, do we?"

"No, the US banned sealing in 1972. You guys have done a great job in protecting marine mammals. But Canada hasn't. Our fishermen kill hundreds of thousands of seal pups each year for fur." I open my binder to an especially gruesome image—hundreds of skinned carcasses abandoned on the ice.

"My God!"

"My God is right. Canada has said it'll end the seal hunt when its seafood industry asks it to. If US chefs, like yourself, stop buying Canadian seafood, our seafood industry will ask."

"You Canadian?"

I grin and hand the chef the pledge form. "I'm proud to live in Canada. I'm just not proud of the seal hunt. Please help us save our seal pups."

As he reads it over, I ask, "Do you know where you buy your snow crab and lobster?"

"Snow crab is from Canada. I'll have to ask our distributor where we get our lobster. I think it's from a variety of places."

"Would you be willing to sign the pledge for snow crab, switching it out for Alaskan or Chilean? You'll be helping to save the lives of hundreds of thousands of two-week- to three-month-old seal pups who, in just a month, will be shot and clubbed by Canada's commercial fishermen, primarily from Newfoundland, where snow crab is their number one export."

I can see his mind weighing the expense of switching his seafood away from Canada with the moral costs of buying seafood from fishermen who battered helpless baby animals into bloody pulps. To an animal lover, it might seem like an easy decision to make. I knew differently. There were contracts to renegotiate, money-saving seafood deals he might lose. He also may be weighing the cost of the effort and time expenditures needed to seek out a new distributor, should his old one fail to accommodate his non-Canadian seafood purchasing resolve. My stomach tightens as I wait for his decision.

When he looks up at me and nods, I breathe a sigh of relief. I watch as he opens the top of the hostess desk, searching through the old menus and seating charts for a pen. I whip one out. Shutting the desktop, the chef lays down the pledge and begins filling in the required information. I watch him scribble his signature on the appropriate line and thank him. I want to give him a hug to show how grateful I am, but hugs can be misinterpreted. I shake his hand heartily instead, and then watch as he returns to his kitchen. Am I imagining that he has a lightness in his step? That he's holding his head higher? I certainly am. Next, I visit several Mexican chefs who have a soft spot for our fluff balls of cuteness.

I drive back to Mom's with four pledges in my white binder, a lightness in my braking foot, and a song by Natasha St-Pier—from the one CD I brought with me—blasting from the speakers. I hastily eat a peanut butter sandwich and head off to the guest bedroom.

"I need the car tomorrow. I have to go grocery shopping."

I fall asleep to the song "Plus simple que ça" quietly playing on Mom's CD player.

I wake early, grab a banana, and walk a block to Trader Joe's, filling my bag with nuts, almond butter, soymilk, and vegan cheese.

I carry my bags into the kitchen and begin to load the soymilk into the fridge. I pull open the cold cut drawer and am about to deposit my soy cheese when I see a package of Nova Scotia smoked salmon fillets wrapped in cellophane, the orange slices smirking from behind their country-of-origin labeling. I begin to steam as I put the last of my groceries away. I grab yesterday's *Palm Beach Post* and sit at the kitchen island, trying to remain calm. At noon, my mother, still in her nightgown, Scotch tape holding her hair in place, steps into the kitchen.

"Can you believe I overslept?"

I put down the newspaper and locomote to the refrigerator. From the cold cut drawer, I lift out the package of salmon. "Mom, where did you get this?"

"What are you talking about?" my mother asks, maneuvering around me to get a bag of 2 percent milk from the top shelf.

"The lox, Mom. The Nova Scotia lox." I wave the package in front of her. "Where did you get this?"

"At Publix, where I always shop. Why?"

"Nova Scotia lox is a Canadian seafood product."

"So?"

I drop the lox on the counter and throw up my hands in exasperation. "Canadian fishermen are the ones clubbing and shooting baby seals!"

"I didn't know." She pours the moo juice into a glass and returns the carton to the fridge.

"Yes, you did. I've told you. What do you think I do all day?"

"I forgot."

"Mom, if you buy Nova Scotia lox, you might as well go to the ice and club a baby seal yourself."

"Don't be ridiculous."

"How are we going to end the seal hunt if my own family is supporting sealers?"

"I don't support sealers."

"Yes, you do." I pick up and dangle the package of lox in front of her.

"Alright. I won't buy it again," she says stiffly.

"Publix Super Markets is part of our boycott. They shouldn't be selling seafood from Nova Scotia anyway."

"Well, I can't help what they sell," my mother says, throwing up her hands.

"Well, I can." I grab my purse from the counter and sprint toward the door.

"Where are you going, Karen?"

"To Publix."

My mother looks horrified. "I don't want you making trouble."

"I'm just going to talk to them. They shouldn't be buying Canadian seafood, and neither should you."

At the frozen fish section, I survey the piles of packaged smoked salmon in the freezer case. Shuffling through the various brands, I glance at their country-of-origin labels: Alaska, Chile, Norway, Canada. I lift a package of Nova Scotia lox from the case and head over to the seafood counter, where I see fresh Canadian snow crab, halibut, and cod. Cod! What about the moratorium?

I'm angry now. "Excuuuuuse me," I holler at the plastic slat curtain separating the seafood counter from the fish butchery.

The seafood manager pokes his head out through the slats. "May I help you?"

I hold up the package of lox and jab it with my index finger. "This is from Nova Scotia!"

He looks bewildered. "So?"

I hand him the package so he can inspect it further.

"Publix is part of the Canadian Seafood Boycott," I say.

"The what?"

"The Canadian Seafood Boycott. It's a campaign to end Canada's commercial seal hunt. You aren't supposed to be selling Canadian seafood. Not Nova Scotia lox or Canadian halibut or Canadian snow crab," I say, waving my hand like *Wheel of Fortune*'s Vanna White at the deceased fish behind the Plexiglas.

"Lady, I don't know what you're talking about."

"Weren't you told?"

"Told what?"

"Canadian fishermen are sealers and they kill hundreds of thousands of baby seals each year. Because of it, Publix is boycotting Canadian seafood."

"No one told me."

"Are you sure?"

"I don't make the decisions on what seafood to buy anyway. That's done at head office. I just stock whatever they tell me. If you want to take it up with head office, be my guest." With that, he turns around and re-enters the butchery.

Has Publix ignored its promise not to buy Canadian seafood? I flip open my cellphone and call Liz. She hasn't a clue who got the pledge. "Call Stephen," she suggests. Stephen is equally flummoxed, so I call one of my boycott colleagues in the United States.

"Publix didn't sign a pledge," she tells me.

"Why are we listing them as part of our boycott?"

"Their VP of seafood promised he wouldn't buy seafood from sealers."

I gasp. "There's no way he'd know who caught his seafood."

My colleague considers for a moment. "I guess you're right."

"So how did he promise? In a letter?"

"No, verbally," she says. "They're such a big name. We were thrilled to get them."

"Big name or not, we need to remove them until we receive a pledge or written agreement. No more verbal promises. They're unenforceable. In writing only!"

Sunday evening, Ben calls while Mom and I are watching *Dateline*. I take my phone into the guest bedroom and sit on the edge of the bed.

"I miss you. I just wish you were home." His voice falters.

Should I say I miss him, too? Would he hear the falseness in my voice?

"How's the hospice volunteer?" I ask instead.

"He's nice. He sleeps in your bed . . ."

"Well, I didn't think he'd fit in your hospital cot."

". . . with Karma." He laughs.

Hearing Ben's laughter surprises me. I haven't heard him laugh in years.

"When *are* you coming home?"

"Four more days."

"It's just like . . . you know, like . . . embarrassing. Robert has to . . . like . . . he has to help me with the toilet, and, you know . . ."

"I know."

"Can't you come home early?"

"Ben, Mom's calling me for dinner. I gotta go."

After I hang up, my shoulders slump. I see Ben—not the angry Ben, but his essence—trapped behind the barricade of his useless muscles, desperate to get out. I lie on the bed, squeeze my eyes shut, and wrap my arms around myself.

In the morning, I hear my mother shouting at Eddie in the bedroom. "Mind your goddamn business. I'd like to see how you'd take care of me if something happened." When she comes into the kitchen, her mouth is set in a hard line. She forces a smile. "Tonight, I'm going to make dinner. A roast. I know you won't eat it. I'll make you something else."

At dinner, I fork the Thai red curry into my mouth as Mom passes a generous plate of roast cow to Eddie.

"I hope you don't mind a TV dinner," she says. "You used to love them."

"I was six."

"The woman at the grocery store said it was vegan." She sloshes a piece of roast moo into gravy and slips it into her mouth. When she finishes chewing, she asks, "Have you spoken with Ben?"

"Yesterday."

"How's he coping without you?" Eddie provokes.

Mom gives Eddie the hot eye, then turns to me. "So, have you thought about what you're going to do when you get home?"

"Work."

"That's not what I mean. You can't keep going on like this. One fight after another. It's no way to live."

"I'll tell you what she should do. She should go back to her husband, who needs her."

"Eddie, stay out of it," my mother snaps.

"I'm not going to stay out of it; this is my house. I can say what I want. She should go back to her husband. He needs his wife. Home. With him. She should never have left. The last time I saw him, he could barely dress himself."

"He probably can't even do that now," Mom says, sighing and pushing back her chair. "Does anyone want more mashed potatoes?" She puts her napkin on the table and proceeds to the mashed potato bowl on the counter.

"That's what I mean," Eddie says as Mom spoons a nibble of mashed potato into her mouth. "He probably can't even wipe his own ass now."

"Eddie, I'm warning you," she says, returning with the bowl.

"Will you both just stop it?" I say, standing up and bringing my plate to the sink. I scrape the remaining noodles down the drain and turn to Eddie. "If you must know, Eddie: no, he can't wipe his own ass. I'm the one who wipes it for him—if it's any of your business, which it's not. But if you care so deeply, be my guest—take over. Get on a plane and go there yourself. I'll give you the keys." I stomp off down the hall to the guest bedroom.

"See what you did!" I hear my mother saying as I close the door.

Three days later, I pack, sliding my twenty pledges into the top pocket of my suitcase, and climb into her Lexus.

As Mom careens down the highway, she reaches for my hand. "I don't want you to leave, baby."

I squeeze her hand, too. "I know."

We sit in thoughtful silence the rest of the drive and in no time at all, Mom swerves into an empty parking spot in front of the Air Canada DEPARTURE sign. I open the passenger door and step into heat hot enough to melt the road tar. I pull my suitcase from the trunk and lift it to the curb.

Mom swivels out of the driver's seat, leaving her oasis of air conditioning. "Gelf is so far away," she frowns, pulling me into a long hug.

I rest my head on her shoulder. "Thanks, Mom, for letting me stay."

"I'm always here if you need me." When she lets go, she holds me at arm's length. "You can come *any* time. But see if you can work things out. Eddie's right. Ben needs you."

I flinch at her words. The night of my fight with Eddie, after my stomping down the hall and slamming the guestroom door, I returned to the kitchen to help Mom clean up. Eddie had retired to the TV room, leaving us to clear the dishes off the table and sponge down the counters. It was then that I told her about my last day with Ben—how he had trashed my office, splintered my desk, and rammed his footrests into my shins. That's what makes her words so painful. It feels like she's abandoning me for Ben and Eddie.

"Goodbye, Mom." I kiss her quickly on the lips, tip the case onto its back wheels, and hurry toward the airport's double doors. Before entering, I stop. What if this were the last time I saw my mom? What if something happened to her, or me, or the world? What if there were never another goodbye? I turn to wave, but my mother is already veering onto the ring road that will take her to the highway.

A taxi picks me up at Pearson and, my head against the glass, I watch as we whiz past the unsightly high-rises and the fields of snow glowing in the moonlight. In no time, I'm wheeling my suitcase through the condo building's lobby, and then down the common hallway to my front door. I grip the keys in my pocket, my stomach churning.

Breathe, Karen. Breathe. I open the door to Ben and his wheelchair.

"I'm so glad you're home," he grins, backing up his wheelchair to let me in.

In the morning, I help Ben out of bed and into his wheelchair. I busy myself in the kitchen making breakfast, while Ben watches *Marilyn in the Morning*.

After breakfast, I approach my office. I didn't have it in me to open the door last night. Now, with my hand on the knob, I try to catch my breath.

For God's sake, you're not going to stand out here all day. Go in.

You're still here! Whoopie! I snark at the Dop.

What? Did you think I was going to Florida?

171

I can almost feel her nudge me.

I turn the handle and step inside. It looks like a murder scene: dead books and binders, their guts spilled on the laminate. My SAVE THE MALES coffee cup is in pieces beside them. A milk crate is on its side, bleeding file folders. I fight for breath.

Just look at this, I say to myself, gesturing at the mess.

You didn't think I was going to clean it up, did you? the Dop says snootily.

Go away. I don't need your help. I should have stayed in Florida and left you both behind.

I can travel, too! she says. *How do you think I got here?*

I hate you both, I say. *Did you see him last night?* I ask, referring to Ben. *He was all smiles when I got home. Like this ever happened.* I swipe my hand at the articles carpeting the floor.

Blah, blah, blah, the Dop says. *Someone's in a mood.*

I spread my hands, so they parenthesize the fallen objects. *I can't deal with this.*

It's not my job to find a solution, she says.

Then go home or wherever you are come from! I silently yell.

The Dop makes no sound.

Just get out of here! I shout again in silence. I've always been able to communicate my thoughts to her without making a sound. But all is quiet. Did she leave? Or is she just giving me the silent treatment, I wonder.

Hmmph, I say. *I can ignore you, too!*

I kneel beside the red three-ring binder. The rings are bent. I try strong-arming them together, but their ends no longer embrace. Still, I reach for the scattered tabs and thread them through the binder rings. I start piling the articles into stacks by their dates, I loop in the 2004s, then the 2005s. Next, I pick up a CBC Radio interview transcript, the pages held together with a small binder clip, and examine the first page. The interview is with the Newfoundland fisheries and aquaculture minister, Tom Rideout. I scan down the page when . . . *Whoa! . . .* my eyes brake. I rub them and squint at the number "C$55 million" I see halfway down. *Fifty-five million!* This is what Rideout tells the interviewer is the value of the 2006 seal hunt.[1] That can't be right. I've been to the DFO's website many times and know that the full value of the 2006 commercial seal hunt is C$30 million,[2] at least according to the site. I decide to turn on my computer and recheck it.

I slide the cursor and click until I come to the "Canadian Seal Landings and Landed Values" page where all the data for 2006 have been recorded. There I find, just as I thought, that the value of the 2006 seal hunt is C$30 million or C$30,090,106 to be exact.[3] I slide the transcript through the binder loops and then start fitting in the rest of the 2006 articles, but do it unhurriedly to make sure I don't miss anything. The value of the 2006 seal hunt seems to be yo-yoing between C$30 million and C$34.7 million, depending on the source.[4,5] It's confusing, and my mind is whirling, and I almost miss the most stunning number of all. Newfoundland minister of fisheries and aquaculture Tom Rideout claims that his province's commercial seal hunt puts "C$70 million into the pockets of people who are normally unemployed every winter."[6]

How could C$30 million turn into C$55 million, and then into C$70 million? Perhaps an alchemist could make it happen, but not Canada's federal and provincial fisheries and aquaculture department.

And what about other years? Browsing through 2005, I find similar disparities. Tom Rideout tells the Canadian Press that the value of the 2005 seal hunt is C$15.7 million. DFO spokesperson Phil Jenkins refers to the 2005 landed value as C$16.5 million. The DFO website claims that the 2005 seal hunt value exceeds C$16.5 million. Roger Simon, director of the DFO's Magdalen Islands section, alleges that the landed value is worth C$20 million, and the Canadian Sealers Association claims it's C$40 million. Why have I not noticed this before? Perhaps in my hurry to absorb information, I missed the finer details. Can it be true that no one in our federal or Newfoundland's provincial government knows the value of the seal hunt?

My head swimming with all the craziness, I call Stephen.

"The numbers are all over the place. If I'm having trouble figuring out what's what, imagine how difficult it would be for the average Canadian. They see 'C$70 million goes into the pockets of the unemployed' and think, *Wow, the seal hunt is economically important. Of course it needs to continue. Of course my tax dollars are going to a good cause.*"

"I always thought that the DFO was pulling numbers out of a hat," Stephen says.

"Could they really be making the values up? And for what purpose? And if they are, why not stick with one number instead of three? The least they could do is explain how they come up with the values. The Canadian public deserves an honest answer."

"I don't think the DFO has a clear grasp of the real economic value. It's not in their interest to know. They want people to think sealing is the one thing standing between poor fishing families and poverty." Stephen directs me to the "Report of the Eminent Panel on Seal Management." "Read it," he says. "You'll see how the DFO couldn't even provide simple information to a panel of experts that the fisheries minister appointed to find out the real value of the hunt."

"If the government is making up the value of the seal hunt each year or even if it has made up the value of just one or two seal hunts, the public needs to know. If the true value of the seal hunt is far less than what they announce, then people should know they are being fooled. They should know their tax dollars are going down the drain!"

"Show how the DFO came up with the numbers. Prove they're made up."

"But how? Do I just walk up to Loyola Hearn and invite him out for a veggie burger?"

"You'll find a way." Stephen says before clicking off the phone.

33

Ad Hominem

October 2006

"I NEED YOU to represent me in a debate," Liz tells me once I've
hung up my coat on an office coat peg and plopped into a chair beside
her. Without looking up from her computer screen and the image of a
pile of dead pit bulls taken at a Toronto animal shelter, she continues:
"I planned to go myself, but the mayor's office just called. They're
squeezing me in." Both her hands do a palms-up as she shakes her head
at a close-up of the carcasses. "Animal Control's killing hundreds of
perfectly wonderful dogs who have never hurt anyone. Ontario's fucking
pit bull legislation." She turns to me, almost as an afterthought. "The
debate's on *Talk Ottawa*."

It takes a moment for Liz's words to sink in. "TV?"

"Local TV."

"Local in Ottawa!"

"Are you up for it?"

My last formal debate was in grade school. I don't remember the topic
or whether I won. I do remember I was terrified.

"What do you think?" Liz asks, backing up her chair to face me. I'm
about to answer when Stephen strides into the room, grabs the back of a
conference table chair, and pulls it across the room, positioning it beside
Liz. "I just told Karen about the debate," Liz tells him.

"And?" Stephen installs himself into the chair. He leans forward; his
eyes meet mine.

175

I close my eyes, bite my upper lip, surrender my fate to the gods, and nod.

"Well, that's certainly good news," Stephen says.

I turn to Liz. "Who'll I be debating?"

"Senator Céline Hervieux-Payette."

Céline Hervieux-Payette! Her name sends my jaw dropping like a free-falling elevator. *Céline Hervieux-Payette*: the pearls, the headband, the blond pageboy hair. Hervieux-Payette is Québec's number one seal hunt fangirl! Her smile may spread across the senate chamber like a rising tide, but when it comes to the seal hunt, you could sharpen a fillet knife on her charm. When a Minnesota mother mailed Canadian senators a letter expressing horror that Canada's "appalling" seal hunt had not ended, and adding that because of it her family would be cancelling their Canada vacation, Senator CHP jumped on the Minnesotan faster than a Saint-Tite rodeo rider onto the back of a terrified bronco. What *she* found "appalling," Hervieux-Payette replied, was the US's "daily massacre of innocent people in Iraq, the execution of prisoners—mainly blacks—in American prisons, the massive sale of handguns to Americans, and the destabilization of the entire world by the American government's aggressive foreign policy. . . ."[1] It felt to me like bashing a puppy on the head with a *Boston Globe* for peeing in the kitchen.

"The seal hunt is almost never debated live by Canadian politicians. That's what makes this debate so important," Liz says.

"Live!" I sputter.

"That's why Stephen's here to prep you." With that, Liz slide-walks her chair back to her desk and begins finger-tapping her computer keys.

Stephen pulls his chair closer. "The main thing you need to know is the seal hunt is not about bringing jobs to rural fishing ports. It's not about protecting cod. It's about politics, pure and simple. No politician could ever get elected opposing it. Doing so would be political suicide."

"There's no politician in Canada who opposes the seal hunt!?"

"Not publicly. David Lavigne and Sheryl Fink of IFAW have spoken to about fourteen members of Parliament who oppose it. But they'd be demolished by their party if they said so publicly."

"What about senators?"

"According to David, there's one. Have you heard of Mac Harb?"

I shake my head. There are 105 senators in Canada's Parliament. If I had to name six of them or die, I'd be writing my own obituary.

"Sheryl and Dave were in Ottawa a few months ago, promoting David Lavigne's book, *Gaining Ground*. They were standing in front of Parliament, and apparently Harb came up to them and told them he wanted to do whatever he could to help end the seal hunt."

"Out of the blue?"

Stephen gives an I-wasn't-there shrug. "The way Dave tells it, Harb had been travelling in Europe for some Canadian and EU parliamentary meeting, and the one issue that kept coming up was the seal hunt and our government's lack of action against it. I suppose that's what motivated him."

"I'd love to talk to him."

"First the Senator Hervieux-Payette debate, then we'll see about Harb."

Back home, I write out the questions the *Talk Ottawa* host may ask me, and then frame my responses. I print them out, stuff them in my coat pocket, and grab Karma's leash.

"Karma, do you want to go to the dog park?"

His head springs up from the sofa. He jumps off and ziplines to the door, tail wagging.

Off Kortright Road is a five-mile stretch of pine forest with walking trails, muddy pools, and a riot of dogs chasing each other, their human companions not far behind. Karma knows where we are even before we turn onto the gravel road. When I open the door, he bounces out, beelining for a red setter, hoping to incite a chase. I pull out my crib sheet and begin to walk, slowly paralleling the racing dogs. I glance at the top question. *Without the seal hunt, how would fishermen control the growing population of seals and the declining population of cod?*

"Seals and cod have lived in harmony for a millennium. The cod decline is because of overfishing and poor fisheries management," I answer in undertones.

Silently, I read the next question. *Animal rights groups collect money from misguided donors. Aren't they using the seal hunt as a fundraising tool?* I sigh. I hate this question, or rather I hate what the question implies. What it implies is that animal organizations only care about animal cruelty because they can profit off it. They think of their campaigns as merchandise they can sell to an unsuspecting public. Instead of selling a mug or a sweatshirt with the organization's logo, they are selling an image, and the more horrible the image, the more it's worth. I inhale a frustrated breath before gathering my thoughts.

But first I glance up from my crib sheet and scan for Karma. I don't see him right away. Then out of the corner of my eye I catch sight of a streak of white clambering up the opposite bank of a gully that runs through the dog park. Karma's paws are thick with gooey mud, the kind that won't wash off easily. At the top of the embankment, he stops to look for me. Our eyes meet. Knowing I am where he expects me to be is the only reassurance my independently minded Karma needs, and then he's off, racing to the edge of the woods, while his former playmate, the setter, trots obediently beside her human companion. I have two choices: I can either give Karma his freedom to run joyfully around his favourite playground, or I can put him on a leash and force him to walk like a prisoner in chains up and down an uninspiring neighbourhood sidewalk. I choose to give him his freedom.

I turn back to the potential debate question and formulate my argument: "When people give money to animal production organizations they trust their donation will be used to fight against an animal practice. Donors can control how much money they give and can stop their donations at any time. They are kept informed about the progress of the campaign they help fund, and they can access fact sheets or more lengthy explanations of the campaign's approach. No one is misled.

"The federal government, on the other hand, does misleads its donors— us, Canada's taxpayers—about where our tax dollars go and about what percentage is used to advance projects or programs many oppose, such as the seal hunt. Canadian taxpayers can't stop their 'donations' at any time. Try and you'll be slapped with fines and late fees. There is little transparency; obtaining government documents is costly and time consuming; and pertinent information is often redacted. Moreover, the true reasons for expenditures are often not revealed, especially when the aim of the funding is political rather than altruistic."

As I walk on, I see a thin, glimmering, jagged line in the sand, no longer than 15 cm, with a white circle at the end of it. I bend down to inspect it and see a flattened snail shell and the sparkling, circuitous course she has taken, and the slime-like mucus she has left in her wake. (Snails are usually hermaphrodites, but I prefer the pronoun *she* instead of *it*.) Ahead, several dog walkers chat, keeping a long eye on their dogs, oblivious to the fragile snails crossing their path. I say a little prayer for the dead snail and move on, returning to my sheet. *"Ad hominem,"* I read, trying to remember what it means. Something about deflection. Like blaming the messenger. I make a mental note to squeeze it into the debate.

The next question is about the economic necessity of the seal hunt. *How will the sealers earn a living if activists have their way?* I know the answer off the top of my head. It's one I've used many times in reply to seal hunt supporters' accusations that the Canadian Seafood Boycott was bent on stealing the food off the dinner tables of hard-working, impoverished fishermen. My reply is that if politicians really cared about improving the lives of impoverished fishermen, then they'd tell them the truth about the seal hunt, which is that the seal hunt is an unprofitable make-work project for fishermen that is funded mostly if not totally by tax dollars. If the federal government genuinely cared about their constituents' livelihoods, they would buy back the fishermen's sealing licences and invest instead in twenty-first-century job creation and retraining programs. The seal hunt is an insulting non-solution to the real financial needs of fishing families.

As I continue along the dog walking path, a snail threads her way across the sandy, dry terrain, heading for the gluey mud and stagnant water of the gully. It may seem more hospitable to an unsuspecting snail traveller, but chances are she would get stuck in the mud, the opening to the cavity of her shell would fill up with silt, and she would suffocate. I pick up the mollusk by her shell and place her carefully in the grass so she won't get stepped on.

* * *

I'm sweating under the hot lights in the *Talk Ottawa* studio as a soundman fits a tiny microphone inside my collar.[2]

"Say something," the sound technician says, holding the mic in front of my lips.

"Something." I laugh nervously.

The woman in a tweed blazer beside me flashes a beauty-queen smile. Senator Céline Hervieux-Payette, I presume.

The lights are hot, the back of my neck itchy. Before I can scratch, the lights flash on and off and a loud buzzing noise lets us know we are *on air*.

"I'm your host, Jenn Geary, and on *Talk Ottawa* tonight we are here to discuss the seal hunt. Our two guests come from very different sides of the issue. Here with us from Québec, Senator Céline Hervieux-Payette, and uh . . ." (she searches her notes) ". . . from the Animal Alliance, Karen Levenson."

"Director of the seal campaign."

"Yes, that's right," Jenn enthuses. "We're glad to have you both. As you know, the seal hunt is a complex issue with two sides diametrically opposed. So, tell us what the seal hunt means to you?"

"Jobs!" The senator raises her chin. "And food on the tables of poor fishermen."

"Cruelty," I say. "And government failure. If the seal hunt is the only way to end poverty in Québec and Newfoundland, our government is failing."

"Some people think the seal hunt is unnecessarily cruel. What do you say?" Jenn Geary nods to the senator.

"Canada's seal hunt is the most humane marine mammal hunt in the world," she says, reading from her notes.

"Have you seen it?" I interrupt. I know she hasn't. (Neither have I, though I've seen the videos and read the witness reports.) But Paul Watson has, and in his face-off with Hervieux-Payette on CTV, he said something like: "You've not been to the hunt or seen a seal killed, have you? You're in no position to claim it's humane."

"Our sealers have regulations to follow. It is the most well-regulated, humane slaughter of marine animals in the world."

I repeat a splendid Paul Watson comeback. "To say it's humane is like accusing [serial child killer] Clifford Olson of mildly abusing children."[3]

Hervieux-Payette's head whiplashes. But I step on the gas: "Veterinarians who *have* seen the hunt say that seals are skinned alive. Is that what *you* call *humane?*"

"It is like any other hunts of animals for food," she says. Then she implies that the way sealers kill seals is no different than the way farmers kill pigs and chickens. She says that farmers must follow codes of practice (which are voluntary and not enforced, although Hervieux-Payette doesn't mention this fact) just as sealers must follow regulations (which are only periodically enforced).

I cannot let her get away with her attempt to soft-soap cruelty. So, I say, "Undercover videos show workers bashing in the heads of pigs, stomping on the backs of chickens. We see the same thing with the seal hunt: sealers club the heads of three-week-old seal pups or stomp on or kick them. Is that humane?"

"They are clubbed on the head so they lose consciousness," she says. "If I have a car accident and I hit my head, I lose consciousness. If the car is burning, I won't feel it. It doesn't look nice. But it is better that I am unconscious."

My eyebrows waggle, but before I can say anything, the senator continues: "We have too many seals. Like we have too many deer on Vancouver Island. If we do not shoot them, they cannot live. They won't have enough food. We must do something."-

"If you want to talk about deer or traffic accidents, I'm happy to another time. But now, let's stick to seals."

The senator opens her mouth, shocked by my directness.

"Killing animals so they can live defies logic," I jab. But before I can decimate the senator's argument further, Jenn Geary interrupts.

"Many people say animal activists are terrorists. What do you say?" she asks the senator.

I admire anyone who can sit beside a senator who calls you a terrorist and respond without wringing her neck. I sit on my hands, waiting for her to finish. What was that word Stephen had given me? *Ad . . . ad hom . . . ad hom. . . .* I look up. Jenn Geary is staring at me.

"Miss Levenson, what do you say?"

"Ad hominem," I sputter.

"Ad hominem?" The senator lowers her chin into her pearls and side-glances me.

"Go on," Geary encourages.

But my head is foggy like after a summer rain, when the heat rises from the ground and makes one momentarily feel lost.

You know this, my Doppelgänger says. *Snap out of it!* And then the fog lifts.

"In a country as rich as Canada, suggesting the seal hunt is the way out of poverty is ludicrous!"

Bravo, the Dop says.

Soon, the debate is over. The technicians begin moving away the tall studio lights and turning them off. The senator and I push back our chairs simultaneously. I side-glance her: she looks like she has morning sickness, though I am certain she's too old. She side-glances me, too. I know the look. It's as if I were a spider she wished to squish. Once she gathers her notes and purse, she gives me a wide berth and heads out toward the lobby. Giddy, I pack up my belongings. As I walk out of the studio, a production assistant gives me a thumbs-up. I grin my widest yet humblest, we-are-all-in-this-together grin, and allow myself a quiet, self-congratulatory chortle.

You are a superstar! I tell myself as I wait in the lobby for my airport taxi.

"Before you leave," the receptionist calls out from the lobby desk, "Would you mind confirming your address? We'll mail you the tape once it's ready."

"A tape?"

"That's right—we send a tape to everyone who comes on the show."

I write my address on the paper provided and the receptionist compares it to the one she has on the computer.

"You're good to go. You should receive it by the end of the week."

When the tape arrives several days later, I can't wait to pop it into my video machine. Ben and I watch it together.

"You're too aggressive," Ben says once the tape ends.

I sit on the sofa, picking the cuticle on my right thumb.

"You come off like a televangelical rooting out evil."

"All women seem aggressive when they stand up for what they believe in," I bristle. But I can't deny the sinking feeling as I watch the tape a second time. Fewer eye rolls and smug facial expressions would have been nice.

34

NO MORE MR. NICE GUY

IN JANUARY 2007, the European Commission rejects appeals for an EU-wide ban on seal trade. Mouthing the words of the DFO, it claims: "Seals are not listed as an endangered species." Nevertheless, on January 25, Belgium becomes the first country to ban seal imports.[1] The Netherlands is not far behind.

"Think about Canadian soldiers who died in Europe during the First World War before slamming the door shut on Canadian seal products," Fisheries and Oceans Minister Loyola Hearn scolds.

Hearn blames activists for their pressure campaigns. Should he restrict observer licences? Ban them altogether? Or should he settle on something less excessive—something that would draw less public ire? He decides to increase the observation distance from ten metres to twenty.

"There was no consultation!" activists fume.

"How can you see anything from twenty metres away?" observers lament.

Meanwhile, snow crab exports to the United States have dropped by 36 percent or US$353.6 million.

On April 3, 2007, the seal hunt begins in the Southern Gulf in what scientists call "the worst ice conditions for more than two decades." They describe ice so thin or nonexistent that the latest cohort of baby harp seals is nearly wiped out. Instead of paying C$105 per pelt as they did in 2006, buyers will now pay only C$55 for a top-quality pelt.

Then, on April 18, the Front's hunt begins against the backdrop of cracking and splitting ice. One hundred sealing vessels become trapped between the moving pans, as do some Coast Guard icebreakers attempting to free them. The Coast Guard dispatches helicopters to drop food, water, and smokes to the stranded seamen and Coast Guard officers. Eventually, fifty crew members are evacuated, though five hundred remain to hunt and kill 221,488 baby seals and 3,257 adults.

While Ottawa tries to convince the EU not to ban seal products, which it claims are economic necessities in Newfoundland and Québec, Newfoundland sealer Desmond Adams tells the *Toronto Star* in an April 23 article: "We all go out [sealing] for the love of it rather than the money."

Rebecca responds. "If the above quote [. . .] is true for even a portion of Canada's commercial seal hunters, allowing the seal hunt to continue [. . .] is an abomination. Economic data from Canada confirm that Adams is right about one thing—sealers earn a very small share of their annual income from the commercial seal hunt."

So which is it: love or money? I wonder. The seal hunt's economic necessity has always been a point of contention between the government and activists. The DFO claims sealers earn up to 35 percent of their annual income from the hunt, while activists claim it is more like 5 percent. Who's right?

Read the Eminent Panel report, the Dop says.

The report?

The report Stephen told you about.

The report! With all the calls, mailings, and email correspondence to US chefs, I've forgotten all about the "Report of the Eminent Panel on Seal Management." *Of course*, it would have some clues. Why else would Stephen suggest it?

The lemony mid-morning sun pierces my office window and refracts off the smudges on my glasses. I wipe the lenses clean with my sweatshirt and adjust the frame snugly on my nose before Googling the 2001 report. The origin of the report traces back to 1998, when Fisheries and Oceans

Minister Herb Dhaliwal assembled a panel of economists and fisheries scientists to determine "the best strategies for management of seal populations in Atlantic Canada." While attempting to fulfill its mandate, the panel discovered that the economic data it had received from the DFO and DFA (Newfoundland's Department of Fisheries and Aquaculture) were "imprecise" and "lacking in consistency." For instance, the DFO reported that in 1998, the total value of the commercial seal hunt was C$5.6 million, C$5.4 million of which resulted from the Newfoundland portion of the hunt. Yet, the DFA reported that in 1998 the value of its portion of the hunt was C$8.75M.[2]

I find the discrepancies mind-boggling, as I'm sure the panel did. Unfortunately, the DFO offered little insight as to why the discrepancies occurred. It told the panel that the data that both agencies provided "[were] derived from purchase slips prepared by buyers and that all products [pelts, blubber, meat] [were] included."

After several rereadings, I latch onto the words *purchase slips*. I've never heard of them, but they seem important. In fact, they seem like the very things I need in order to determine the value of the 2006 and 2007 seal hunts. Who should I call to get them? Although the DFO manages the seal hunt, it's the DFA that has the most vested interest. Ninety percent of the sealers come from Newfoundland and it's where seventy percent of the seal hunt takes place. I call the DFA and am put through to the department's access to information and privacy (ATIP) coordinator.

"The Eminent Panel report says that you and the DFO determine the value of the seal hunt from purchase slips," I paraphrase to the ATIP coordinator.

There's a notable silence. I continue. "The Eminent Panel report— you know, the 2001 'Report of the Eminent Panel on Seal Management' . . . Herb Dhaliwal, fisheries minister. . . ."

"Yeah?" the coordinator says.

"The purchase slips are the way you determine the value of the hunt, right?"

"That's a while ago, eh, 2001?"

"Six years. If the Eminent Panel is right, I'd like to see them."

"Purchase slips?"

"Yes."

"We don't got no purchase slips."

"Then how do you know the value of each year's hunt?"

"The buyers call it in."

"Call *what* in, exactly?"

"What they've paid for."

"Paid for?"

"The pelts."

"Each buyer tells your department every year by word of mouth how much they paid for the pelts?"

"Not our department."

"Then what department?"

"The Department of Fisheries and Oceans."

"So I need to call the DFO?"

"Yes."

"And they'll have the purchase slips?"

"No. It's all word of mouth, I told you."[3]

"The federal and Newfoundland fisheries departments take the buyer's word just like that?"

"Just like that."

"With no proof?"

"We've got the proof. They tell us."

"But not physical proof."

"Why would we need it? It's pretty casual," the coordinator affirms. "The department has a good relationship with the buyers, so there's no reason not to trust them."

How can fisheries departments be so careless? As disappointing as the information is, I believe it's true. In the June 15, 2006 Standing Committee on Fisheries and Oceans transcript, the DFO's assistant deputy minister,

David Bevan, states: "We know how many animals are taken as a result of the fact that we have a good working relationship with the buyers and processors, etc. We have a good handle on that."[4]

I call the DFO.

The chief statistician confirms that the data from the purchase slips are used to determine the value of the seal hunt.

"Can I get them?"

"We don't have them."

"Who does?"

"The buyers."

I click off the call and stare into my lap. If the buyers are the only ones who have the purchase slips, I'll never get to see them. Buyers are private companies; they don't have to turn over documents to the public.

A colleague at Sea Shepherd suggests I call one of the Newfoundland regional staff officers at the DFO.

"He's a good guy," says my colleague. "Any time I have a question about how things work, he's always been helpful."

Surprisingly, it doesn't take long to reach the Staff Officer. After explaining who I am, I start with the basics. "How does the government arrive at the annual value of the seal hunt?"

"Sealers are required to maintain logbooks and orally report—it's called *hailing in*—the number of the seals they take each day, and once they sell the pelts, the buyer gives the DFO a copy of the receipt."

"The buyer gives the DFO a physical sales record—on a piece of paper?"

"Yeah, it's called a *purchase slip*. It's a receipt that lists the quantity of pelts the buyer purchased and the agreed-upon purchase price and the total amount of the sale. Buyers are required by law to provide this information."

"So, it's not just word of mouth!"

"That's right."

Then, it dawns on me. If each sealer gets a purchase slip, and the DFO gets a copy of each of them, all I need to do is request copies of the purchase slips from the DFO. That way, I can find out what each sealer earned during the hunt, how many pelts he landed, and how many sealers set sail in 2006 and 2007.

"Hold on," the Staff Officer cautions. "Not all sealers receive a purchase slip for the pelts they landed. The captain of the boat usually hands over all the pelts. He's the one who would receive the purchase slip."

"You mean, there's only one purchase slip for each boat, even though four or five sealers might have landed the pelts?"

"A copy is given to the captain of the vessel, one to the DFO, and one stays with the buyer."

"Who does the captain deal with? How do all the sealers get paid?" I ask.

"Depends on how the processing companies are set up. A company representative might meet the captain at the dock; or the captain might have to deal with the head office."

"A company representative from each purchasing company is stationed at each of the docks, waiting to count the pelts and hand out the money?"

"There's no one specific way," the Staff Officer replies. "Maybe the sealing vessel lands at a port where a buyer is already there, and the captain negotiates the price. Or if there's already a purchasing agreement, then the buyer takes the pelts, counts them, and issues a purchase slip and the cash. The captain divvies up the payment he receives with his crew, minus his expenses and a percentage of the total haul."

"How much were seal pelts going for in 2006?" I ask.

"In 2006, all the buyers agreed to an 'across-the-board' price of C\$105 per pelt, irrespective of grade and age class."

"Was that unusual?" I ask.

"There's not often a blanket price. The pelts are usually graded at the processing plant: A, B, or C. An A pelt is worth more than a B and a B pelt is worth more than a C."

But in 2006 there was a blanket price. All I need to do is add up the total number of pelts from each purchase slip and multiply that number by 105 to get the value of the commercial seal hunt. My next step is clear. I must get those purchase slips. I decide to file a request to the Access to Information and Privacy (ATIP) Office.

35

Giving Me the Slip

I SPEND THE next ten minutes clicking through the DFO's website until I come to the Access to Information form. I request every document the DFO uses to determine the value of Canada's 2006 commercial seal hunt. I also include the John Kearley quote confirming the existence of purchase slips. I address the envelope to the DFO's ATIP office and mail it on my walk with Karma.

Thirty days later, I receive a call from the DFO.

"We received your Access to Information request," a woman with a heavy Québécois accent says.

"Great. When will I receive the information?"

"We don't understand it."

"Don't understand what?"

"Your Access to Information request."

"What's not to understand?"

"Your Access to Information request," she repeats.

"You mean *no one* at the DFO understands my Access to Information request?"

There is silence so long that for a moment I think I've lost her. Finally, she says, "We can't make head or tail out of it."

"You don't have the purchase slips mentioned in the November 6 Standing Committee record?"

"We don't have that information," says the woman, whose name is Nicolette.

"So you're saying, Nicolette, that Mr. Kearley, the manager of Carino Company Limited, Canada's largest seal processor, lied to the Standing Committee on Fisheries and Oceans?"

"No," she says.

"I hope not. Because here are his exact words." I read them into the phone.

Nicolette stammers, "I have to ask my supervisor."

"You do that." I click off my cellphone.

The next morning, Nicolette calls me. "*Bonjour,* Ms. Levenson."

"*Bonjour.* Did you find the purchase slips?"

"You'll need to reword your request."

"What!?"

"You'll need to reword it. No one understands it."

"It took a month for you to tell me I need to reword my request?"

"I will help you write it. I'll send you my suggestions by email," she promises.

I hang up, fuming in my swivel chair. I wonder how long I'll have to wait.

Breathe, says Grandma. *And don't grind your teeth. You'll wear them down.*

Calm down, says the Dop. *You have heart disease in your family.*

I inhale and exhale several times to breathe out my frustration. I need a massage. It's covered by our benefits. But there's no time for one. I log in to Gmail. Sitting at the top of my inbox is an email from the DFO. I click it open. Damn! Nicolette is fast! A quick read leaves me feeling deflated, but I rebound quickly. "Oh no, Nicolette, you're not going to screw with me," I say into the air, as I dial her phone number.

"You don't like it?" she says, surprised.

"It's convoluted. No one will understand it. I'll never get what I want."

You won't get what you want anyway.

What? Did I hear correctly? Did Nicolette say, "You won't get what you want anyway"? Or did I imagine it? I give my head a shake.

"But you must rewrite it if you want the information," Nicolette says.

"Okay, I'll rewrite just like you suggest. Just tell me how long it will take."

"We respond within thirty days of receiving your request."

"You already received my request."

"That was the old one. We don't have your new one."

My teeth grind. "Fine! I'll send it now!"

"*Bien!*" she says.

Merde! I think.

I cut and paste Nicolette's suggestion into the waiting cell of the ATIP form, print it out, and stuff it into an envelope. Am I making the right decision? Should I have fought harder for my version or requested a guarantee that I'd receive the purchase slips? What would Nancy Drew do in my place? She wouldn't use a sharp tone and a French swear. She'd . . . she'd . . . I pull *The Mystery of the 99 Steps* from my bookshelf, open to a random page, and read: "After she put down the receiver, the young sleuth sat staring into space."

I stare into space.

"She was perplexed by this turn of events."

I'm perplexed by the turn of events.

"Nancy had so hoped to warn her father that Monsieur Leblanc was being hoodwinked by an alchemist's trick!"

Am I being hoodwinked by a DFO trick?

* * *

"Nine hundred dollars! What could possibly cost nine hundred dollars? I'm not asking you for the keys to the DFO," I shout into the phone. It's a month and a half since I reworded my request. Now Nicolette tells me if I want the documents, I must pay nine hundred dollars. "For purchase slips?"

"It is not for them. Those are free. It is for the labour."

"The labour! It costs nine hundred dollars for someone to pull purchase slips out of a filing cabinet?"

"There are many slips of paper. Someone has to photocopy each one."

"Photocopies!"

"You do not think we give you the originals?"

Nine hundred dollars of our donors' money! Would seeing the purchase slips be worth it? I can't approve such a large sum on my own. "How can I be sure you'll send me the information I want?" I challenge Nicolette.

"You'll be able to inspect it at our Burlington office when it's ready."

The DFO has a Burlington office? I'm amazed. Even with my mid-level grasp of Canadian geography, I can't think of an ocean anywhere near Burlington.

* * *

On September 26, 2007, after learning that Austria, Britain, France, and Germany are all considering laws in support of an EU-wide seal trade ban, Ottawa contacts the World Trade Organization (WTO) to file a formal complaint. On November 11, Ottawa sends delegates to dispute Belgium's and the Netherlands' seal product bans and circumvent Germany's imminent one.

* * *

The September leaves are vibrating on the branches of the cherry trees outside as Karma and I return from our morning walk in the dog park. I make him his breakfast—a mix of cut-up veggie dogs, carrots, and rice— and pour it into his food bowl. He looks at me, crestfallen, and nose-nudges the bowl away.

"Eat it," I say, pointing to his food bowl. Karma sulks out of the kitchen and flops under the table where I feed Ben, hoping to find tasty droppings.

After calling Miami chefs all morning, I switch gears and read the November 6 Standing Committee evidence again, hoping to find something I've missed. As the sun heats up my office with its midday furnace, my head rolls forward on my shoulders and my eyelids droop. I'm ready to head for the bedroom for a quick snooze when my eyes fish out a paragraph in which Carino's general manager, John Kearley, explains how the company makes fiscal decisions. I put my hands to my face, rub, yawn, push myself upright, and read:

> [W]e make decisions as a company on how much we're going to pay for seal pelts, based on the entire TAC being taken. We know what the TAC is to be [. . .] and we compete with other processors to get [it] all. [. . .] If the TAC in a certain area [. . .] is not taken, then the decisions that we make may be bogus, in that we would not be able to procure sufficient animals to go to our buyers. Then we have buyers who are not pleased because we couldn't fill their order, so then it affects us in the future as to what they would probably pay for seal pelts.[1]

Bogus! Did Kearley say "bogus"? I read the paragraph again, this time slowly. As far as I can tell, Kearley is explaining how Carino determines what it'll pay sealers each year prior to the hunt. Is Kearley suggesting that what it decided to pay sealers in 2006 was a sham? I find Carino's price list for 2006 on its website. Carino had paid C$105 for each pelt. But as I reread the Standing Committee paragraph, it seems to imply that their decision was the result of a guessing game. Can that be right? Clearly it was, because Kearley tells the committee that the company guessed wrong, and because they had already committed to paying sealers the C$105 per pelt, they lost money.

It's important information. I can't risk losing it in the bottomless pit of my seal campaign folders. But where can I store it? An idea occurs to me. I head to the kitchen and search through drawers and cupboards full of dishtowels, cruelty-free cleaners, and shoe polish. I find what I'm looking for: a skein of twine Ben bought years ago. I pull it out, grab a pair of scissors, a roll of masking tape, and a handful of clothespins, and hurry back to my office. I unroll enough twine to affix one end to the far corner of my office with a line of masking tape. I unroll the skein some more, allowing the twine to unravel a good length. When I'm sure I have enough, I cut the twine and tape the cut end to the opposite corner of the room. With the twine above my head, I cut out the quote from Kearley and pin it to the centre of my makeshift clothesline. I fold my arms across my chest and give myself an appreciative nod. This must have been how my grandfathers felt when discovering a reusable widget at the dump.

36

OH SHIT!

I FLY TO Miami for the boycott a few weeks before the 2008 seal hunt and spend a week rustling around South Beach, Biscayne Bay, and Coral Gables, speaking to world-renowned chefs at high-end restaurants and luxury hotels. At the Palme d'Or, the internationally esteemed French restaurant at the Biltmore Hotel in Coral Gables, I meet French chef Philippe Ruiz. He welcomes me into his restaurant and overwhelms me with his kindness and generosity. Without hesitation, he signs my pledge and offers me small plates of vegan food. Out of all the pledges by South Florida chefs who sign on to the boycott, his means the most to me.

While I'm away, the DFO cuts sealing quotas to 270,000 due to climate change–based pressure from marine scientists as well as fear that the EU will implement a union-wide seal import ban. Pelt prices tumble to C$25 for a Grade A pelt; it's a 400 percent fall from 2006.

In London, seal-costumed protesters parade through the Canadian Embassy. In Hamburg, naked bodies painted red position themselves on the ground imitating a pile of seal pelts. Speculation is mounting that the EU will adopt a union-wide seal import ban.

Upon my returning home, depression whacks me like the swinging doors of a restaurant's kitchen. The drive from Toronto's Pearson Airport to Guelph is as appealing as gravel on the roadside. The sky is grim, and cars on the 401 are so jammed together that, from above, we must look like glued-together Lego pieces. And although the direct flight from Miami to Toronto is a cakewalk, to save Animal Alliance money, I booked the cheapest round-trip ticket, which meant two layovers. As I step out of the taxi in front of my building, I wobble on the skateboard of jet lag.

"What are you going to make for dinner?" Ben asks as I unpack my suitcase. I can feel my back automatically stiffen. Making dinner is the last thing I want to do. My cells are demanding a quick shower and bed.

I mush down the lumps of the minute oatmeal, hot from the microwave, and serve it steaming. At the table, I add a splash of cold soymilk and a swirl of maple syrup. It's not the tongue-tantalizing garlic rapini from the award-winning Biscayne Bay Restaurant, but it has its own culinary charm.

"Lumpy," Ben complains, staring into the bowl.

I look inside his bowl, pinpointing a few anorexic lumps. I clobber them with Ben's spoon and drizzle in more milk.

I scrape a quarter spoon of the gruel onto Ben's spoon, and he opens his mouth wide.

"Cold," he says.

I scoop a spoonful of oatmeal into my own mouth and have to agree: I'm off my oatmeal-cooking game.

I reach for his bowl and head into the kitchen.

"What are you going to do with it?"

"Heat it up."

"Can't you make me something else?"

"Like what?"

"Stir fry?"

"I'm not going to make stir fry now. I've had a long day." I indicate his bowl in my hand. "If you don't want it, I'll eat it."

Ben's eyes blacken, but seconds later he capitulates. I put his bowl in the microwave and press the minute timer button.

Ben is halfway through his coffee when Karma, standing at the front door, barks. He trots over, nudges my thigh, and barks again, staring at me with hyperfocus.

"I'll take him out and heat up your coffee when I get back."

"Jesus Christ, Karen!"

"Jesus Christ what? He has to go!"

Karma dances urgently, back at the front door.

"I can't even finish a goddamn cup of coffee."

"Fifteen minutes, tops," I say, tossing on my coat.

Our neighbours' lawns are sodden with end-of-March, shoe-sinking mud, rimmed by crusty snowbanks covered with car splash. Wet seeps through the torn rubber soles of my boots and my socks sop it up. I start jumping over the puddles one by one, pulling Karma along until we are in front of a neighbour's lit windows. I linger on the sidewalk, peeking inside, as Karma sniffs their old maple tree. Inside the house, I see a couple sitting so closely on a sofa their thighs touch. A flannelled arm wraps around a grey-turtlenecked shoulder. On the TV is an image of an overturned sealing boat sliding off an ice pan.

What's happened? Why don't I know about this? I answer my own question. I've spent the entire day calling chefs, too focused on accumulating pledges to pay attention to the news or dwell on the fact that today is the first day of the seal hunt. Was anyone hurt? Suddenly, my arm wrenches and Karma tugs me across the mucky lawn. Before I can stop him, he squats and a string of poo unravels, just as Flannel Shirt rises from the sofa and looks casually out into the night. Pulling Karma with me, I duck behind the old but portly maple. Flannel Shirt says something to Grey Sweater. I hold Karma's collar, pulling him onto the sidewalk in case Flannel Shirt sees us. But she is heading away from the window to the kitchen. The tightness releases in my chest and I release my grip on Karma's collar. He's ready to trot on and I am too, until I see . . .

"Shit," I say, staring at the steaming poo. I reach into my coat for poo bags. My fingers circle empty pockets. "Shit, shit, shit." Karma looks from me to the poo and wags his tail.

"What did the dog walker let you eat while I was in Florida? Rabbit poop in the dog park? The decomposed flesh of a deer leg in the woods?" No matter, I can't leave the dissolving mess on the neighbour's lawn. With the heel of my boot, I scrape a runnel in the thawing snow and toe the shit in, covering it with snow.

Back home, I hang up Karma's leash and remove my boots in the foyer. One look at Karma's backside and I rush into the kitchen and grab a paper towel roll. I wipe his poo-crusted anus and the poo matted beneath, then toss the soiled towels into the garbage before scouring my hands in the sink. Only then do I notice Ben is not at the table where I left him.

"Ben? I'm back."

"I'm in the washroom," he calls.

I tap the door then open it. Ben is struggling to raise himself off his wheelchair cushion and onto the toilet seat.

"What are you doing?"

"What does it look like?" he says.

"Let me help you."

Ben lets himself fall back, exhausted, onto his wheelchair cushion.

"How long have you been here?"

"You said fifteen minutes! I had to go."

I lever the wheelchair back from the toilet, then turn it off. Steadying my feet apart and bending my knees so my shoulders align with his, I sling his arm around my neck and hoist my 240-pound husband out of his chair, turning him slowly to ease him onto the toilet.

"Okay?"

He twists his head away and stares at the wall tile.

"I'll give you some privacy. Call when you're done." I close the door.

Somewhere in my back, a muscle twinges. I place my hand beneath the spot and with one foot forward and one back, I stretch it out and rub at the contraction with my knuckles. Thank the universe that chiropractors are covered in our AAC benefits package. I slump into my swivel chair and squeeze my eyelids shut. But I can't dispel the vision of Ben struggling to reach the toilet or the image of the overturned boat sinking into the water.

The capsize happened miles off Nova Scotia. A sealing boat became trapped between two ice pans and a Coast Guard vessel came to tow it. But something went drastically wrong: an awkward pull of the tow lines, the inattention of the helmsman. Divers found three drowned bodies; a fourth body was not recovered and was presumed dead. Two other sealers miraculously survived. I close my eyes again for just a minute and feel my head listing to the side. Suddenly, I jerk awake and my eyes flash open. I stare down at Levi, who is poking my thigh with his paw, wanting to be picked up and cuddled. I gently shoo him away and rub my eyes. How long have I been asleep? Then it dawns on me: Ben must still be in the washroom. My chair slides back as I stand up and I head down the hall with Levi following at my heels. Cocking my ear to the door, I try to hear inside. Through the door I hear muffled moaning.

"Ben? Ben, are you alright?" I don't wait for him to answer. I throw the door open wide and see that Ben is still sitting on the toilet. His face is scarlet as he strains and grunts and a flatulent odor hovers.

"How's it going?"

"It's not."

"You're kidding!"

He strains again, only his words squeezing out. "It's been five days!" And then he crumples.

"Five!" I place my hand on his shoulder. "Let's get you up." I help Ben back into his chair. "Do you want to go to bed?"

He shakes his head.

"Come, then. Let's watch TV."

Ben's tears well, but he can't wipe them away. I pull a towel off the paper towel roll and gently wipe his eyes.

"Don't worry. You can try again later."

* * *

On the second day of the hunt, forty miles east of Ingonish, Cape Breton, the Coast Guard vessel *Des Groseilliers* rams the *Farley Mowat*.[1] A crew member videotapes it, but when officials seize the ship, they confiscate the tape and arrest the captain and first officer. During a news conference, Hearn melts down like a mannequin on fire at Madame Tussauds. He condemns the *Farley Mowat*'s crew as "a bunch of money-sucking manipulators" and Paul Watson as "gutless."

My anger boils like a pot on a volcano. Hearn's hatred for activists (in my opinion), his lack of control at news conferences, and his mischaracterization of events when activists' lives are put in danger by fisheries officers or the RCMP pervert his ability to make good decisions. I write to Prime Minister Stephen Harper, calling for Hearn's removal.

* * *

The next morning, I pull open the blinds in Ben's bedroom to the morning's felted dreariness.

"Wakey, wakey! It's already ten."

"I'm up," Ben moans.

"How are you feeling?"

"Sharp pains."

His face is pale green.

"Is it continuous?"

"On and off. Every fifteen minutes."

"Want me to call an ambulance?"

"No. I want to get out of bed."

I lower the cot's sidebar and pull his blankets down past his feet. That's when I see his stomach, bloated to the size of a basketball.

"Oh my God, Ben, is it gas?"

In too much pain to answer, he moans, "Bend my legs over my stomach."

I hoist his legs up, bend his knees, and guide them over his abdomen. Ben groans, squeezing his eyes shut. But as hard as Ben strains, no stomach gas exits.

"Stop! Put my legs down!" he cries in pain.

I guide his legs back onto the cot.

"Press my stomach."

I lay my palms below his belly button and press.

"*Awhhhh!*" he grunts. "Not in the middle. On the sides."

My palms firmly bear down on either side. His body stiffens; his toes point.

"*Auuuuuhhh!*" he howls.

With all the pressing, I expect to hear an explosion of fetid wind. But the basketball refuses to deflate. "What about sitting upright?" I maneuver his body to the cot's edge and fold him into a sitting position. Holding him in place, I turn on the wheelchair, but soon realize there's no way to move it and hold Ben. I lay him back down and toggle the control lever, inching the wheelchair closer, before flicking the switch off. Returning Ben to sitting, I adjust his body so I can lift him up, then tiny-step him around and into the chair. Our first stop is the washroom. I arrange him on the toilet and wait outside, massaging my sacrum. I'm about to head to my office for a longer wait when Ben calls. Except for an ounce of urine, there's nothing to flush. I wipe the tip of his penis and reverse my actions. I follow him to the living room and turn on the TV. He groans again, his eyes finding mine.

"Do you *want* me to call an ambulance?"

"No."

An hour later, he says *yes*.

When the paramedics arrive, two navy-uniformed women lift Ben onto the gurney and secure his body with a strap.

"*Uuuuuhhhhh!*" Ben protests as the gurney bumps over the lobby threshold.

"I'll be right behind you," I shout before the double doors of the ambulance close.

In the emergency room, Ben lies in one of the small rooms behind a green curtain at the far end of the row. I slide the curtain open and am about to step inside when a plump nurse edges in front of me. "The doctor's ordered morphine for your pain," she tells Ben. Turning toward me, she says, "He told me he has ALS."

"Yes." I tell her.

"We'll have to call his neurologist, then."

She pulls a notepad from her pocket and scribbles Dr. Ryan's name. Then she assures us, "The doctor will be in shortly." A second later, pea-green scrubs and a navy bandana poke in.

"I'm Dr. Kabango," he says, studying Ben. "You're dehydrated." He turns to the nurse, "Get the IV."

Once the nurse has left, Dr. Kabango steps up to the bed. He reaches for Ben's wrist and silently counts the beats of his pulse, then shines a penlight into Ben's mouth, stethoscopes his heart, and has him breathe in and out.

"Heart good. Lungs good." He touches Ben's stomach.

"*Ahhhh,*" Ben cries.

"What about here?" Kabango says, and then places his hand on another spot, and then another.

Ben groans each time.

"When was he diagnosed with ALS?" Kabango asks me, his eyes still on Ben.

"About ten years ago."

Kabango's eyebrows raise. "Ten years!"

"At first, they thought it was . . ."

Kabango cuts me off. "We're going to take some X-rays, then probably surgery to remove some of the blockage."

"What's wrong?"

"As ALS progresses, people find they can't be as physically active, so the abdominal and pelvic muscles weaken and are less able to push waste out." He leans over the edge of Ben's cot and asks, "When did you start having trouble?"

Ben groans.

"About a week ago," I tell Kabango.

"Three weeks," Ben groans.

"Can you fix it?" I ask.

"With ALS, his muscles will only get weaker. Bowel blockages will become more frequent."

"It's not life-threatening though?"

"Put it this way: he probably won't die of a collapsed lung. It'll be a bowel blockage that will kill him."

I move in closer to Ben and hold his hand as the doctor ducks out and the nurse wheels in the IV pole with a fluid pack hooked on. I step aside so she can insert the IV needle into a vein in Ben's wrist.

"Why don't you go home, dear," she suggests, likely reading the horror in my face. "You can't do anything for him now. We'll call you when he has a room," she says, tapping the tube with the back of her index finger to make sure the fluid is flowing.

At home, I'm clumsy-tired. I stumble to the sofa and fall onto it, my coat and boots still on, and begin to hyperventilate. Karma lays his head on my lap, his eyes looking up at me, while Bella lounges on the armrest and Levi settles behind me on the back cushion. As I breathe and breathe, I think of Ben's lungs collapsing and his abdomen muscles dissolving like sugar in the rain.

* * *

Hypoxia (oxygen loss) has created dead zones in the Northwest Atlantic where marine species, including cod, can't survive. One theory gaining traction is that decomposing plant and marine life, including the rotting carcasses of slaughtered seals, has caused bacterial counts to rise and oxygen to decline, so that small prey species that cod rely on for food die off. Oxygen is the life force of the ocean; hypoxia is what kills it.

* * *

I race through the sliding doors into the waiting area and skid to a stop at the ER reception window. "I got a call my husband's in surgery! Ben Ouellette!"

The receptionist types into her computer, studies the screen, and then speaks through the open reception window. "You might as well take a seat. Looks like he'll be a while." I flop into one of the waiting room chairs in front of her window. The wall clock's long arm lowers and rises twice before the receptionist tells me I can go up to the third floor.

Ben is in the ICU; his curtained stall is across from the nurses' station. Not only is he hooked up to an IV monitor, but he also has a nasogastric tube running up a nostril, down his throat, and into his stomach. Another tube leads to a plastic jug hooked to the cot's bottom frame, and it is filling with green sludge. When the jug is full, a nurse will unhook it to take away, but before she does, she will hook on a clean one.

"Chances are he won't wake up for a while," the nurse confides. "The doctor gave him some morphine." I notice another needle in his vein, with a tube leading from another fluid pack. I sit in the visitor's chair and contemplate a crack in the yellow-painted wall as Ben sleeps. Hours later, his eyes open and he blinks at me. Then he falls back asleep. Eventually, I return home. I spend the latter part of the afternoon in my office, sorting articles into my red notebook and putting together packages of boycott information to courier to chefs in the US. When my cellphone rings, I brace myself, expecting the doctor.

"Hello?" my voice wobbles.

"Guess what!" A woman's voice speed-skates down the length of her sentences. "A DFO official just admitted that the commercial seal hunt is not well regulated or closely monitored!"

It takes me a long second to recognize that the voice belongs to Bridget Curran, founder of the Atlantic Canadian Anti-Sealing Coalition in Nova Scotia. I snap to attention.

"Oh my God! Tell me!"

"I just got off the phone with a fisheries supervisor in _____.[2] He said that in his detachment, dockside monitors are never present during the hunt!"

"How can it be well managed if there's no dockside monitoring?"

"I asked the same question. He said, 'Sealers aren't required to have a dockside monitor count their pelts, and that in their DFO detachment one is never present during the hunt. All sealers need to do is hail in the number of pelts they've landed.'"

"And the DFO just takes their word?"

"Apparently."

"Nobody confirms the number of pelts?"

"They do a few random spot checks. But other than that, he said, 'We don't look over their shoulders.' But maybe they should. The reason I called him in the first place is I got a call from a resident who saw eight to ten sealers driving ATVs and Ski-doos that were hauling wooden box-sleds piled high with seal pelts, and the sealers took them right to a sealer's home."

"Did you tell the supervisor?"

"Of course. He just repeated that they don't look over sealers' shoulders. That most of the guys are honest."

After clicking off the phone, I call the detachment supervisor, hoping to corroborate Bridget's account of their conversation. Surprisingly, he picks up and, without hesitation, confirms almost verbatim what Bridget told me.

Nevertheless, the DFO refers to its Dockside Monitoring Program as "the main and sometimes the only way it receives the information it needs to manage the fisheries." Later, I check with another industry source who confirms that "dockside monitors are never present" in his area.

* * *

Three weeks after his surgery, Ben's health improves. He's moved to the step-down unit. A week later, as I walk past the nurses' station on my way home, the night nurse says, "You'll be happy your guy's going home soon."

"What?"

"The doctor plans to sign his release papers on Thursday."

Thursday? It's Tuesday! My stomach sinks. "He can't come home!" I gasp.

The nurse does a double take. "Why?"

"What if he falls? What if he chokes? I can't lift him. The last time he needed the washroom, I had to call 911. They sent a fire truck! He needs a nursing home."

"Nursing home staff aren't equipped to care for someone in Ben's condition."

"Neither am I."

"Hmm!" The nurse taps her pen on the page of an open ledger, thinking. "We could see if there's a chronic care bed somewhere."

"What about St. Mark's? It's just a few blocks from where we live."

"There's a waiting list a mile long."

I throw up my hands in exasperation. "Well, he can't come home."

"There's others nearby we could call. I'll make a note for the day staff."

As I walk to my car, I wonder how I'm going to break the news to Ben. How can I tell him he's not coming home?

When I return to the condo, I flop on the sofa and begin searching for the right words. I make several bumbling attempts, but none sound right. There's no good way to tell him, or at least I haven't found one.

Just blurt it out, the Dop suggests, dropping by out of nowhere.

It'll devastate him.

He's going to find out sometime.

Don't forget to breathe, my grandmother weighs in. This is the second time they've visited me at the same time. Had they come together, perhaps in my grandmother's old Buick? I wonder if that's still kicking around, too. I had no idea they knew each other.

In the hospital's step-down unit, a level below the ICU, Ben sits up in bed in his room across from the nursing station. I sit on the edge of the visitor's chair, trying to stop my knees from nervously yo-yoing.

"What's wrong?" Ben asks.

I slide back into the chair and lean forward, resting my elbows on my thighs. Unaware that my fingers are steepling as if for quiet prayer, it's only when I feel my fingers tenting against my lips that I say a silent one. *There's no way through but forward*, I tell myself, urging myself on. "Ben, you won't be able to come home. I'm sorry. I can't take care of you. The nurses are looking for a place."

I brace for his anger. But, instead, his face softens.

"I know."

"You know? How? Did one of the nurses tell you?"

He shakes his head. "I know you can't take care of me. I can't do anything for myself. And once they remove the catheter. . . ." He looks down at his lap and hangs his head. "I'll have to wear a diaper. I can't expect you to. . . . It's no life for you."

Guelph General sends Ben to a chronic care hospital in Kinlie, half an hour away. The December sky is as grey as despair as I drive up Highway 6. An umbrella of clouds menaces the white-brick hospital set on a street of towering oaks, lanky pines, and sprawling Victorian homes. Ben's room has four beds, separated by curtains suspended from ceiling tracks. The hospital is too small to separate patients by their impairments. Cancer patients sleep beside Alzheimer's patients who sleep beside paraplegics. As I step into the room, I see Ben's wheelchair folded against the heating unit. As I go further, I hear Ben's laugh. I walk toward it, and peek through the openings of the curtains until I find Ben's bed, the last on the right. He's not alone.

"How do poets say hello, Bennie?" asks a woman with a loud, husky voice.

"I don't know," Ben chuckles, a sound I haven't heard in ages.

"'Haven't we metaphor?'" the woman guffaws.

Ben snorts.

"Last one. Then I gotta go. I at least need to make it look like I'm working. Okeydokey?"

"Okeydokey," Ben says. I can hear the smile in his voice.

"Here goes: Yesterday, I saw a guy spill some Scrabble letters on the road."

"Go for it," Ben urges.

"I asked him, 'What's the word on the street?'"

"That's the worst joke I've ever heard!"

"Bennie! You don't mean that."

I peek through the opening of the curtain into Ben's cubicle. Sitting beside Ben's bed is a female version of the Hulk in teddy bear scrubs. She lifts a tray off the overbed table and sidles along the narrow space between his bed and the wall. From where I stand, I can see a gravy-stained plate, a soda cracker wrapper in an empty soup bowl, and an open milk carton heading my way. I step aside, trying not to be seen.

"Bye, Bennie," the Hulk says over her shoulder, and then steps through the curtain opening. That's when she notices me.

"Bennie, you got a girlfriend?" She opens the curtain for him to see.

Surprise flashes in Ben's eyes.

"Hi!" I wave.

"Hi!" He smiles. "It's my wife!" he tells the Hulk.

"Well, I'll let you two get at it then. Don't do anything I wouldn't do, Bennie." The Hulk winks. She gives me a penetrating glance, nods slightly, steps around me, and vanishes out the door.

Despite his bleak surroundings, Ben's cheeks are rosy.

"You're looking better. You at least have colour."

"Don't call the *Guelph Mercury* yet. I still feel like shit."

I glance at the bottom frame of his cot. "No catheter?"

"No. I've graduated to diapers."

"Oh, Ben! I'm so sorry."

"It's okay. We knew this was coming."

"You seem chipper! I didn't expect you to be so happy here."

He pats the space on the bed beside him. I hoist myself up and reach for his hand. We sit silently until he says, "I'm so glad you're here."

I stare at the cuticle I'm picking, avoiding his eyes. "I'm sorry I couldn't get here before today. . . . It was really snowing. I was afraid to drive."

"I know it wasn't safe. You did the right thing."

I look around at the cinderblock walls painted putrid green. There's a cold, depressing light coming from the only window. It overlooks a treeless common, as small as a postage stamp.

"Nice digs," I lie.

"Four-star!" Sadness spreads like a vapour over Ben's smile.

"What about a TV? I can order one. You can watch *Law & Order*."

"I don't want a TV."

"There must be something I can do for you."

"I just want you to visit."

"Well, I'm here."

* * *

Tuesday night I sit on a paint-splattered stool working on my seal painting. Despite the peeling linoleum, the paint-splattered table, and the unpainted plywood separating our studio from the one the stained-glass artisan uses, I love being here, smelling the turps, the oil paint, the pleasantly musty air, and taking comfort in the navy-blackness of the night outside. As we're packing up, April suggests we go for drinks at the Aberfoyle Mill.

Sitting around a table under rough-hewn beams, the four of us guzzle beers in the pub's shadowy light and discuss entering our first art show.

"We're ready," Brynn says.

"How many could you show?" Murray asks her. "We can't have a show with just one painting each."

Brynn, who comes to the studio every night, says, "I could put in six."

"Three," says April.

We all turn to Cal. "I don't want to get my head messed up with a show." He leans so far back in his chair, I'm afraid his head will fly off his shoulders and bullseye the hub of the antique bicycle hanging on the wall behind him. "I just want to enjoy painting."

"What about you?" Murray inclines his head toward me, his eyes sparkling more than friendship.

My quick thought is that I'm sure not going to get much painting done with Ben in the hospital. All I have right now is my unfinished seal painting. "Hmmm," I hesitate, ignoring the heat coming from Murray.

"Why don't I buy you another drink while you think?" Murray stands up and heads to the bar before I can stop him.

"Let me pay for it," I say, when he returns with my beer. I search my wallet futilely for the ten dollars I know the beer costs. With work and Ben, I haven't had a chance to go to the bank. And the truth is, funds are tight. All the money we have coming in now is from my paltry salary.

Murray holds his hand up, either because he wanted to pay for my beer or because he sees from my expression that I don't have the cash.

"You buy me a beer sometime," he says.

WTF! Were those sparks? the Dop says as I drive home. *He's into you.*

I don't answer. It's winter and I'm concentrating on the road.

* * *

On the weekend, as I turn right at the elevators and follow the red painted arrows to Ben's room, an impressively sleek, dark-haired man turns into the corridor ahead of me. I watch him speed down the aisle, his white coat whipping behind him, caught by an imaginary hospital breeze. He stops in front of Ben's room and enters it. Is he visiting Ben or one of the other patients? I hang back, not wanting to intrude. A few minutes go by before I stick my head through the doorway, trying to hear who he is speaking with. When I'm sure it's Ben, I step inside the room. Ben is in bed in his blue hospital gown and the dark-haired man stands at the foot of the cot, studying what looks like a medical chart. The doctor clicks and unclicks an expensive silver ballpoint as he reads through the notes, flipping over one page after another.

"You say your back hurts. Is it all the time?" he asks Ben.

"Mostly when I'm sitting."

"What about leg pain?"

"Tingling."

"I'd like to see your legs," the doctor says, throwing back Ben's blanket. Ben's legs look like two brackets. The doctor prods the left calf. "Do you feel that?"

"Yes," Ben says.

The doctor prods the right calf. "And that?"

Ben nods.

"Have you always had this wasting?"

"Since I was in my twenties."

The doctor clicks his pen in deep thought.

"Can I come in?" I ask, stepping further into the room without waiting for a response. "I'm Ben's wife."

"Hi," Ben says, with happy surprise.

"Yes, yes. Come in, please. I'm Doctor Aadesh Prajapati from the neurosurgery department. I'll be taking care of your husband while he's here."

I hold out my hand. He shakes it, and then he turns back to Ben. "The tingling in your arms, when did that start?"

"My right arm, the last couple of years I was driving truck."

"How long ago was that?"

"Six or seven years."

"And the left?"

"A few years ago, maybe."

I nod.

"Hmmm!" the doctor says, stroking his chin. "I want to send you for X-rays and a bone scan."

Two days later, when the results come back, Dr. Prajapati holds up a radiograph so we both can see it.

"What we're looking at is a breakdown of Ben's vertebrae," he says, tapping his pen at a cross-section of a bone in Ben's spine that looks like the disintegrating banks of a pond. In healthy people, bones get remodeled all the time by efficient home contractor-like cells called osteoclasts that remove the old and damaged bone and reabsorb it.

I like the home improvement analogy. Mom would like it, too. Interior design is her thing. These cells replace the old and damaged bone with new bone. Kind of like remodeling an old house. But in bodies with bone diseases, the remodeling doesn't take place. The fixer-upper never gets fixed.

"Isn't that because of the ALS?" I ask.

Prajapati shakes his head. "It has nothing to do with Ben's original diagnosis."

"It's something new!?" I say, horrified.

"Paget's disease of bone," Dr. Prajapati says. "It's probably what's causing the tingling in your arms and legs and why your legs look the way they do," he tells Ben.

"So how can we fix it?"

"There are drugs. They all come with rather unpleasant side effects. The drug I'd recommend," he turns to Ben, "you might experience some bone pain . . . nausea . . . dizziness. Some patients find they develop lesions on their faces, exposing the bones in their jaws."

My eyes go wide. I look over at Ben and see his eyes have gone wide, too.

"I don't want drugs," he says, shaking his head.

Good choice, I think. There's nothing like side effects to make one opt out of animal-tested pharmaceuticals and home improvement projects.

* * *

Europe's members of parliament remain concerned about the seal hunt's cruelty. To allay their fears, Loyola Hearn invites them to Newfoundland to witness the seal hunt. The MPs arrive in early April 2008, ready if not excited to witness the brutal hunt. But instead of climbing into survival suits, they are told to climb into boardroom chairs to watch presentations on sealing's fiscal benefits or, to add some local colour to their visit, they are taken on a tour of seal-processing plants.[3]

On April 19, 2008, an Ipsos Reid press release is sent to the media. It recounts the findings of its latest poll, commissioned by IFAW, which shows that only 39 percent of Canadians support the commercial seal hunt.[4]

In another blow, later that year, a 2008 veterinary report by the European Food Safety Authority (EFSA) on the animal welfare aspects of sealing confirms that effective killing does not always occur, animals may suffer pain and distress, and sealers often do not comply with the regulations. The results of the EFSA findings are consistent with studies on the animal welfare aspects of the seal hunt, conducted in 2002 and 2007.

In July, I land a forty-restaurant chain spanning seventeen US states. The boycott is still going strong. For a break, I pull out the November 6, 2006 Standing Committee minutes and head into the living room for a scenery change. As I read and sip coffee on the sofa, something catches my eye. John Kearley, Carino's general manager, admits that Carino regularly breaks US law:

> When we ship samples of our product to our parent [in Norway], we have to disguise the description of what it is, because it may be seized by US Customs. We have to disguise what we are shipping. Just recently I shipped samples of our seal oil for analysis and I termed it marine oil so that people looking at the document would not know whether it was lube oil or whatever. You have to do these things. It's unfortunate that we're selling a legal product yet have to disguise it as something else.[5]

Holy shit! I call US Customs and Border Protection. Soon, I'm informing a customs officer of Kearley's November 6 fraud admission and emailing him the Standing Committee passage.

"If this is true and Canada has been sending marine mammal products into the country, they're breaking the law. We'll check into it, I can promise you that," the officer says.[6]

When I ask if he'll keep me informed, he tells me that he can't reveal the results of an investigation.

37

MRS. VESPA

"HAPPY NEW YEAR," I say, scooping vegan cake into Ben's mouth, following it with champagne that Ben sips through a plastic straw from a paper cup. "You make any resolutions?"

"Only to get into St. Mark's. You?"

"To get you out of this place." Since Ben's arrival, the cancer patient in his room has died; the Alzheimer's patient sits strapped daily to a chair by his bed; and the twenty-something paraplegic in the cot beside Ben, a drunk driving accident, has brain damage and only two words left in his vocabulary. "Nice knockers!" he says when the nurses check on him.

"I'll call St. Mark's this week to see where you are on the list." I begin to clean up, tossing the paper plates and cups in the bin in his room, taking down the HAPPY NEW YEAR letters I've taped onto the bed frame, and sweeping up the confetti on the floor.

"You've got to go now, love?" he says, resigned.

"I don't want to be out with the drunks on the road." I look around the room to see if I've missed anything, then I pull my coat off the back of the visitor's chair, put on my scarf and hat, and then lean over Ben's bed to kiss his cheek. "I will call St. Mark's. I'll let you know what happens."

Two days later, when I call, I'm told five people are ahead of Ben. I make an appointment to speak to the intake officer, and the next day, fueled with adrenaline and purpose, I speed over the calming bumps in the parking lot and screech into a parking space. At the reception desk, I give my name. Within minutes, a large bald man in a navy striped umpire jersey strides over.

"Hi, I'm Bill," he says, extending his hand. His grip has enough heft to lift and lower me with each shake. "I'll take you over to the intake office." I follow him down a long corridor, quickstepping to keep up. "Ever been here before?" he asks as we turn the corner.

I nod. "My husband and I took a tour a couple of years ago." I remember Ben wheeling around the halls excitedly while I trudged behind fighting back tears, unable to contemplate Ben in this waiting-to-die place. Now, after Kinlie, St. Mark's isn't so bad.

We stop outside a tiny office, just large enough for a single filing cabinet, a wooden desk, two chairs, and a tiny Filipina with pursed lips, thick-rimmed glasses, and a black mole that beetles out of the left side of her chin.

Bill introduces her as Mrs. Vespa. She waves me into the empty chair. I fold my coat on my lap and get right to the point.

"Ben cannot stay in Kinlie."

"Why not?" she asks. Her hands are resting on a closed file folder in front of her. Is it Ben's? I wonder.

"Have you seen Highway 6? It's a half-hour obstacle course of snowdrifts and whiteouts. Last Thursday, there was a snow squall and I nearly ran off the road."

Mrs. Vespa takes off her glasses and carefully lays them beside the file folder. She looks at me down the Heartbreak Hill of her nose. I flash her a winning smile, radiating as brightly as a florescent light bulb. Mrs. Vespa wrangles on her glasses, drops her eyes back to the file folder, sighs out a sliver of air, then opens it.

"Your husband doesn't fit the requirements of complex care," she sniffs. My head snaps back in disbelief. "Are you nuts?" I want to say, but Mrs. Vespa, with her beetle-moled chin, holds all the hospital intake cards.

I gape at her. "I'm not sure I understand,"

"He's too self-sufficient. The patients we admit have multiple physical health barriers. For instance, they can't feed or clothe themselves, or do any of the self-care tasks needed for daily life."

"Ben can't do any of the self-care tasks needed for daily life! His muscles are atrophying, he's just been diagnosed with Paget's syndrome, and his bowels need a permanent plumber!"

Mrs. Vespa rises from her chair and walks over to the metal file cabinet. She pulls open the bottom drawer and shuffles through a small batch of files, sliding four out to read the names on the labels before tucking them back into place. "There are three people ahead of Ben waiting for a bed," she says, shutting the drawer.

That's better than the five I was told were ahead of him when I made the appointment. Had two of them died? Never mind, I am here for Ben. "Ben can't feed himself, or change his clothes, or get up from the toilet. I've had to call the fire department just to lift him off. He wears a diaper, for gosh sakes!" Unmoved, Mrs. Vespa takes her glasses off again and we sit staring at each other.

"You have to take him. I'm at my wits' end."

"I'm sorry," she says, looking at her watch.

I am not going to win this battle with words, I realize. So I do what any self-respecting, desperate wife who is not getting her way would do: I cry.

"I can't take it anymore. I'm so exhausted," I sob, willing drops of moisture to fall from my eyes.

Mrs. Vespa slides over a box of tissues and I dab. Then she rolls back her chair, stands and squeezes herself past her desk to the door, and holds it open. "Well, we can't do anything today, can we?" she says, waving me to the door.

"Ben is the poster child for complex care," I sniff as I leave her office.

In March, speculation mounts that the EU will adopt a union-wide seal import ban. Seal-costumed protestors parade to the Canadian embassy in London. Naked, blood-painted PETA supporters pile themselves on top of each other at the embassy in Hamburg. Maybe I should parade through the halls of St. Mark's with a protest sign that reads LET BEN IN or chain myself to a revolving door at the lobby entrance. In the end, I don't need to go to extremes. When Canada's sealers return to the docks like victors in a battle, St. Mark's calls. Ben has a bed. Two weeks later, an attendant loads Ben and his wheelchair into the back of an ambulance and drives him to St. Mark's.

* * *

Ben has only been in St. Mark's a few weeks when I tell him I'm heading for Miami. The HSUS is going to host an opening for a gallery of photographs of Canada's harp seal nursery taken by a famous fashion photographer, along with a cocktail party for the local chefs who have joined the boycott. Since many of my pledges have come from Miami chefs, I'm asked to help.

"I'll be back before you know it," I assure Ben.

As I step through the doorway of the Miami gallery a few days later, the first thing I see is a photograph of a baby seal nose to nose with her mother; they look like they are kissing. It is the most tender photograph of a mother seal and her pup I have ever seen. There are many other photographs, all in beautiful colour: a baby seal just beginning to moult; a beater pup rolled on her back in the turquoise snow; a baby seal with tears in her eyes.

(Many people think that the eyes of harp seals well up because they are crying. That's not it at all. There is a biological reason for the tears. Vision is the harp seal's most important sense, so their eyes tend to be larger than those of mammals who rely on other faculties. To protect their eyes from the salt water that surrounds them, their lacrimal glands produce a constant flow of tears. However, harp seals lack tear ducts, which means they are physically unable to drain away their tears.)

Still, the images tug at my heart. They show so much vulnerability and tenderness I want to cry. I pull myself away. I am here to mingle and thank the chefs for joining the boycott campaign. They all look dashing in their white culinary uniforms and dough-boy hats. Many stand near the bar, drinks in hand. There's my first celebrity chef, from the Biltmore's Palme d'Or Restaurant in Coral Gables; and the rapini master, whose culinary prowess with the green vegetable brings me to my knees and whose mastery over seduction makes me stay several feet away; and the cranky James Beard chef, who agrees to do complimentary hors d'oeuvres for the event but skimps with only two platters. As I mill around, I overhear conversations on venture capital, restaurant makeovers, and visionless restaurateurs. Yet I'm drawn back to the photograph of the mother and her baby, whom I allow my fingers to caress above the glass. "Hello," I whisper. "I'm trying to save you."

"You like that one?" I turn to see the fashion photographer, who's come up beside me, a glass of white wine in her hand.

"Very much. I wonder if the pup survived the hunt. Probably not."

"We won't ever know, will we?"

"No, but in your photograph of this baby and her mother, their love shines through. You've immortalized them. They are the reason I give my all to end the damn hunt."

"I know what you mean," the photographer says, and she is about to say something else when HSUS's vice president of wildlife, standing in the centre of the gallery, calls everyone to attention: "I want to thank you for coming here tonight and for supporting our campaign. . . ." I try to focus on his words, but all I want to do is be with the baby and pray she's not dead.

* * *

It's late Saturday afternoon when I return home. After I pay the pet sitter, I climb into bed and sleep well into Sunday. Later that afternoon, I visit St. Mark's and tell Ben about the frisky-handed chef, the fashion photographer, and the baby seal and her mother. The next morning, I read a press release from Carino's managing director, Knut A. Nygaard, and general manager, John C. Kearley, explaining why, after such high prices in 2006, the market took a downturn in 2007:

During 2006 we paid a very high price of seal pelts as it seemed that the world market had not yet seen the top level for sealskins prices, in comparison to other furs. When the high-priced sealskins from 2006 hit the markets, sales became difficult, but some did sell, but by the year end 2006 all sales stopped. Sales prices have had to be reduced twice since January 2007 and we see no signs of being able to increase prices during the next few months. Unfortunately, there has been a severe downturn in the prices for sealskins on the world market.

I pin the press release to my clothesline and stand back. It goes on to explain that because Carino only processes seals, unlike other buyers, who also process all kinds of fish species, they are unable to use the profits from selling other species to offset their losses when the pelts don't sell:

The world demand for sealskins does not come automatically, a large share of our margins on sealskins would go to marketing, in fact we have been leading the field with marketing of sealskins worldwide during the past several years and feel at least partially responsible for the fact that there is such a market today.[1]

Reading the press release jars my memory. I submitted my ATIP request eons ago. So where the hell are my purchase slips? I call the DFO.

38

LOST AND FOUND

THE DFO'S BURLINGTON office is a five-story building with a black-and-grey rectangular façade. There is nothing nautical about it. As I pull into the parking lot, my skin tingles at the thought I'll soon be looking at the purchase slips. Five minutes later I'm in the lobby taking the elevator up to the floor of the Fish and Fish Habitat Protection Program at the Ontario regional office of Fisheries and Oceans Canada.

"I'm here to review purchase slips for 2006 and 2007," I tell the receptionist, giving her my name.

She leans down and picks up a bulldog size box from under her desk and sets it on top of the modesty panel that hides the unsightly computer wires. "Do you want to check the documents first to see if they're what you want?"

"Yes," I say.

She takes a cutter and slices open the packing tape and lets me look inside. I lift out the rumpled newsprint, cushioning the piles of paper, and shuffle through the box, noting that there are two stacks of photocopies, thousands in each stack, and each stack is for a separate year, one for 2006 and one for 2007.

"Seems to be all here."

"Okay. Let's get you set up in the conference room. Let me just tape this back up." She pulls out a roll of packing tape and affixes a length across the top of the box that she opened. She carries the box for me, and I follow her down a series of hallways. We turn left, right, left, and stop at the entrance to a dark room. She flips on the lights. In the centre, I see a conference table long enough to moonlight as a superhighway. Leatherette swivel chairs congregate around its perimeter. She lays the box on the table.

"Can I get you anything else?" she asks.

"I'm fine. Just excited to finally get a look at these." I nod at the box.

"I'll let you get at it then."

After she leaves, I sit down in one of the chairs and half-swivel, taking in the beige walls, a projector tucked in a corner, and the white marker board beside it. If I listen, I can hear the buzz of the government employees in cubicles down the hall, the guttural growl of a photocopy machine, and a ringing phone.

I turn back to the box. My hands glide over the smooth cardboard. I stick my thumbnail under the lip of the tape and pull it up. I reach in and remove the first slip from the box and study it. It has a mix of columns and rows. At the top of each column are headings: one for the quantity of seal pelts sold; another for the age classes of the seals killed; and others for the grades, prices, and values of the pelts. Then there are rows for the name of the sealing licence holder, his address, the vessel name, and the area where he (or she) sealed. There are also rows for the dates the vessel left the dock and when it returned, and for the killing gear used. There are more rows for the buyer's name and address. So many headings! So many spaces for information! But as I take out more slips, I see that much of the data has been redacted or not entered at all.

I lift out more pages and spread them on the table. What can I make out of these data-devoid purchase slips? Likely nothing. All that work to get the slips and the long wait for them to arrive, all for naught! I slump in the swivel chair and contemplate getting on my hands and knees under the table and screaming.

What the hell do you think you're doing?

It's the Dop! Dammit! *What does it look like I'm doing? I'm getting ready to concede that the DFO has won.*

Giving up already? I didn't suspect you'd give up this easily!

I sit up in my chair and hold out a few purchase slips so the Dop can see them. *Look at this!* I slap the slips in the air. *What am I supposed to do with these?*

What are you talking about?

All the information I asked for is redacted or left out. I jab an index finger at the blank grade, price, and value columns. I show her another slip, and another. *These slips are shit.* I slap the pages on the table and fold my hands across my chest.

Stop whining! The Dop points to something written under one of the description headings. *What's that?*

It says "seal pelts," Big deal. I know these are purchase slips for seal pelts. It's the age classes I wanted: raggedy jackets . . . beaters . . . bedlamers! And the grades of the pelts, and what the sealers got paid for them, and what the buyer thought was the pelts' estimated value. All that is supposed to be listed here. I smack the back of my fingers against a page.

What is that? The Dop pokes at the same page.

A sealer's name!

Uh huh! And what does that say?

Rifle.

So there is information, just not the information you were looking for.

What good will that do me? I don't need the sealers' names or their gear. How am I going to add up the quantities of pelts and the prices paid for them if the information has been redacted or purposely left out? How can I reveal the real economic values of the 2006 and 2007 seal hunts when I don't have any monetary evidence? How can I prove the proceeds are inflated when I have nothing to go on?

Did you ever wonder why the information you asked for is missing?

Duh! They don't want me to see it, obviously.

Ask yourself why. It makes no sense. All one needs to do is pick up a newspaper to read of a DFO or DFA spokesperson bragging about the number of seals killed and what the value of the hunt was that year. So, how do they figure what the value is if so much of the information is left out?

I suppose the buyers tell them. At least, that's what the Newfoundland Staff Officer told me.

Tell them what?

I don't know. The number of pelts landed and their estimated values.

Why aren't they listed? It would seem to me that the perfect time to fill out all the information is when the buyer is at the dock when you've got the sealers right there to ask any questions.

Maybe there's something we don't know.

Anyway, if the government is so cautious about giving away confidential information, why do they list the names of the sealers? Again, she points to a purchase slip on the table and then to another one. *Your thoughts?*

How should I know? I shrug.

Figure it out! And with that, the Dop is gone.

I rummage through the slips on the table and snort. Not only are the names of the sealers visible, but some of their addresses and occupations are as well. I'm changing my opinion of the Dop. She may be crusty, patronizing, and bothersome, but she has a good eye for detail. And, in her own way, she's trying to help.

Outside the conference room someone shouts from down the hall, "See you tomorrow," and then someone else shouts, "Have a good night." I hear drawers opening and closing, chairs rolling back from their workstations, and the photocopier shutting down. The clock on the wall says 4:30 p.m. on the dot. The government office workers are going home. Our taxpayer dollars at work! I gather up the loose purchase slips and restack them in the box, which I carry past the emptying offices to the reception desk, where the receptionist awaits me.

"Do you want to take them?" she asks.

"Absolutely."

I hand her my AAC credit card and watch as she inserts it into the payment terminal. Amid the noise of the transaction, I mentally see C$900 draining from AAC's bank account.

As I walk out the door of the DFO building, I raise my chin and smile. If the cardboard burden in my arms were not so heavy, and the twinging muscle in my back not so intrusive, I might strut and revel in my accomplishment.

Driving back to Guelph, I wonder now that I have the purchase slips what I will do with them. There's not enough room in the condo to line them all up, edge to edge, to compare them. They will need to be organized. But how? What would Rebecca or Stephen or Liz do? Or better yet, what would Nancy Drew do?

The next morning, I pull out a handful of purchase slips and lay them out on my office floor. My eyes glance down the length of them. Each time I look I see new things that twig my interest. For instance, on one I read the name of the buyer is the Fogo Island Co-op.[1] Fogo Island is a tiny spot off Newfoundland's northeast coast. I pull out another handful of slips and then another. Fogo Island Co-op, founded to protect local islanders from corporate fishery monopolies, like Carino Company Limited and the Barry Group, is the only processing company listed on any of the slips. Why wasn't its name redacted or simply left out as were the names of the other processing companies? Is it too small? Or is it not powerful enough to command the DFO to protect it from nosy animal rights activists?

As I unload the box of purchase slips onto the floor and shuffle through them, I see other interesting things. On some slips, the address of a small business is scribbled above the sealer's name. Does the sealer work at the business outside of the fishery when he's not sealing? "Professional commercial sealing licences may be issued only to full time or bona fide fishers registered with the DFO." These exact words are from the *Overview of the Atlantic Seal Hunt 2006–2010*, published on the DFO's website. If a sealer works at a business other than one in the fishing industry when he's not sealing, he's not a full-time, bona fide fisherman. Does it also mean he's not struggling? Struggling fishermen is the reason the DFO gives to justify the seal hunt.

I Google the name of one of those businesses, and up pops a fibreglass company. I Google the name of another; it's a sawmill. I Google some more. One is a fire department, another is a school academy, a third is a general contracting company. Does this mean that sealers are not just fishermen, but other things as well: fire fighters, school staff, builders? Do sealers have other jobs outside of the fishing industry? According to the slips, the answer is *maybe*.

I randomly Google Earth a few sealers' home addresses and nearly faint. The homes are one-story saltboxes or two-story, multi-gabled dwellings, with expansive front and back yards along tree-lined streets. I feel a twinge of envy. Are these the homes of poor fishermen who can't put food on their tables?

The DFO claims sealers derived up to 35 percent of their annual income from sealing. I call a colleague to ask if she had ever received evidence backing up the 35-percent claim. She tells me that she had filed an Access to Information Request with the DFO, seeking out such information, but had received no supporting evidence confirming it. In fact, she tells me: "In one of the documents I got back, the DFO admits it doesn't have any supportive back-up documents!"

The more I study the slips, the more questions I have. Under the heading *gear used*, the words *rifle* and *hakapik* are most common. However, I note that a few of the slips list *pots* or *nets*, two exceptionally cruel killing contraptions that were outlawed in the 1960s. Have the sealers using pots or nets been arrested? I wonder how I can find out. I can't investigate sealers' arrests now, however. I must stay focused on the purchase slips.

The words *hailed in* have been scribbled at the bottom of some of the purchase slips, but not all. The Newfoundland Staff Officer told me that hailing in is a must. Officials subtract the number of seals hailed in each day from the total number of seals available under the annual established quota. Yet, as I search among the slips, only a fifth of them from 2006 indicate sealers hailed in. In 2007, almost no sealer did. Was it a clerical error? Or a failure of sealers or dockside monitors to follow DFO protocols? Or was it the result of not having monitors at the docks at all? How could the DFO determine when the TAC had been reached if they didn't know how many seals were killed each day?

As I stare at the thousands of purchase slips helter-skelter on the floor, my eyes glaze over at the enormity of the task in front of me. What do I do with all this information?

Create a spreadsheet, input the data, and note what's missing, Nancy Drew communicates silently.

Nancy! You're here! And you've modernized your approach to detecting. I don't remember you using spreadsheets in Mystery at Lilac Inn *or* The Secret of the Old Clock. Nancy doesn't answer me, but, of course, she's right. If the DFO has not compiled the data into a meaningful document, I will. I stack the 2006 and 2007 purchase slips into towers on my desk. A few clicks and two new Excel spreadsheets pop up; I title one "2006" and the other "2007." Next, I label about a dozen columns with headings borrowed from the purchase slips. I make new ones too, since information like *hailing in* and *fisherman's count* are scribbled on the slips as well.

Hey, wait a minute! Monitors are supposed to count the pelts the vessels bring in each day. But because dockside monitors aren't always present, or if they are, they might only do a few random spot checks, it's up to the fishermen themselves to be honest and record the real number of seal pelts landed.

Something jogs my memory. I remember speaking with Bridget Curran, the founder of the Atlantic Canadian Anti-Sealing Coalition. She told me about a situation in a small fishing village where a resident had observed sealers landing pelts at one of the sealers' homes, rather than at the harbour dock, which they had done previously. The resident had said the dock was only minutes away from the home. The incident seemed fishy. Had the sealers hailed in their pelts that day? Or were the pelts taken under the radar of the DFO? The DFO claims its commercial seal hunt is well regulated. But it doesn't matter what regulations the DFO puts in place if there's no one ensuring the regulations are being followed. I take a deep breath and blow the air out through my lips.

* * *

February 14, 2008: Valentine's Day. I reach into my purse to pull out the Valentine's card I bought Ben in St. Mark's gift store.

"You got a great ass," Ben says.

The card drops from my hand. I whip around to face him.

"Ben!"

"What?" His eyes twinkle.

"I came here to visit because it's Valentine's Day, and I didn't want you to feel lonely. Not so you could make inappropriate comments."

You didn't come to see Ben because he's lonely, a voice scoffs. Startled, I look around, expecting to find some know-it-all nurse coming to tell me off. But no one is there. *You came for one reason only.*

Oh no. It's the Dop! Why does she have to show up now? And why does she contradict everything I say?

Because you're lonely.

Not true. I'm not lonely. I'm being thoughtful, I snap, glancing down at the card on the floor.

Lonely. You're so pathetic and lonely, the Dop sings, sounding like Bobby Vinton.

Okay! I didn't want to be alone on Valentine's Day. I sit on the visitor's chair and rub my hands over my eyes.

So, do you want to be out of your relationship with Ben or not?

I want to be out. You know that.

Well, if you want to be out, stop sending mixed messages.

What mixed messages?

Visiting him on Valentine's Day. Buying him a card.

After a moment of thinking, I metaphorically slap my forehead. *How come I didn't see that I was sending mixed messages?*

I wait for the Dop's response. But then I can feel the energy in the room changing, and I realize she's gone. But, like always, she's spot on! It is time I clarify my situation, not only for Ben but for me. I slide the visitor's chair up to Ben's bed.

"Ben, we need to talk."

"Sorry I didn't get you a card, love," Ben says.

I shake my head and wave his apology away. "Ben, it's not that. I have something to say." It's my tone that grabs him, and the fact that I've just picked up the card off the floor but haven't given it to him.

"I want to be a better husband. You're the love of my life." He often says this when he feels his hold on me slipping. "I just want you to know that I'm very committed to our marriage, and to looking at my shadow side."

He knows the words to say. And I believe he means them. What I don't believe is that he will be able to sustain any changes long-term.

"Ben."

"I've changed since we lived together. I've been thinking. . . ."

"Ben."

"What?"

"I don't love you anymore, not like a wife." The silence is so loud, I want to fill it. I bite the side of my lip to keep from talking.

He blinks.

"I'm still going to visit you. But things need to change between us."

"Like what?"

"No more commenting on my body, okay?"

"Okay," he says.

"No more complaining about my work."

He nods.

"No more acting like we're a married couple."

"You are still the love of my life."

"And you're like a brother to me."

It can't be this easy, can it? I feel a lightness and exultation I haven't felt in years as I walk out the door of St. Mark's toward my van. But driving home, I think about how alone Ben is; without me he has no one. I reach for a tissue in my purse and my knuckles brush against the Valentine's Day card. That's when the tears fall.

* * *

Two months later, the CBC breaks a story about four sealers who are facing seventeen charges for violating the Marine Mammal Regulations in the Gulf of St. Lawrence during the 2007 seal hunt. Ten charges concern the sealers' failures to administer the eye-blink reflex test, and the other seven are brought because the sealers used "improper instruments for harvesting seals." Are these the sealers who used the pots and nets? I wonder.

In response to the breaking news, Dwight Spence of the Canadian Sealers Association tells the reporter that the eye-blink test is a waste of paper.

"If you shoot a seal, usually the head is blown off it. So, where's the eyes . . . ? They're covered with blood, so you don't see them anyway."[2]

Why the hell did it take so long to charge these guys?

39

RUN, KAREN, RUN

MID-JULY 2008, STEPHEN and I meet at a Guelph restaurant with prayer flags fluttering outside. Inside, a silver Buddha sits cross-legged on the fireplace mantle and the aroma of soy sauce and sesame oil fills me with hunger when I step through the door. Stephen is waiting at a table, mulling over the menu, his Tilley hat on the table beside him.

After I have a chance to look at the menu, Stephen says, "How's the boycott?"

My eyes widen in disbelief. "You don't know?"

"I know the trade data. But I want to hear it from your end."

"We've landed over 3,500 restaurants and grocery stores, and we've signed up some of the top chefs in the US, and about 100,000 individuals have pledged to boycott Canadian seafood."

"Sounds good," Stephen says, shutting his menu. With Type-A impatience, he searches the empty restaurant for a waiter.

"But still, we haven't ended the seal hunt. Volunteers call every week, wanting a definitive end date."

"We can't give it to them. Winning doesn't happen overnight."

"But Stephen, we said it'd take us a year or two. It's been four years now. The DFO isn't caving."

"It's only after you enter a campaign that you truly find out how challenging it is."

The waiter arrives for our orders and then brings us pots of green tea and small cups to pour it into. Once he is gone, Stephen leans back in his chair and continues. "Everyone wants an easy win. I've been following the trade data on Newfoundland's seafood exports to the US. Since we started the boycott, the value of snow crab has declined significantly."

I pour my tea and take a thirsty gulp. "The DFO claims the boycott is having no effect," I say, my mouth twisting in dismay.

He lifts his eyebrows. "What do you think they're going to say?"

I give a half shrug. "I guess you're right. No one at the DFO is going to shout from the rooftop, 'snow crab value declines due to boycott.'"

Soon the waiter arrives with our food; he sets plates of steaming tempura, kung pao vegan chicken, and vegan crab in the middle of the table for us to share. Green pepper and chunks of vegan chicken and shrimp dance beside roasted peanuts and hot Sichuan peppers, all on a bed of snowy-white rice. I take a bite of crab. The sauce is sweet, sour, and savoury all at the same time.

Between forkfuls, Stephen says, "Ottawa knows Newfoundland's snow crab is being hit because of the boycott. Restaurants in the US are just not willing to buy it. And the more restaurants and grocery chains you sign on, the more it's going to hurt." Stephen holds out the dish of kung pao chicken. I stab my fork into a piece and stuff it into my mouth. A small radio plays in the background. I can hear the scratchy voice of Leonard Cohen singing "Hallelujah." I take it as a good omen.

"The reason I asked you here isn't to talk about the boycott." Stephen puts down his fork and wipes the napkin across his mouth.

I put my fork down, too, and take a nervous sip of tea. When I look up, I see Stephen studying me.

"Liz and I want you to run as a candidate for the Animal Alliance Environment Voters Party."

"What?"

"A by-election has just been called in Guelph."

I nod. Guelph's member of parliament retired a few days ago, leaving a vacancy in the House of Commons. A by-election has just been called to replace her.

"We want you to run in that election. But there's also a good chance that the Governor General will dissolve Parliament by September, and if that happens, a national federal election will be triggered. We want to run four candidates federally, including you and Liz."

"Run! You've got to be kidding!"

"Liz ran in 2006. It was a trial run. Just to see what was required. We learned a lot in that election. We now have a perfect opportunity to take what we've learned and run more candidates."

"I've never run for anything in my life."

"You don't need to win. You don't even need to get many votes. We're not interested in forming a government. We're interested in challenging the status quo on animals."

"I don't know. I need time to think."

A few days later, I walk into the Guelph Elections Canada pop-up store and look around. It's empty except for the returning officer, a small dark-haired woman in her sixties, sitting behind a folding table.

"I'm here to sign up as a candidate for the Animal Alliance Environment Voters Party of Canada." I hand her my AAEV endorsement, then reach for the pen on the table waiting for her to hand me the sign-up sheet I expect I'll be asked to sign."

"You won't be able to fill anything out today," she says.

"Why not?"

She hands me a package of forms inside a plastic envelope. "Before you can run for office, you'll have to get the residents of Guelph to consent to your candidacy. Here are the Electors Consenting to Candidacy forms. You'll need to get at least a hundred names, along with their addresses, telephone numbers, and signatures. Anyone who signs must be an eligible Guelph voter, currently residing in Guelph. Then you'll bring the signed forms back to me and I will send them to our Elections Canada office in Ottawa to be confirmed, and then if everything is hunky-dory, I'll call you and you can fill out these candidate information forms."

She hands me another plastic envelope with more forms and tells me that once I return them I'll be able to take an oath attesting to my obligations under the Canada Elections Act. "From there, you'll be put on the official list of candidates to run in the 2008 election. Election day is October 14th."

It's a lot of information to digest at once. Recognizing that, she says, "Call me anytime if you have questions. And good luck. I'm glad there's a political party for the animals. It's about time."

"Thanks," I say. I am about to leave the office when I realize I haven't a clue how to get the signatures. "Can I just walk up to people and ask them to sign? Or do I need to go to their houses and knock on their doors?"

"Get them any way you can, honey, as long as it's legal."

Early next morning, I slip on my running shoes, sling over my shoulder my AAC tote bag containing my clipboard, endorsement forms, and our party's campaign flyers, and set out to the dog park. While driving there, I work on my spiel.

The first person I approach is a woman I know because we walk our dogs at the same time every morning. This morning, however, I decide to take Karma out early, so he wouldn't interfere with my signature collection by jumping on a potential endorser.

"I'm running for the Animal Alliance Environment Voters Party of Canada," I tell her. "We're a new federal party for animals. In fact, we're the only political party in Canada that singularly focuses on animal and environmental protection. I intend to give animals a voice and to speak about the policies we need to protect them and the environment. But our party is also about protecting people, because policies that are bad for animals and the environment are also bad for humans."

The woman reaches for my clipboard and is the first to endorse my candidacy. My next signature comes from a guy with a perfectly groomed white Pomeranian. I fuss over the dog while he reads the party's information flyer and signs the endorsement form.

By 8 a.m. the dog-walking rush is over, I've got twenty-five signatures from people whose dogs know how to sit, stay, and heel. On the weekend, I get the signatures of nine Louise Penny booklovers during my book club. Later that week, at the vegetable case at Zehrs, I get a signature from the tomato lady, the field greens guy, and a college student grabbing a bag of pistachios. At the checkout line, I get another three signatures, and try not to annoy the paying customers. Outside the Ultra Food & Drug, I hand my clipboard to customers entering or exiting the store and score ten more signatures.

The lunch crowd downtown is pickier.

"Why in the world would you want to run for office?" one asks.

"What makes you think you have the experience?" says another.

"You know you're not going to win," says a third.

"It's not about winning, though I'll give it my best shot. It's about giving animals a voice during elections," I say.

I get six endorsements outside the vegetarian Cornerstone Restaurant, four outside the bank, and ten outside the bookstore. Back to the dog park several evenings later for the after-work and before-bed dog runs: I score thirty. Finally, I schlep through the doors of my condo building and stand outside the elevator. Howard signs, David, and Joan, too.

"I'm not going to vote for you," Betty tells me as she wheels her shopping buggy out of the elevator.

"You don't have to vote for me. All I need you to do is endorse my candidacy." I hold out my clipboard and offer her a pen. Instead of taking it, she white-knuckles the bar of her buggy.

"Don't we have enough candidates already? We don't need a lot of fringe parties muddling up things."

"We're a democracy, Betty. Thousands of people in this city care about animals, as I'm sure you do. They should be represented. Let *me* give them a voice."

"Hmm," she says, undecided. She looks from me to the flyer I have given her, and then seeming to make up her mind, she takes my clipboard and pen, and after expelling a disgruntled sigh, she signs. "Don't expect me to vote for you," she says. "I'm okay with you running and I'm an animal lover, but people come first."

* * *

The DFO announces the results of the 2008 hunt around mid-summer. Out of a 275,000 total allowable catch, 217,857 seals have been slaughtered. Although the full TAC has now been reached, activists take little comfort. Over 200,000 seal pups will never swim in the ocean, learn to feed themselves, or give birth to their own babies.

* * *

As the evening sun peeks through the studio's cloudy windowpanes, I prop up my easel beside Cal's. Reaching into my satchel for the candidate endorsement forms, I pull the clipboard out.

I clear my throat to get attention. My studio mates turn their heads toward me. "Excuse me, everybody. I want to run in the federal election, but I need one hundred people to endorse me. Would you mind signing my endorsement form?" I wave the clipboard in the air.

"Your what!?" Cal bellows, like a *Saturday Night Live* sketch comedian.

"My endorsement form."

"Give me that." Cal grabs the clipboard and holds it up an inch from his eyes. "Huh hum," he says, scanning the instructions. Finished, he looks at me with knitted-browed seriousness and lowers his glasses.

"Give me that pen." He prints his name and address, and with a grand flourish, he scribbles his signature. "There, you have your first signature!"

"I already have most of them, Cal," I say, flipping up the top page.

"Oh!" Cal huffs indignation. "Anybody got whiteout?"

"I've got titanium white," Murray says brightly, holding the paint tube in the air.

I glance at Cal and swipe the clipboard away from him. "Would anyone else like to sign?"

"I always vote NDP," says Brynn.

"I don't know who I'm voting for," says April. "Who are you voting for, Murray?"

Murray grins. "When it comes to voting, I believe in the sanctity of secrecy."

I hold the clipboard out to Brynn. "It's just your endorsement of my candidacy. You don't have to vote for me."

"I've never had anyone ask me this before. It's interesting," she says, looking the form over. She fills in her information, signs, then hands it to April. April puts her brush down on her easel tray and signs. When she is finished, she holds it out to Murray.

"I never vote for anyone. I always vote against," Murray says.

Cal's eyes go wide. "What?" he says with pretend surprise.

"'Never give a man an even break or smarten up a chump.' W. C. Fields!"

Cal grabs the clipboard from April and shoves it at him. "Sign," he orders.

"What do I get if I sign?" Murray asks, raising his eyebrows at me.

"Will you listen to that!" Cal booms. "If that isn't the most selfish, insensitive, cockamamie, son-of-a-gun bunch of malarkey anyone has ever heard! Go ahead and sign before I smack you one," he mock-grimaces, then winks at me.

"What about cutting my federal taxes?" Murray asks.

"She's not running to lower taxes, you dolt. She's running to protect animals." Cal folds his arms across his chest, rolling his eyes. "God, the work I have to do around here."

"And the environment," I say. "Think of your grandchildren."

"I don't have grandchildren, just three children who couldn't give up meat or horse racing if their lives depended on it."

"Meat is bad for you," April says.

Brynn furrows her brow. "Red meat. I don't know about chicken."

"What about seals? I hear they're delicious," Murray's eyes glint.

I glare at him. "Your children bet on horses?"

"Adult children. I wouldn't let them go as babies."

Cal motions to the clipboard. "Sign it already, for God's sake. Karen will be ninety before you get your name on that form."

Murray takes the clipboard, fills in his contact information, and signs the form with an artistic flare, returning it with a grin.

By the end of the week, I have more than a hundred endorsements. I return to Guelph's election office and am sworn in as a federal candidate of the Animal Alliance Environment Voters (AAEV) Party.

Liz and I celebrate over the phone.

"We're making history. People will look back and say, 'That's when everything changed for animals.'" I raise my glass in a silent toast. I can almost hear our imaginary glasses clinking.

"Don't get carried away," Liz says. "We'll be lucky to get fifty votes each."

"Isn't that how all parties start?"

"We'll see, honey bunny."

40

CANVASSING 2008

NOW THAT I'M an official candidate, I load my Animal Alliance tote bag full of flyers and map out my route. In front of the bank, downtown shoppers and end-of-shift workers wait for the bus. I hand a flyer to a man with dusty jeans and the smell of cows. He skims it, then looks pointedly at me.

"It's a wasted vote. I've been around a time, young lady, and as far as I can tell, no one's ever voted for a moose, or a whale, or an owl."

"Policies that protect animals and the environment protect people too," I tell him.

"Don't see how a political party for animals is going to take off. People are for people."

Nine parties run in Guelph, including the Communists, Marxists, Libertarians, the Marijuana Party, and AAEV.

"The Animal what?" a woman asks, leaning on the doorjamb of her bungalow. A green terrycloth bathrobe is cinched tightly around her waist and a cigarette smokes between her fingers.

I hand her a flyer and slowly repeat the party's long name.

"Well, that's a mouthful," she laughs, sucking on her cigarette and exhaling a fog of nicotine exhaust. I cough demurely into my elbow. She takes a step back and looks like she's ready to shut the door.

"Today there are parties in Germany, Italy, Spain, the Netherlands, and Australia focused on creating legislation to protect animals and the environment. They're not fringe parties, they have seats in government—making lives better for animals, their habitats, and humans. Now Canada has one. I represent that party, the only party in Canada that will protect animals, humans, and the environment, upon which we all depend."

She folds her arms across her chest. "Hmmm! I'm not interested."

"Gosh, it's hot out here," I say, wiping my forehead with the back of my hand. "I'd love a glass of water."

She hesitates, squinting at me, "Ssssure." She steps inside, lightly closing the screen door behind her, and heads for the kitchen. I quietly open the door and tiptoe inside, shutting it with barely a sound. I hear a faucet run and the pressure lock of a freezer pucker open. To the right of the hall is a sitting room with a green upholstered chair. I lunge for it as the crack of a metal ice cube tray separates ice cubes. I plop into the chair and fold my hands in my lap. Green Bathrobe, glass in hand, looks out the screen door; she can't find me. As she starts back to the kitchen, she catches me out of the corner of her eye. I smile sweetly.

"Hope you don't mind me sitting a second. I'm just a bit dizzy. It's the heat." She hands me the glass and sits down on the sofa while I take a sip.

"It's going up past 30°C today. Tomorrow, the same. You'd better put on sunscreen."

"Thanks."

"I don't remember it getting this hot when I was a kid."

"What do you think of climate change?"

"Well . . . I don't have green grass anymore. And the birdbath out back: I fill it in the morning, by lunchtime it's dry."

"That's horrible and frustrating because the main-party candidates won't talk about climate change. Maybe they care more about Alberta's tar sands than your poor birds and grass. Sadly, Canada has the worst environmental and animal protection record in the West. It's not just fossil fuels; it's Big Ag, forestry, mining, land development. Chemicals in our food, water, air. All contributing to cancer, lung disease, the death of the planet."

"You know, when you think about it, it's really scary."

"That's why Guelph needs a candidate who is committed to protecting the environment and animals and people. But it's up to you whom you vote for." I take another sip of water, then drain my glass. "Thank you for the water, and your time."

"You've given me something to think about. Good luck," she calls after me as I head out the door. "Don't forget sunscreen."

In the centre of town, I approach a woman whose children are playing around the penny fountain.

"Your kids are adorable."

"Thanks." She checks over her shoulder as her son reaches in to fish out pennies. "Aiden, don't lean over the edge. I'm warning you."

"I'm running in the federal election for a new party, the Animal Alliance Environment Voters Party of Canada. AAEV for short."

"Like the Greens?"

"No. Better. We want to end federal policies that destroy our children's future." I tilt my head toward her kids and nod. "They need healthy food, not food grown with toxic, cancer-causing pesticides, where farm animals are raised in deplorable conditions and filled with antibiotics and growth hormones that affect people's health. We need healthy water, not water ravaged by E. coli."

The woman's eyes dart from me to her kids playing in the fountain and then back to me. I reach into my satchel and pull out a flyer. "Here's some information."

"Okay," she says, taking it and then turning back to her children. "Leslie, don't drink the water!" She shouts. "Aiden, out of the water, now!"

* * *

I'm excluded from Guelph's first all-candidates debate, so I raise my hand after each candidate speaks. At first, the moderator is happy to give me the microphone.

I address the candidates. "I'm the AAEV candidate who wasn't allowed to speak here today. You talk about the need for jobs. Yet Canada's commercial seal hunt—the largest and most brutal marine mammal slaughter in the world—provides no real jobs for sealers; sealers hunt a week at most, which our taxes prop up. Will you oppose the commercial seal hunt if elected?"

The Green Party candidate says, "Yes."

The NDP candidate says, "No. The seal hunt provides food and a sacred culture for the Inuit."

"No one's trying to end the Inuit subsistence seal hunt," I counter. "It's the commercial hunt I'm talking about. Sealing is never going to end poverty in rural fishing villages. It never has and it never will. The only thing that will end poverty in these communities is twenty-first-century jobs and infrastructure!"

The Conservative candidate says the seal hunt is humane, sustainable, and economically important. I wish I had videos and pictures to show her. "How do you know?" I reply, "DFO officers are almost never present, which means there's no monitoring. Recent activist videos show sealers skinning babies alive or leaving them to die in their own vomit."

The Liberal Party candidate says, "When my wife and I traveled to India, we saw a man machete-ing a live snake into pieces. It's part of a cultural tradition that we aren't part of. It's the same with the Inuit. The seal hunt may seem cruel, but who are we to judge?"

"The commercial and Inuit seal hunts are two distinctly different hunts! We don't oppose Inuit sealing. It's the tax-funded, commercial seal hunt by fishermen that needs to end." I'm about to say more when the moderator grabs the microphone.

I speak at several all-candidates debates, however: one at the University of Guelph; one hosted by the Guelph-Wellington Coalition for Social Justice; and one for the Cable-Satellite Public Affairs Network (C-SPAN).

"You did really well," the Liberal candidate tells me after the C-SPAN debate. "If you were a real candidate, you know, from one of the main parties, I'd be worried."

41

VEGGIE BURGERS

A FEW DAYS later, I walk through the automatic doors of St. Mark's on my way to visit Ben. As I make my way through the lobby and turn right through the doors of his wing, the stench of soggy, grey cafeteria food and the reek of industrial floor cleaner hit me immediately. In the two and a half months I've been away campaigning, I have forgotten how they assault my sense of smell. I hold my breath until I reach Ben's room.

Ben lies on his cot, curled to one side, his body shaped like a question mark. Nurses slide their hands like slender forks beneath him, tugging at his hospital gown. Hands shimmy off his diaper with its egg of poo inside. A nurse wipes his anus. A second one folds a clean diaper between his legs. The intimacy is too much. I feel like a creepy voyeur and step into the hall. Just as I do, Ben notices me and his eyes light up.

"Hi, I didn't expect to see you."

"Do you want me to wait in the visitors' lounge?"

"No. They're almost done," he says, indicating the nurses.

"What's new?" he asks as the nurses adjust his gown, drop their soiled gloves into the hazardous-waste bin, and leave for another patient. I slide the visitor's chair up to the bed.

"What's new with you?" I respond, my hand waving at his hot-orange bed head sticking up at all angles. "You dyed your hair!"

"I needed, like, some colour in my life."

"Neon orange? Brave choice."

"It was either that or blue. Maybe next time."

"So what's up with you, outside of the orange hair?"

"I had chicken cutlet for dinner and French fries."

"You won the lottery!"

Ben's nose scrunches up.

"Not good?"

"Hardly any chicken, mostly batter. The French fries were cold."

"How about if I bring you a veggie burger next time?"

"How about a McDonald's hamburger—a Double Double? I haven't had one of those since I left home."

"How about a veggie burger?"

"You can't deny a dying man his one last wish."

"You're not a dying man. And I am sure this won't be your last wish. Ask someone else to get it."

He looks downcast, like a forlorn puppy.

As I walk back to the van, my head throbs. I have a campaign to run. I have doors still to knock on, votes to get. I'm running for Canada's goddamn animal protection party. I can't go to the Golden Arches! I just can't. How can he even ask me?

Several days later, I pull out a ground-up cow from a white takeout bag. She steams inside her whole-wheat, sesame seed–sprinkled coffin.

"It's not a Double Double!" Ben frowns. "I asked you for a Double Double."

I break off a small piece and hold it out to him. He opens his mouth and I gently push it in. As he chews, ketchup dribbles down his chin and into the runnels of his beard. A drop of it falls onto the bed's white sheet before I can catch it. I pull out a napkin from the bag and dab his mouth and beard. He recoils.

"You should be happy I got you this dead, ground-up cow patty, in this fucking cow coffin." I lift off the top half of the bun, holding it so he can see the ground-up flesh. "I'm never doing it again, ever." I'm still furious that Ben asked me to get the burger knowing my views about eating meat. But I feel more furious at myself for giving in. I turn my head away, so I don't have to see Ben with the ground cow bits between his teeth or the ketchup sticking several strands of his beard together. That's when I notice the walls of Ben's room are covered with animal photographs: gorillas in a torrent of rain, a chicken grooming in a farmyard, a calf standing beneath her mother's belly, a baby seal on ice.

"What's this?"

"What do you think?"

"I don't know. Animal pictures." I shrug my shoulders. "Why?"

"I've become a vegetarian."

"A vegetarian!? You've just eaten a cow!"

"My last."

"You asked me to get you a fucking Double Double. How could you?"

"I thought you'd be pleased."

"Pleased? About buying a piece of a cow?"

"No. About my becoming a vegetarian."

"You just decided, like what, now? Just like that?" I snap my fingers in the air.

"I've been thinking about it for a while."

"You couldn't call me and tell me you'd decided to become a vegetarian? No need to kill another cow."

"I'm still going to eat yogurt. The dietician says it's good for my gut."

"I've killed a cow." I flop into the chair and let my head hang.

"You didn't kill it. It would have died anyway. Someone else would have eaten it."

"*Her.* Not *it. Her.* And everyone who eats a cow kills one. Why didn't you tell me?"

"I wanted to see what you'd do."

"It was a test?"

"This will be the last hamburger I will ever eat. I promise."

"A fucking test!"

"I thought it would make you happy."

I propel myself off the chair so furiously its wooden legs screech across the linoleum.

"That was one of the meanest things *anyone* could ever do to me. It was despicable—you asking me—and insane that I did it." I grab my purse and glare at him before striding for the door.

"You're leaving?"

I stop and turn toward him. "Fuck you."

In my van in the St. Mark's parking lot, I stare out the window, both hands white-knuckling the steering wheel. I just broke my twenty-seven-year-long commitment to never buy meat. Why? Why did I do it? I picture the terrified eyes of the cow in the transport truck. Her being forced into the stall at the slaughterhouse, slipping on the blood and fecal matter on the floor from the dead and dying cows before her. The captive bolt flying from the gun to her forehead. Piercing the bone. Her collapsing.

"Bastard! Fucking bastard!" I scream. I turn my key in the ignition, clutch down from PARK, and drive.

42

RED BRICK CAFÉ

MY EYES MOVE off my call list of Minneapolis chefs to the case of muffins on the counter of the Red Brick Café. What I wouldn't give to dive headfirst into a muffin, gluten and sugar drowning the anxiety in the pit of my stomach. *Muffins are fattening*, I tell myself as I try to quell my emotional hunger. I can see the butter and eggs glistening off their skins. *I'm a vegan*, I add and pull my eyes away.

I count the chefs on my list whom I've already called today. Six. Not one agreed to sign the Canadian Seafood Boycott pledge. Minneapolis would be difficult to win over, Stephen warned me. Minnesota borders Canada. Restaurants and grocery stores would be reluctant to give up Canada's Great Lakes' trout, yellow perch, and sturgeon to save the seals, who live more than two thousand miles away. What's in it for them? The good feeling of helping to save a seal's life? How does that compare to losing trout- and sturgeon-loving customers? Getting Minneapolis restaurants on board would be a big win for our campaign, however. It would send a message to fishermen in sealing provinces that all of America is behind ending the seal hunt.

I call a buyer for a Minneapolis restaurant chain. I get her on the first ring. I explain about the boycott and the seal hunt. She doesn't hurry me off the phone like some of the other chefs I've called. She asks me to call back later, once she's had time to discuss the boycott with her distributors.

I thank her and click off. It was the most promising call of the day, but still, I have no pledge to show for it. How can we end the seal hunt if I can't get pledges? My eyes flit to the muffin case and I find myself walking over to where the muffins are—two rows of them—their freshly baked banana smell knocking at my nostrils.

"I'll have those muffins," I say, tilting my head in their direction.

Don't do it, the Dop says. Of course, only I can hear her. *Do you know how many calories those are? And they're not vegan.*

"How many?" the woman behind the counter asks.

"All."

"All?"

"All. In a bag." In my mind's eye, I can see the Dop cringing.

The woman puts them in a brown paper bag. I pay for them and head into the washroom. I pull out a muffin and take a huge bite. I watch myself chewing in the mirror.

What are you doing?

Go away.

Eat them all. It won't change things. You're still upset about Ben and the hamburger thing.

I plop the toilet seat down and sit on it, stuffing a quarter of the muffin into my mouth. I swallow it quickly and then shove in the rest. Once I've masticated the entire muffin, I pull another out of the bag and break it in half. I shove it into my mouth, chewing and swallowing at the same time.

What are you doing? the Dop asks. *Stuffing your face won't bring in pledges.*

What am *I doing?* I ask myself. I stand and look in the mirror at the crumbs sitting on my lips, the banana smear on the edge of my mouth. I already look five pounds heavier. I turn on the cold water and splash my face. I let the water fill my cupped hands and take a gulp. I gargle and spit the banana remnants into the sink and wash them away. I grab a paper towel and wipe my face. I toss the rest of the muffins in the trash. I straighten my shirt and return to my booth. Just as I sit down, I hear a voice.

"I heard you talking about the seal hunt," a young woman says, approaching my table. She has thick brown hair tied in a heavy bun.

"I'm sorry. Was I too loud?" I ask, a wave of embarrassment skimming above the muffin mash in my stomach.

"I wasn't trying to listen, it's just that, well. . . ."

She shifts from one foot to the other, and folds and unfolds her arms.

"Sit," I say, waving my hand at the chair opposite.

"No, I couldn't. I'm interrupting."

"I'm taking a break."

She hesitates, then sits. I wipe at my mouth with my fingers, making sure there aren't any more muffin crumbs clinging to my lips.

"I'm sorry to bother you. I heard you talking about the seal hunt. It's starting soon, isn't it?"

I nod.

She turns her head and looks out the window, tears welling. "When I saw the seal hunt for the first time on TV, I had nightmares. I couldn't get it out of my head—those little black-eyed babies, bawling for their mothers. It makes me so angry, I don't know what to do."

"You can vote in the next election."

"For the Green Party?"

"No. Animal Alliance Environment Voters."

"There's an animal party?"

"I'm running."

"That's fantastic! I'll vote for you. What's your name?"

After I tell her, she's momentarily silent. "I work for that new coffee shop in the South End. A lot of animal people work there. If you have any information, I'd be glad to put it out."

I pull out some flyers from my Animal Alliance tote bag and slide them across the table. She takes them, stands, and holds out her hand. "By the way, my name is Natalie."

"It's nice to meet you, Natalie."

"I'll tell my husband. He'll vote for you, too. Stop by the coffee shop. They all love animals."

After she leaves, I pack up my phone and my call list and head for the door. It's been a good day after all.

The rest of the summer, I knock on doors, pass out campaign literature, compose speeches, memorize talking points, and call more chefs.

* * *

Liz has rented a Sutton Place Hotel suite to watch the votes come in. There are five AAEV candidates: four in Ontario, including me; one in British Columbia. We fix our eyes on Elections Canada's website on Stephen's laptop. When one of us receives a vote, we all go wild, hooting and hollering and jumping up and down. Popcorn flies into the air like confetti and parachutes down onto the royal-blue rug. How fitting that we're back at the Sutton Place, where our boycott campaign began.

Liz's votes continue to rise, topping a hundred. A second candidate is not far behind. I'm in third place. By the end of the night, I've won twenty-seven votes.

It doesn't matter, the Dop reminds me. *You still got the message out. You still changed twenty-seven minds.*

* * *

In the Trafalgar painting studio parking lot, I fit my painting of the seal pup and her mother into an empty space in the back of my van. As I do, I hear someone racing up behind me.

"Hey! Want to get a coffee sometime?" says Murray, his boat painting held tightly under one arm and the handle of his paint box gripped in one hand. "So, would you? Want coffee?"

I look at him strangely. "Why?"

"'There comes a time in the affairs of man when he must take the bull by the tail and face the situation,'" he explains in a voice sounding like W. C. Fields's. He sets his paint box down by his feet and leans his canvas on it.

Danger, danger, Will Robinson, the Dop says, using a phrase from the TV show *Lost in Space.*

What did the Dop just say?

I said, "You don't know what you're getting yourself into."

"Why?" I ask the Dop, then realize I've spoken aloud.

"Why? Well . . . I admire your passion."

Will you listen to that drivel! Passion! This is a guy who paints boats. All he paints is boats, she says.

"Well, all I paint is animals," I say, throwing up my hands.

"I know. You have a natural talent for them," Murray says.

What's going on? I'm talking to the Dop. Why can Murray hear me?

"So that's a *yes*?" Murray asks.

"I guesssss." I furrow my brow. I have to ask him. "Did you just hear what I said?"

"You said, *yes,* or at least *I guess,* which, call me hopeful, seems like it's closer to a *yes* than a *no.* Plus, it's just a coffee. Not a lifetime commitment."

"No, I mean before that." I can see Murray is confused. "Never mind," I tell him.

"How about Williams?"

There's no "just a coffee," the Dop says.

I can make my own decisions, I hiss at the Dop.

"If you want to go someplace else, that's fine by me," Murray says.

"No, Williams is perfect."

"Good! How about Friday?"

Murray jumps up and down like a teenager. I find it charming. But I also find something is odd. How can Murray hear me when I'm talking to the Dop? No one's ever been able to hear our conversations before.

"I'll see you." He points a finger at me. "Seven o'clock?"

I nod.

Haven't you forgotten something? says the Dop.

Murray turns and looks around, and notices his paint box and canvas, which he is about to leave behind. "You're right!" he says, embarrassed. He picks them up and then, beaming at me, he walks backward a few steps before turning toward his car.

I stare down at the wedding band on my finger and give it a twist. What have I done? No matter what I've told Ben, I'm still married!

43

SNAKES ARE PEOPLE, TOO

"GET ME MY iPhone," Ben says, grinning as I enter the room. "I have something to show you."

It's been a month since I have seen him. In that time, his hands have become shakier and his cheeks have begun to hang.

"Look, I'm sorry I got angry at you the last time I was here. Buying the hamburger was my decision. I shouldn't have blamed you."

"Water under the bridge." He turns to the night table beside his bed and looks at his phone.

I grab it and put it into his left hand. His fingers wobble as they attempt to fold themselves around it. A shaky right index finger aims for the ON button. It waggles over the keys like a plane hanging in the air before crashing. But then his hands give up the exertion and collapse on the bed.

"Type in *what is my spiritual animal*," he says. "One of the nurses showed me this website."

After the site opens, I see renderings of animals on its home page: a wolf baying at the moon, an owl staring from a tree branch, a tiger skulking through jungle underbrush.

"Natives believe in spirit animals, you know, like guides, mentors. They bring you messages from the spirit world," he says.

"Which nurse?" I feel a twinge of jealousy and turn away to hide it.

"Nadia."

Pulling the visitor's chair from the far corner up to the bed, I face Ben. "Nadia? Is she native?"

"Russian, I think. But she's into angel cards, and auras, and she goes to sweat lodges. I don't think you've ever met her. She was working upstairs, but they moved her down here 'cause they're short-staffed. We're just friends."

I smile. "I want you to have friends."

"I can't rely on you for everything, right?"

"You can rely on me for some things, but not everything."

"You have your own life and I'm like . . . you can't live here with me."

"No, I can't."

"I need other people. I have so much time on my hands. I just can't watch reruns all day. I've decided I'm going to eat dinner in the cafeteria, go to the sing-alongs, and I'm going to make friends."

"That's great!"

"Anyway, Nadia and I talk. She showed me this test to find your spirit animal. It asks you questions, and then you choose from four options."

"Interesting. Who's your spirit animal?"

"I was disappointed at first. I imagined I was going to be, like, a tiger or a bull."

"Go ahead. You can tell me."

He lowers his eyes.

"You're embarrassed by your spirit animal?"

"No. Not really."

"Go on, tell me."

"The rabbit."

"What's wrong with the rabbit?"

"The rabbit is always afraid, always running away. But the more I started reading up on it, you know, maybe I *am* a rabbit."

"Read it to me."

I find the page and hold the phone in front of him. "Rabbits live close to the ground where they can easily hide. . . . Rabbit is a sound navigator, having perceptions that pilot him through darkness. . . . Rabbit also symbolizes those moments in life when we must 'hop to,' even in unfamiliar surroundings, using our inner light for direction."[1]

"Wow, I like that. You *are* a navigator; you *do* find direction. I don't mean because you were a truck driver. Look how you're navigating here, deciding to make new friends. I think the rabbit is perfect."

"Okay, now it's your turn."

I click the START button and up pops my first question. *What's your favourite weather?* I click on *rain*. *Which would you rather do?* I click on *read a book*. After several more questions, my spirit animal appears. "Maybe I should take the test again," I say.

"Read it," Ben says.

I frown. "It's the snake."

"You have to be open."

I begin to read aloud. "The snake is a symbol of life, change, and longevity," I read aloud. "Snakes symbolize healing and transforming your life. If you're working to heal animals or the earth, this is an excellent symbol to embrace. Snakes shed their skin as they grow, so ask yourself, 'What do I need to shake off, so I can expand my horizons?' Snake speaks heavily of old, outmoded ways of thinking and living that will hold you back until you're ready for release. Once you do, the Snake's metamorphosis process can begin within and without."[2]

"Wow! That is so cool."

Ben grins. "See, it fits, doesn't it?"

✳ ✳ ✳

Murray sits across from me at a table at Williams. Around us, students type into their laptops. A Joni Mitchell tune plays in the background. I study his hands resting on the table: trim nails, long fingers, smooth skin. I imagine them clasped around my own.

He smiles and then I do.

"When did you start painting?" I say, noticing his white hair has shades of lilac and light grey running through it; the colour of a whitecoat seal pup's hair in shadow. I want to touch it to feel whether it is coarse or silky.

"'Never try to impress a woman, because if you do, she'll expect you to keep up the standard for the rest of your life.'"

I grin. "W. C. Fields?"

"'If you can't dazzle them with brilliance . . .'"

"'Baffle them with bull,'" we say together, laughing.

"That's the only W. C. quote I know."

His denim-blue eyes smile and arch his brows above his silver-rimmed glasses. "'I wrote books and gave lectures.'"

"Enough W. C.! I can't keep up with you. I blame myself. I've obviously not had a proper W. C. Fields education."

He half-smiles and shifts in his seat. "Yes, you're right. I've taken it over the top, haven't I?"

I stare into my lap.

"To answer your question, painting is something I've always wanted to do. I was in a special class for gifted students in high school."

"*Impressive!*"

His cheeks flush. "I'm not sure how impressive it was or, rather, how impressive I was in it. I hardly went to class. But my favourite subject was art. A high school teacher saw some of my drawings and recognized I had some talent and got me into a summer drawing program at the Ontario College of Art."

"What happened?"

"Life took over," he shrugs. "Got married. Had kids. A job in computers. Eventually, my own company. I was making lots of money." He closes his eyes for a second, then opens them. "But I should've been an artist. That's what I really wanted. But you can't raise kids on an artist's income, unless you're Robert Bateman or Damien Hirst."

"So now you're making up for lost time."

"You could say that. . . . What about you?"

"My grandmother was an oil painter. When I was little, she used to make painting smocks for me out of brown paper grocery bags? She'd cut out holes—one for my head, two for my arms. She gave me my first canvas board to paint on."

"You must have been a cutie."

"It was a special time being with my grandmother. She taught me about painting and dance and the theatre. She took me to see *Swan Lake* and the *Nutcracker*."

"She sounds like a special person."

"She was. You know, my first painting was a sailboat."

"I knew we'd have something in common. Boats are my specialty."

I look down at my hands and twist the ring on my finger. "You do know I'm married."

"I was wondering," he says, glancing at my ring. "I've never heard you mention him."

"Ben's at St. Mark's. He has ALS. I visit him."

We both look at the table in awkward silence. I turn my head and gaze around at the students huddling over their tables, the loud din of their chatting and typing mixes with the lyrics of Ferron's folksong-y, Bob Dylan-ish "Slender Wet Branches."

"I love folk music," I say.

"I'm more of a Beatles' fan. Have you always loved politics?"

"No," I shrug. "Never. Until now."

"Why now?"

"For the first time, politics matters. I can stand up for animals."

"Why animals?"

"They don't have a voice." I tell him about the seal campaign and my research on the government.

"You're a seal-hunt detective. Kind of like a female Hardy Boys."

"Kind of," I smile.

44

BLAME GAME

"HI, MARLENE. I haven't received your pledge. Did you send it?" I sit at a booth at the Red Brick Café. Around me, customers sip coffee and slice and butter muffins. The one server rushes from the cash register to the kitchen and then to a table, and back again. She has yet to wipe my table clean, although I nabbed it more than ten minutes ago. Crumbs litter the surface and I swipe a swath of them onto the floor.

The Minneapolis seafood buyer is worryingly silent on the other end of the phone. As I wait for her to speak, I stick-handle a muffin crumb with the end of my pen, as if I were Sid the Kid. *Left, right, left—she shoots!* I propel the crumb off the table onto the floor beside my booth. *She scores!* The Red Brick Café's muffins today, I notice, are cranberry, big as fists and pumped full of egg and butter. Their warm, cakey berry-ness tempts me; but I will not let myself succumb as I did before. I recalibrate my concentration.

"We spoke about Canada's commercial seal hunt. Remember? I sent you information several weeks ago about our boycott."

"I've read your information." Marlene was friendly on our last phone call, but now her voice is cold.

"Great! What do you think?"

"You've been misleading me."

"What? How?"

"You told me it's the fishermen in Canada who are killing all the seals. You said they were the cruel ones. My people tell me it's not the fishermen at all."

"Who do they say it is?"

"The Indians. They're the ones killing the baby seals in the snow and ice. They're the barbarians, not the fishermen."

Indians! I cringe at the word. "Who told you that? Was it someone from the Canadian Department of Fisheries and Oceans?"

A boycott colleague mentioned a while back that some of the chefs she had signed on in Boston had been visited out of the blue by Canadian fisheries officers. Each told the same story: the fisheries officers had pressured them to discontinue their support of the boycott and resume buying Canadian seafood. (The chefs didn't budge.) Most surprisingly, the chefs said the officers told them that the problem of cruelty during the seal hunt was not due to fishermen but the Inuit. Has one of these officers gotten to Marlene?

"I won't hurt fishermen."

"It would help to know where your people got their information."

"That's not important."

"Marlene, whoever spoke to you got their information wrong. I believe your people were referring to the Inuit subsistence hunters, who are not the focus of our boycott and are not responsible for the on-ice brutality."

I wait for Marlene's response, but there is none.

"Marlene, traditionally the Inuit have *not* hunted baby or even juvenile harp seals and they don't hunt seals on the ice; they hunt them in open water. Commercial fishermen are the ones who hunt the seal pups on the ice. The hunt has become a race with fishermen competing against each other to kill and skin as many pups as possible before their area's quota is reached. It's a mad dash to kill seal pups, and because of it, the fishermen race from pup to pup, clubbing and skinning them, often without checking to make sure the pups are unconscious or dead."

Silence fills the void between us.

"Whoever told you the Inuit . . ."

"I don't have time for this," she says and hangs up.

Stephen once mentioned something called "the Inuit card." At the time, I didn't understand what it meant. Later, I looked it up and found it's not a physical card but a deliberate plan to blame the Inuit for the offences of commercial sealers.

When I return from the café to my office, I search the Internet again for the phrase. I find a 2001 Department of Foreign Affairs and International Trade memo, which was originally leaked to IFAW.[1] Can a seven-year-old memo be relevant? The author of the memo, Mark Saigeon, "recommended Canada play the Nunavut Inuit card as leverage" to convince the United States to open its doors to commercial seal products, after having banned them in 1972. I search some more and find a September 6, 2006 *CBC* article, "EU Politicians Push to Ban Canadian Seal Product Imports," reporting that 368 EU lawmakers signed a declaration demanding the EU ban seal products in Europe in protest of Canada's seal hunt. Trying to prevent the EU-wide ban, Canadian officials whipped out their Inuit card, but used it in reverse, not to claim the Inuit were at fault for anything, but to claim how vital the seal hunt was for "the survival of Aboriginal peoples in the Arctic."[2] The Inuit card was alive and well in Canada.

* * *

On December 30, 2008, the DFO tweaks its MMR, adding a "dead before skinning" rule. EU lawmakers suggested such legislation years before, but Canada ignored them. Now, Ottawa hopes that the rule will stave off the ban.

45

CODSWALLOP

"WE DON'T HAVE a budget for the seal hunt," the DFO budget officer tells me. I grab a stuffed seal pup toy from the shelf above my desk and, in frustration, hop it back and forth on its tail as I listen to why he can't send me a list of the 2006 and 2007 sealing expenditures. I want them because if I can determine the cumulative spending of research, maintenance, assistance and rescue operations, government missions abroad, and any other subsidies used to prop up the seal hunt during these two years, I can deduct those expenses from the government's announced sealing values for each year. By doing so, I might be able to come up with a reasonable assessment of the real worth of the 2006 and 2007 seal hunts.

"You must have a sealing budget."

"We have a fisheries budget."

"But seals aren't fish. They are marine mammals. Surely you have a sealing budget somewhere." *You're not a fish are you?* I say silently to the stuffed seal toy.

"We have one budget. It is the same budget for the snow crab fishery, the lobster fishery, the cod fishery, and any other fishery we manage. All our expenses are consolidated into one fisheries budget."

"If the DFO considers seals to be fish, what about narwhals, and walruses, and whales?"

"If we manage them, they're in the fisheries budget."

"Okay, that's what I want, then: a list of all items spent on harp seals within the fisheries budget."

"We don't list out what's spent on the seal fishery."

"That can't be true. There are seal hunt expenses that have nothing to do with other fisheries. What about the seal hunt rescue in 2007? The costs of deploying icebreakers, and helicopters, and officers who got trapped in the ice. Surely those expenses are listed."

"Nope."

"Why not?"

"The Coast Guard already owns those vessels. They're employed in all the fisheries, not just the seal hunt. And those officers are getting paid whether they're out rescuing sealers or not."

"But the seal hunt is the only 'fishery' that operates at that time of year. The fishermen who seal are the only ones out on the ice."

"And, like I said, there are no separate items in the budget for the seal hunt."

"Can you send me the fisheries budget then, so I can see it with my own eyes?"

"You'll have to file an ATIP request. But I doubt you'll get it. The fisheries budget is confidential."

"Codswallop!" I say once I've hung up. I look down at the toy seal pup in my hand. Those expenses exist, and I'm going to find them, I tell her. Maybe it's my imagination, but I swear she winks.

My red binder has almost every article ever written on the seal hunt since 2004. In other binders, I've stored DFO press releases and dozens of website documents. Standing Committee transcripts and parliamentary reports are fat suckers, so the only place to store them is in piles on my floor. Nevertheless, no matter where they are stored, inside those articles, reports, and transcripts are dozens and dozens of references to sealing expenditures. I had found them before in my general reading and at the same time saw no immediate purpose for marking them for later reference. I'll find them again.

I start with the 2006 and 2007 Standing Committee transcripts. And heeding Nancy Drew's advice once again, I formulate a spreadsheet. I will add any expense I can find for these years. In good time, I fill the spreadsheet with dozens of items. Grants for new seal product research and development, the costs of search and rescue operations during the 2007 ice disaster, the funds for trade missions and delegations sent to Europe to garner seal hunt support.

And then, as we say in the detective business, the trail goes cold.

What do I do now? I wonder. It doesn't take long to come up with the answer. I push back my chair and walk over to the Nancy Drew section of my bookshelf. *The Hidden Staircase* calls to me. I pull it down from the shelf, open it to a random page, and start reading.

"Even though we can't get inside Riverview Manor," Nancy tells her friend Helen, "we can hunt through the outbuildings [. . .] for the entrance to an underground passage."[1]

I mull over Nancy's sagaciousness. To the average person, Nancy's words would mean nothing, not least regarding the investigation of sealing expenses. To me, however, finding this passage is reason to do a little swivel chair–sitting victory dance, accompanied by a big "Woohoo!" The girl detective does it again! The clue may not be visible to some, but it is to me. Just like Nancy, I can't get inside the place I want to (the DFO sealing budget), but I can go through its outbuildings—all the federal departments that may be hiding sealing expenses. I know the Department of Foreign Affairs and International Trade provides some funding for trade missions and delegations outside the country, but is it the only one? Likely, it takes a village to prop up the seal hunt—a village of government departments I have yet to uncover. But which ones? And where can I find the clues to lead me there? I wonder if another Nancy Drew can help me. I stand and glance over the titles.

Are you simpleminded? the Dop asks with her usual pleasantry.

Was she here all the time, or did she just pop in for tea or torture?

No, I'm not simpleminded, I scoff. *I was one point away from* summa cum laude.

Will you cut this summa cum laude *shit? It was three decades ago.*

Why are you here? Just to annoy me?

No. To help you. Listen: the government has always maintained that it didn't subsidize the seal hunt after 2001, right?

Yes. And your point?

Good God! Do I have to spell it out for you?

You came to me. I was floundering very nicely on my own.

Sit down on your swivel chair, put your fingers on the keyboard, and shut up.

I do as I'm told, settling my fingers in the typist's preferred position, and suddenly they start moving. I stare down at my hands. It's like watching an Ouija board contacting the dead.

Up comes: A partial list of Canadian government sealing industry costs and subsidies (1995 to 2001). My fingers skid to a halt.

But I don't need 1995 to 2001. I need 2006 and 2007.

Shush. Before you start objecting, look.

"DFO and Coast Guard costs on the ice for the seal hunt in Newfoundland, 1995–2001," I read. My eyes bore into the screen at the exact place where the costs are described: *support to seal operations, icebreaking, search and rescue,* and *enforcement.* I look at another column and see that the funding agencies for the project were the DFO and the Coast Guard, and the price tag—C$5,957,000. Yikes!

"Yikes" is right. Keep reading.

The next project listed is for Québec. I glance at the price tag: C$1,820,000! A few rows down, there's Federal Seal Meat Purchasing Subsidies—C$2,523,000, and Provincial Seal Meat Purchasing Subsidies for Newfoundland—handing out C$1,918,000 for meat no one wanted. Winston Waye the Sausage Man got C$95,700 for equipment and consulting. He was supposed to provide seal meat products for export. The money was dished out by the Atlantic Canada Opportunities Agency and the Canada Foundation for Innovation.

But try as I might to find him using Google, it seems Winston Waye the Sausage Man has disappeared off the face of the Earth, or at least off the face of the Internet. And for all the C$95,700 spent on seal sausage development, they are hardly a foodie consideration today, except for the most perverted culinary minds. It *appears* that C$95,700 went up in a puff of smoke.

It's all very interesting, but I need the 2006 and 2007 subsidies, not the 1995 ones. What does the Coast Guard do today?

Icebreaking, search and rescue.

So where does all that money come from? the Dop asks.

My jaw drops. If I want to find today's subsidies, I should start looking at all the funding agencies that subsidized the seal hunt yesterday. I have found my passageway!

Indeed, you have. Good show! she says, a bit like Mary Poppins.

I spend the next couple of days tracking down all the departments that funded the seal hunt between 1995 and 2001. Most are still in existence.

Days later—some may call it serendipity or coincidence, I call it the seal hunt–hating gods at work—a Toronto lawyer calls me out of the blue. At first, I wonder, What have I done now? But as I listen, I realize he's talking about the seal hunt. Apparently, Murray Teitel, family and civil litigation lawyer, hates the seal hunt about as much as I do. And while stewing about it in his office between billable hours, he decides to track down the DFO's sealing subsidies, even if the DFO pretends they didn't exist!

"What are you going to do with them?" I ask.

"I'm going to write an article for the *Financial Post*."

"You're on staff—like a lawyer-journalist-seal-subsidy detective?"

"No. But I get how they think."

"They won't publish it. The media have been so negligent on this issue. We've sent out press releases reeking with information about the seal hunt, and they've all ended up in limbo."

"The thing about the *Financial Post* is they hate government waste," Teitel says. "I thought I'd tackle it from a taxpayer's point of view. I'm pretty sure they'll print it."

Wow! I'm usually wary of lawyers, but I really like this guy. So I tell him about how I single-handedly found a way to get to the subsidies that supported the seal hunt, albeit it fifteen-plus years ago.

"Interesting," Teitel says. "I should mention that I've spoken to the DFO about sealing subsidies and they told me there weren't any. Of course, I didn't believe them. One just needs to look at the news to know the seal hunt is heavily subsidized. Half of the 2007 seal hunt's *economic opportunity* [economic value], which was C$12 million according to the DFO's website, had to be eaten up by expenses. There was the disaster last year with those boats getting trapped in the ice, involving ten vessels—from icebreakers to helicopters to patrol planes."

I tell him about my own conversation with the DFO's budget office. "The budget officer claims it costs nothing because the DFO owns the boats and aircraft, and because the crew was on salary."

"That's like saying it costs nothing for the City of Toronto to put out fires because it owns the fire trucks and the firefighters are on staff."

"There was the C$7.9 million Ice Compensation Program directed at the sealing industry to subsidize the repairs of boats damaged in the 2007 ice," I add. "There was the capsizing of the trapped boat that was rescued and then tipped over by the Coast Guard vessel towing it to dock."

"The lawsuits and legal bills alone would have cost C$6 million," Teitel says.

Leave it to a lawyer to think of that.

"Don't forget all the trade missions to the EU to counter the seal product bans," Teitel reminds me. "It all comes out of taxpayers' pockets."

Shortly thereafter, Murray Teitel concludes: "I have to run. I've got a client coming in a half-hour from now and I haven't even had lunch yet."

"Good luck on your *Financial Post* article," I respond, as we say goodbye.

On April 17, 2008, Murray Teitel's article, "The Millions Ottawa Spends Subsidizing the Seal Hunt," appears in the *Financial Post* under *FP Comment*.

Alas, I need to get back to the boycott. I set aside my subsidies research and begin, once again, to call chefs. Yet, as I wait for the chefs to come to the phone, which can be a long wait at times, I continue to browse through random Standing Committee transcripts. In the one dated April 14, 2008, I find an interesting comment made by Peter Stoffer, an MP from Nova

Scotia, to a colleague, which adds fuel to the subsidies' fire. Stoffer directs his colleague not to use the word *subsidy*: "I would eradicate that from your vocabulary and use the word *investment*. *Subsidy* scares government people off. I think *investment* . . . sounds much better."[2]

I copy the page, cut out Stoffer's comment, and pin it to the clothesline. Stepping back, I am pleased to see that my clothesline is just about out of room. I'll soon have to get new twine and new tape so I can extend it down the hall.

Just then, my cellphone buzzes.

"Hello? Who's this?" I ask. My jaw drops upon hearing the answer.

46

STATE OF PLAY

ON JULY 1, 1867, Canada became a nation. Neither at its inception nor at its hundred-year anniversary would Canadians have ever dreamed that one of their lawmakers would attempt to topple its sacrosanct commercial seal hunt. Flash forward almost 150 years. On Friday, February 27, 2009, Liberal Senator Mac Harb, representing Ottawa Centre, sends a letter to all senators announcing his intention to introduce a private member's bill to amend the Fisheries Act. This proposed legislation, Bill S-229, if enacted, would "prohibit the commercial fishing for seals in Canadian fisheries waters and [. . .] disallow the issuance of commercial licences for seal fishing." Indigenous Canadians with treaty rights would be exempt.

A few days later, on March 3, Senator Harb reads the bill in what amounts to its first reading in the Senate. Once it's read, the Speaker pro tempore (the presiding official) asks when the bill should have a second reading. The one-word answer spoken by all those senators present is *never*. Harb's bill is dead on arrival.

In my office, I Google the transcript and read for myself the demoralizing record of how an entire senate chamber clubbed democracy. Reflecting on what happened, one senator told reporters that in his decades in the Senate, he'd never seen a bill so totally unsupported.

On March 23, Rebecca Aldworth sums up what Harb's bill means for Canadians who have opposed the seal hunt for over five decades: "This is the first time that Canadians have had a potential piece of legislation to rally around—and we have to show overwhelmingly that Canadians want the seal hunt to stop. Finally, we are being given a political avenue to do that," she tells the *Georgia Straight*.[1]

Not only does Senator Harb clear the way for the introduction of legislation to end the seal hunt, but he is also, as far as I know, the first Canadian politician to witness the seal hunt first-hand. Late in March, he accompanies IFAW to the hunt. As photographers capture him sitting on a mound of snow next to a whitecoat, he smiles for the camera, yet there is no sparkle in his eyes. As I study the photograph online, I wonder if he is contemplating the fate of the curious seal pup who has sidled up beside him as the cameras click and click.

Before Harb's visit to the nursery, the European Union began to consider a ban on the trade in seal products. The consideration causes the market for seal products drops considerably.[2] Dion Dakins, manager of NuTan Furs, one of Canada's premier buyers of seal pelts, warns sealers to ensure they have buyers before leaving dock. Three years earlier, in 2006, sealers banked C$105 for each pelt they sold. Now, they are looking at C$15 a pelt, along with a scarcity of buyers.[3]

"I'm not going this year," Newfoundland sealer Ray Newman tells the *Nor'wester*. "There's no way you can make a buck off it."

I'm thinking the same thing as I read the words of Newman and others. A fleet of sealing vessels, usually heading for the ice by now, remains docked. I print the April 24, 2009 *Nor'wester* article "Pelt Prices Keep Some Sealers Home," and kick my feet up on my desk, raising my chocolate soymilk in a toast.[4]

Getting cocky is premature, however. If the EU doesn't ban seal imports, prices will increase and sealers will resume hunting. News of the EU's decision is supposed to come any day. On Wednesday, May 5, I read the headline. "Disastrous EU Seal Ban Casts Gloom Over Summit."[5] For an anti-sealing campaigner like me, victory is a vegan cherry pie of sweetness, and right now I'm a ten-year-old sugar junkie sticking my finger in the pie's still-steaming centre and angling the cherry filling into my mouth.

✳ ✳ ✳

Across the ocean, the EU alerts Canada and all other sealing nations—
Norway, Russia, Greenland, and Namibia—that their seal-trading days
in Europe are over. Ottawa insists Canada must receive a seal product ban
exemption and threatens to launch a WTO complaint.[6]

47

DNR

DROPS AS BIG as grapes drench maple trees and fill the asphalt ruts of St. Mark's parking lot. I dodge the puddles and dash through the front doors into the lobby. My wet sneakers squeak on the linoleum as I head to Ben's room. He lies in bed, wearing the sweatshirt with the neon fish that my mother and Eddie brought him back from Aruba last winter. Like a voyeur, I observe him unnoticed. As he turns to the window, his pillow bunches around his head. Does he see any of the baby rabbits who live in the shadows underneath his window ledge? Days before, they hop-walked for the first time. It's June 2009. Ben has lived at St. Mark's for two years now. As I step into his room, he turns toward me.

"We need to talk."

"No 'Hello, glad to see you'?" I smile.

"I'm serious." A knot of tension contorts his forehead.

I nod. "Okay."

"Shut the door," His face is as grim as I've ever seen it—not angry, but something I can't define. I close the door.

"Okay, what's up?" I settle into the visitor's chair and crabwalk it closer to Ben's bed. My stomach corkscrews as I wait for him to talk.

Karen, don't forget to breathe, I hear my grandmother say.

"You look upset," I say.

He stares into my eyes. "I haven't shit in ten days."

"You told me you were having problems two days ago, but you were hoping to wait it out. Do you think it's another bowel blockage?"

"Nadia wants me to get an X-ray. She called Dr. Chakrabarti this morning."

"When is Chakrabarti going to see you?"

"She's supposed to come tonight."

"I wish St. Mark's had their own doctor. They shouldn't have to rely on a doctor in Buffalo."

"She'll get me into Guelph General if I need it."

I knit my brows and twist my lips as I think about Ben returning to Guelph General. "I'm sorry, Ben. I wish there were something I could do."

Ben fights back tears. "I've made a decision."

I nod several times, waiting for him to tell me.

"If I do go back to Guelph General, I want it to be for the last time."

"But what if you need to go back?"

"I've signed a DNR order."

"What!"

"'Do Not Resuscitate.'"

"I know what it means. I just don't know why you'd do something like that. You can still breathe and swallow on your own. You're not going to die soon."

"Remember what the doctor told us? I probably won't die from ALS. It'll be from a complication like pneumonia or a bowel obstruction."

I want to say something comforting, but all I can think of is: "Oh God."

"I'm just saying: if something happens, I want the doctors, and you, to let me go."

"Ben. You're scaring me."

"If I die at the hospital, I don't want anyone trying to bring me back."

I sit on the edge of the bed and take his hand. We sit in silence until a nurse's aide brings in his dinner tray. She sets it on the bed table. I unfold a serviette and tuck it under Ben's chin, then stand ready to feed him.

"I'm not hungry," he says as I move his tray table closer.

"At least see what you got."

"I know what I got. I got a cheese sandwich; it's the only thing the kitchen staff know how to make that's edible and vegetarian."

"Cheese is constipating."

Ben shrugs.

"That could be part of your problem!" I lift the plastic lid and glare at the sandwich. "Do you want it?"

He shakes his head. "I'm not hungry."

"You must eat something. I can go to the cafeteria and get you some crackers."

"It won't stay down."

"Are you nauseous?"

He nods.

Lack of appetite, nausea, a green tinge to his skin—I know the signs. Most likely, he has a bowel obstruction. I push away the tray table and sit on the edge of his bed, holding his hand.

After a moment, he moans.

"Do you have cramps?"

He blinks. Then moans again. "Sharp pain." He fumbles for the call button the nurses have tied to the bed frame beside him.

"You're calling the nurse?"

"You should go." He inclines his head toward the door.

"Let me sit with you."

"The nurse will call you if anything happens."

A nurse aide strolls into his room. "What's up?" Then she sees the pistachio-green colour of his face. She places her fingers on Ben's forehead. "You feel hot."

Ben moans.

"Cramps?"

He can now barely nod.

"Do you want something for the pain?"

The answer fills Ben's eyes.

"I'll be right back," she says and rushes from the room.

"Oh God, Ben."

"Go home."

"How will I know if you're going to Guelph General?"

"The nurse will call you."

As I turn to leave, the nurse's aide brushes past me with a small paper cup and I watch as Ben opens his mouth, and the aide tips the pill in.

The nurse calls me a few hours later. I rush to Guelph General and run down the hall to his room. The rotten egg smell hits me first, filling my nose and making me want to gag. I detect its source. A network of tubes connects to various machines: one drains green sludge out of Ben's bowel and tunnels it into a jug attached to his bed; another runs from his nose to the back of his throat, siphoning the mucus out of his lungs. He sleeps. I sit in the visitor's chair beside him, folding and unfolding my hands.

When he wakes, I stand beside him. "How are you feeling?"

"Wadder. Ma throa' hur's."

Before I entered Ben's room, a nurse grabbed my arm. "He can't have any water. You can give him some ice chips. There's some in the Styrofoam cup by his bed."

"The nurse says, 'no water'! I can give you some ice chips."

Ben opens his mouth and I spoon a few in.

"Ah can' wallow."

"You can't swallow?"

"Ma 'ose is dippin' in ma throa'."

"Your nose is dripping?"

He nods. "Hur."

"Wait here." I stride over to the nurses' station across from Ben's room. "My husband's in pain!"

When the nurse fails to respond, I lean over her desk. "Helloooo!"

"What's the matter!" she asks, continuing to stare at the report in front of her.

"His throat hurts."

"That's because he has a tube down his throat," she says, lifting her head to look at me.

"Can't you do something?"

"If we remove the tube, his lungs will fill up."

"He says his nose is dripping into his throat and the tube hurts."

"The only thing I can do is call the respiratory technician."

Half an hour later, a woman in peach-coloured scrubs enters with a small kidney-shaped tub and an aspirator, which she shelves on the tray table.

"Open," she says to Ben. She peers down his throat, then jiggles the tube.

A scream claws its way up from the bottom of Ben's throat. "*Aaauuuuuwwww!*"

"It hurts him," I say.

"It's not draining as well as it could. I'll have to pull it out," she tells us both. "This might hurt a bit," she says to Ben.

"*Aaaahhhhcck!*" Ben gags as she slowly eases out the tube. When it's fully out, the technician wipes off the mucus clinging to it, then loops the tube around like a garden hose. Next, she reaches for the tube and lays it on Ben's chest under his chin. The motor of the aspirator looks like a cement mixer, only smaller. A plastic tube the size of the one that was down Ben's throat connects to the machine and another conduit runs from it to what looks like a child's sippy cup. When the technician flips the motor's switch, it begins to *ghirrrrr* away. Soon, the aspirator suctions a sticky mass from his throat. I watch it slide into the sippy cup.

"How's that feel?" the technician asks as she removes the aspirator's suction tube.

"Better," Ben says, almost normally.

"Good. Now let's get this tube back in and see how you do." She unwinds the tube she pulled from Ben's throat earlier and eases it back one of Ben's nostrils and threads it into his throat.

"*Auuuuuhhhh,*" Ben chokes.

Just then, the intercom calls: "Respiratory technician needed in room ten."

"Can't you leave it out?" I say.

"He'll drown in his own mucus," she says, wiggling the tube back and forth to make sure it has wormed its way down as far as it should go.

"It will just clog again," I say.

"I'll check on him shortly." She grabs the aspirator and hurries toward the door. "Hang in there," she tells Ben before disappearing down the hall.

The next time the technician checks in, about two hours later, she brings a codeine tablet to help Ben sleep.

"Guh hoe slee," he says a few minutes later, his lids barely open.

"I'm not going home. I'll sleep here." I wake up blinking half an hour later and look around to see where I am. I wipe the back of my hand across my eyes.

"Guh hoe," Ben says.

I look at Ben in surprise. "You're up?"

"Cud no eep. Nor."

"I was snoring? I'm sorry."

"Guh hoe," Ben says.

"Okay," I stand. "I'll be back in the morning." I kiss the top of his head. "You'll be alright," I tell him, silently hoping he'll make it through the night. "Please call me if anything . . ," I tell the nurses' station nurse.

"Of course," she says.

Six hours later, I return to Ben's room. He's sleeping without the tube up his nose.

"Ben had a very bad night, despite the codeine," the morning nurse says.

"Why's the tube out?"

"The doctor thinks it was aggravating his throat and causing the mucus." Even without the tube, Ben has a high fever, she tells me, and suggests I run a facecloth under the sink's faucet to bathe his face. A few days later, Ben's bowels move by themselves. He eats without throwing up. After a week, he sits up in his bed, then in his wheelchair. Soon he returns to St. Mark's.

48

ROSALIE

"I CAN'T INVITE you in," I tell Murray at the end of our date. We sit in his car in front of my condo building. Entrance lights cut into the darkness.

"I'm not a CSIS agent," he jokes.

"I know. I should never have told you about CSIS. Still, I can't invite you in."

"The only problem is I have to pee," he says, squirming in the driver's seat.

I've heard better lines than that.

"I'm not looking to get into your pants," he says. "I really do need to pee."

"I'm sorry, my house is a mess."

"I can go out in the back of your building if you'd rather. But in the next five minutes, I'm going to have to go somewhere."

"It's just that I haven't cleaned."

"I don't care about cleaning. Do you have a toilet?"

"Of course I have a toilet."

"Does it work?"

"Of course it works."

"Can I use it?"

He really does look like he needs to go. "I have a husky-malamute," I warn him as he steps out of the car.

"I love dogs," he says, hurrying to the front door.

I notice his navy wool jacket as I pull out my keys. "He's white and he sheds."

"Toilet?" Murray urges.

I unlock the lobby door. We ride the elevator and hurry down the hall. As I open my front door, Murray bounces as he tries to keep his legs pressed together. I say a mental prayer. "Please don't let him see . . ." But before I can finish, Karma hurls himself off the sofa and bounds toward Murray.

"He's gentle," I say as Karma throws his paws up onto the shoulders of Murray's jacket.

"Hey, Karma, nice to meet you. But if you'll excuse me, nature calls."

I point him toward the washroom, and without bothering to take off his coat, he strides down the hall, with Karma trotting behind him.

Unable to accompany Murray into the washroom, Karma wanders into the bedroom. My bedroom door is open. I forgot to shut it!

Cluck, cluck, cluck! comes from inside. Then *woof, woof.*

Sliding my hands down my forehead, I head down the hallway, hoping that Murray hasn't heard a thing. But, as I near the washroom, the toilet flushes and water comes out of the faucet. Just as the handle of the washroom door turns, and the door opens, the clucks get louder and I know I'm too late. Murray steps from the washroom and I barrel into him.

Cluck, cluck, cluck, cluck, cluck.

Ruff, ruff, ruuuuuf, Karma replies.

Murray looks at me and then at the open doorway of the bedroom. "What is that?"

"Rosalie," I say. "She's a *who.*"

Cluck. Cluck. CLUCK!

Ruff.

"Who is Rosalie?" Murray leans into the room.

"Please don't look," I say.

But that doesn't stop him. His eyes go wide. "There's a chicken in your bedroom."

I nod.

"There's a live chicken in your bedroom."

I nod again, faster.

"Does she live here?"

"Only for a time."

"She lives here!"

"She's a rescue."

"A rescue! You rescued a chicken! From what? A farm? Did you steal her?"

"No, I did not steal her!" I shake my head. "She came to me in desperation. Do you want to meet her?"

Murray thinks for a moment and then shrugs. "I guess I'll have to."

Rosalie nests in straw inside Karma's puppy crate. Her leftover corn niblets are scattered on the floor.

"I found her walking around with twine tied to her leg."

"When?"

"When I was walking Karma a few nights ago."

"Did you ever think she belonged to someone?"

"It was cold and sleeting, and I couldn't leave her wandering the streets with a piece of twine around her leg. She'd freeze to death," I shrug.

Murray nods, weighing my words. "What do you intend to do with her?"

"Bring her to a sanctuary."

"They're willing to take her?"

"We go tomorrow."

"We?"

"Rosalie and me, and probably Karma. He hates being left behind."

Murray sighs.

I turn my face away and rub the back of my neck. "Well, it's late."

Checking his watch, Murray says, "I didn't realize the time!"

"Well, it does pass quickly when one is being introduced to a chicken."

"A desperate one," he says.

My lower lip trembles. "Yes, a desperate one."

Murray follows me to the front door. In the hallway, he looks at me. I raise my shoulders and shake my head from side to side. "What?"

"Do you know you're a nut?"

"If a nut is rescuing a chicken from a sleet stor . . ."

"But a good nut," he says, cutting me off. A grin spreads across his face. "Can I see you again?"

"I didn't think you'd want to after Rosalie and Karma. And you haven't even met Levi and Bella. They've been hiding from you."

"More chickens?"

"No. Cats."

"Anyone who'd rescue a chicken from a sleet storm is a good egg in my book."

A moment sits awkwardly between us. "Well, then . . ," I shrug. I reach for the door handle behind me.

"Good night," he says.

"Good night."

He turns his head toward the elevator and looks down the hall, as if he is about to step away. But whether he changes his mind or it's what he intended, he turns back to me, leans closer, and kisses me: at first, a light peck, and then with more intensity, with his arm pressing against my back. Releasing me, he steps back, cocks his head, and smiles, before walking backward down the hall.

I watch him enter the elevator and as the door closes I brush my finger against my lips.

The next afternoon, Rosalie, Karma, and I drive to the sanctuary.

49

MISHEGOSS

THE EU BAN takes effect in August 2010. Canada and Norway file a joint complaint at the World Trade Organization (WTO), claiming that the ban violates trade agreements. Without waiting for a response, Canada decides it won't end the seal hunt, even though the loss of EU markets means that most of the year's pelts will be stored in warehouses.

Diminishing sea ice and non-seal hunt–related pup mortality are bringing new questions about the harp species' survival. Fisheries and Oceans Minister Gail Shea (2008–2011), noting fewer boats are participating in either the Gulf or the Front, extends the hunt in Newfoundland to May 31, well past its usual May 15 closure. Despite Shea's efforts to prolong the hunt, sealers fail to slaughter enough seal pups to fill their quota. Only 67,000 seal pelts are trucked to seal-processing plants such as those in Dildo, Fortune, Marystown, Burin, and Carbonear, Newfoundland. Prices continue to drop and the promised markets in China have yet to appear.

* * *

In the spring, I squeeze myself into tight jeans for a miniature golf date with Murray. The next weekend, Murray joins Karma and me for a walk around Guelph Lake. The 30°C temperature melts my makeup, which streams down my forehead and into my eyes, forcing me to wipe it off with one of Karma's unused biodegradable poo bags. Another weekend, we go to an art show, and the next we travel to a little lake town up north.

During the week, I stare at the last few purchase slips waiting on my desk and the 2,500 rows which have already been entered for the "2007" seal hunt. But my thoughts couldn't be further away. Murray is visiting his mother, sister, and nephews in Guernsey. Every few minutes, I catch myself thinking of him and wondering if he misses me.

Lost in my thoughts, I sit in front of the computer screen and think about our last weekend together before I dropped him off at Pearson. It was such a simple weekend. No big do. No exciting moment of passion. We had dug up his lawn. A simple mention from me that I loved to garden, and he said: "It's yours to do with what you want. I can help you dig." The next moment he was thrusting a spade into the earth.

"I must check for worms. I don't want them hurt while you go digging about."

"We can't dig a garden while searching for every worm in the ground, so they won't get hurt. We'll never get anywhere."

But we did. And that was all that mattered. He was willing to scrape his garden-gloved fingers into the dirt to search for worms to protect them.

"Don't go forgetting me," he said in the airport's departure lounge, pulling me toward him for one last hug.

"Just you be safe," I remember saying. "Don't get on a flight with any plane-crashing terrorists on board."

"No. I promise," he said as he was called into the boarding line.

Nose to the grindstone, the Dop says, trying to snap me out of my reverie.

Reluctantly, I turn back to the last purchase slip and fill in my spreadsheet with its final ominous but boring details. Now that I am finished, I will need to begin analyzing the data. And then what will I do with it? A report maybe? Stephen had suggested it. But what then? Who would read such a report and what conclusions could I make?

The one question I still don't have an answer to is how the DFO uses the purchase slips to figure out the value of the commercial seal hunt.

I thought all I needed to do was get the purchase slips to find out the values of the 2006 and 2007 hunts Then I thought all I needed to do was organize them in some readable manner. But now I realize there is much more to it, but what good are the purchase slips if there are no numbers to add up? Is it all a *mishegoss*, as my grandmother would say, waving her hand in the air, whenever there was something she could not understand? How could I find out?

Days later, while cleaning up my office, I come across a study that I had read several years previously. "The Newfoundland Commercial Seal Hunt and Economic Analysis of Costs and Benefits" measures the economic benefits of the 1996 seal hunt. Clive Southey, its author, was an economics professor at the University of Guelph when he wrote the report for IFAW with one of his students. If anyone can help me figure out the values of the 2006 and 2007 seal hunts using the purchase slips, I imagine he can. I use my Nancy Drew detective skills to find his phone number and a photograph, taken decades ago, of the dashing economist with wind-whipped hair.

When Professor Southey greets me at the door a few days later, I'm momentarily stunned. A man with wispy grey hair stands before me in his pajamas and bathrobe. "Tea?" he asks, then leads me to the kitchen where I watch him heat the kettle and prepare the cups in the typical ritualistic manner of the British. The Japanese were not the only ones to have developed a tea ceremony.

While he stuffs the tea leaves into the strainer, and then inserts the contraption in the pot, he tells me of his years travelling and working for the Kenyan government as its senior economic advisor on the environment. I tell him of my longing to travel to Kenya. Sensing a kindred spirit, he takes me into the living room, which is filled with African artifacts: wooden bowls, carved totems, and ferocious masks.

"This is amazing!" I say, admiring a shrunken head sitting on top of a pillar. "Is it real?"

"The real one is at Pitt Rivers in Oxford. This is just a cast," he says. "Do you know Pitt Rivers?"

I shake my head.

"It's one of the most important ethnological museums in the world, and they have quite the collection of shrunken heads."

After showing me his collection, he motions me to the sunroom—a screened porch with comfy, mismatched chairs—and returns a moment later with our tea. Once settled, I explain my purpose.

"I have thousands of purchase slips from 2006 and 2007 sent to me from the DFO. I was told that they are the documents the government uses to determine the value of the commercial seal hunt. But I can't see how they can determine anything when so much information is missing."

"Have you brought them?" Professor Southey asks.

I pull out a half-dozen slips from my Animal Alliance tote bag and hand them to him. He leans back in his chair and studies one, and then another, between sips of tea. I sit on the edge of my chair, bouncing my foot, awaiting his assessment.

"Well," he says, taping the pages into a straight pile. "I'm sorry to disappoint you, but these are useless."

"You're kidding!" I take the documents back and stare at them. "Are you sure?"

"They don't tell you anything. Not a thing."

A part of me thinks he must be wrong. I reach into my tote bag and pull out a copy of his report. "Then how did you come up with your report? Didn't you use purchase slips?"

"I've never seen a purchase slip in my life until you brought them here."

"What did you use then?" I hand him my copy of his report.

The professor lays the report on his lap and scans its first and second pages. "Here it is," he says, pointing to a section of references. "All the information we used came from the DFO's internal documents, which we listed here."

"Yes, but, if the purchase slips are what the government uses how could you. . . ?"

"Nope. We didn't need to look at purchase slips. The government gave us the information we needed, official memos, reports, whatever we used we listed right here," he says, smacking the listed references with the back of his hand. "Of course, they didn't give us the information out of the goodness of their hearts. We had to request it through the Access to Information legislation."

"Could you explain it to me, then, how you came up with your findings?" I pull up my chair beside his and he begins to explain how he used the information he had to calculate the value of the 1996 commercial seal hunt.

"You see here, there are three sectors that profit from the seal hunt." He points to a small chart on the second page. "There are the sealers, the processors, and the transporters. We totaled what each of their revenues were in 1996, and came up with the value of C$8.96 million."

"But that wasn't your conclusion, was it? You concluded that the real economic value for 1996 is. . . ." I wave my hand at the report, which he returns to me. I let my finger slide down the first page to the bottom, and stop at the last line. "Yes, there it is: $C2.91 million. That's what you concluded the value of the commercial seal hunt to be."

He chuckles. "A far cry from the nine million that they tried to lead us to believe."

"But how did you come up with it? The C$2.91 million?" I hand him back his report.

He pushes his glasses up the bridge of his nose and reexamines the report. "We began to subtract the inputs from the outputs."

"Inputs? Outputs?"

"Yes. The DFO hadn't subtracted any of the factors of production, the resources needed, the inputs, if you will, to operate the hunt. You see, each of the sectors has their own particular inputs."

"What would those be?"

"I can't know them all because they weren't all provided. But let's assume, and it's not too grand an assumption to expect, there are costs for sealers to go out to the ice to hunt the seals, their seal licences. . . ."

"Oh, that's nothing," I say. "A sealing licence costs five dollars a year to renew."

"Then there are the rifles and ammunition, the purchase of those ghastly clubs they use, any clothing specific to the hunting of seals, their rations while they're hunting, any boat maintenance or repair. Not an exhaustive list, surely, but it will do for our purposes. Then there are inputs for the two other sectors as well. Someone must be at the dock to represent the processor, to do whatever needs to be done."

"There's someone to count the pelts and weigh them, I believe," I say. "Though I'm told they aren't always present."

"Still, at some point, that has to be done. Whether at the dock or at the processing plant. And there are other costs to process the pelts, to remove the fat, to preserve the hides, and whatever else is done to them. There is machinery to be bought and maintained for such a purpose, the salaries of the workers must be paid, the plant itself, which has likely been purchased, and there are insurance costs, and lawyers, and accountants, and all sorts of expenses in the seal pelt business. Not to forget the insurance outputs. And, what happens if the pelts are not sold right away? They must be stored."

"Yes, in warehouses," I say.

"But there are also transporting inputs. Someone must transport the pelts from the docks to the plants and once the pelts have been uhm . . . what do they call it?"

"Finished," I say. "I believe that is the term they use."

"Yes, finished. Once the pelts are finished, they would either be transported to the warehouses for storage or to the docks for further travel to the fur merchants, who will then sell to buyers within the fashion industry. There are also inputs for fuel, driver salaries, and truck maintenance and repair costs that must also be subtracted. All these inputs, and likely more, must be subtracted from the final outputs that each of these sectors claim."

"But they're not?"

"No. And that's not even all the outputs we were able to find. Look here, the government offered the sealers a meat subsidy to insure they brought back . . . what was it?" His index finger roams the page. "Here we go. We were told 6.5 million pounds of meat were processed."

"I read about that! The sealers were paid so much a pound to collect the meat. A transport company had to transport it to a processor to process it, and then what? Were there any markets for it?"

"It's not a very edible meat, is it? I can't say I've tried it."

"No, neither have I."

"So, we have to ask ourselves: 'What happened to the meat?'"

"I imagine they would have had to dump it," I say.

"The cost of dumping it would have been huge."

"I suppose some of it could have been used for animal feed," I say.

"I can't tell you what percentage they dumped," the professor says, "but the point is that because there is no document revealing anything to do with the dumping, we can suspect that whatever the cost has not been subtracted from the industry's output."

I rub my forehead. "And this must happen every year in some way, shape, or form. I mean the specifics might change, perhaps there are no meat subsidies, but there would be inputs that the public might never know about and they likely wouldn't be subtracted."

"And we haven't even gotten to the penises. There are inputs there as well as outputs. Oh, and look, it appears that the outputs from the transportation industry have been counted twice."

"Yikes."

"Yes, yikes," says the professor. "And now you see how we arrived at the figure of C$2.91 million. That is the best we could come up with for Newfoundland."

"So the value of the commercial seal hunt of 1996 is not nine million dollars as the government would have led Canadians to believe, but only C2.91 million!"

"And the benefit to all of Canada was zero," the professor says with finality, handing me back my copy of his report.

I slap my thighs and stand, shaking my head. I feel as though all the work I did on the purchase slips is as useless as the carcass of a dead seal pup thrown overboard. I throw up my hands. "The purchase slips are pointless. I was on a wild goose chase." I reach for the handle of my tote. "Thanks for your help, Professor Southey. I'm sorry to have wasted your time."

"Wait a minute. You wanted to prove the value of the commercial seal hunt wasn't what the government claimed, right?"

"Right."

"Then I don't see why you're so glum. The purchase slips were a dead end, but didn't you find out what you came for?"

"I suppose."

"What can you tell me about the outputs of the 2006 and 2007 seal hunts?" he asks.

"Nothing. We didn't even get into them."

"Think!" he says. "What did you learn?"

"Well, I guess, what I learned is that every seal hunt has outputs and inputs."

"Yes." Professor Southey urges. "And?"

"And more than likely the inputs aren't ever subtracted from the final output of the industry in any given year."

Professor Southey nods, then stands and walks me to the door.

After I descend to the bottom of the stairs, I turn around. "Thank you, Professor Southey."

"You're welcome," he says, smiling.

* * *

In October 2010, the federal government of Canada develops a website for the purpose of warning financial institutions and law enforcement agencies that out-of-country terrorist organizations are laundering money through domestic terrorist groups like animal and environmental organizations. It's nonsense. What the government hopes to do is conflate animal and environmental protection groups with extremist groups like Al-Qaeda in the hope of decreasing public support for them and in doing so decreasing their effectiveness. Such an effort was also undertaken in the US between 2005 and 2005. While the most affected organizations would be those with head offices outside of Canada, such as in the United States or the UK, and those which operated branch offices in Toronto and other Canadian cities (as did HSUS and IFAW), the ramifications of such conflation would be felt among all animal and environmental protection organizations. The public would cease to trust us.

"If animal protection groups are conflated with terrorist organizations like Al-Qaeda and Hezbollah," one of the AAC board members says, "donors will be afraid to support our campaigns."

"Let's see what happens," Liz says. "If the government takes this any further, we'll go to court."

I am no stranger to the government's tactic, I remind my AAC colleagues. "It's exactly the tactic CSIS used when the two agents interrogated me last year. 'Do you know of anyone who might make a bomb or use a bomb— maybe not you, but anyone in your group?' That's what they asked me. They believed that I might be a terrorist or that I might know terrorists."

"It's nothing new. About ten years ago, CSIS started looking into the Animal Liberation Front," says Liz. "There had been some break-ins at mink farms. Minks were released. The fur industry pressured the government to crack down. It became ridiculously hard to do anything meaningful without being suspected of being a terrorist."

As I listen, I begin to wonder if CSIS has a file on me.

50

WHO WOULD YOU SAVE?

AN UNSEASONABLY WARM October breeze wrestles my hair, whipping it in all directions, as I sit in the passenger seat beside Catarina, who is driving us in her 1969 lemon-yellow Camaro convertible to a funky country café for a coffee and a chat. Cat has put the top down and Diana Ross & the Supremes are harmonizing on the radio. Neither of us can remember all the words, but we sing along, partly in tune, making up our own words as we go along, our bodies swaying and grooving to the music.

Catarina's silver rings tap out the tune against the steering wheel. When the song ends, she turns off the radio. I ask her about her grandchildren, and she asks me about Karma, Murray, and the seals.

"Have you told Ben about Murray?" she says.

I turn to her and shake my head. "I'm trying to find the right time."

"You must tell him if you and Murray are getting serious."

I stare down at my fingers and smile.

"It's getting serious, isn't it?"

"I don't want to hurt Ben."

Cat puts her hand on mine. "I'm happy for you. You deserve to be happy."

I grasp her hand and hold it.

"So, how about Murray? Does he like Karma? Or more importantly, I think," she says, smiling, "does Karma like him?"

"Karma likes him a lot better than he likes me. I don't give him dog treats every time I see him."

"I have a question for you," Cat says.

I turn toward her. "What? You're not going to ask me something more intimate, are you? Like what undergarments he likes me to wear in bed?"

"No, nothing like that."

"Then what?"

"How does he feel about the way you feel about animals?"

"What do you mean?"

"The way you love them more than people."

"I don't love animals more than people. I love them as much as I love people."

"No you don't. Be honest."

"I am being honest."

"Okay, then. If Karma and I were both trapped in a burning building, who would you save?"

I turn to look at her, my mouth open. "You're kidding."

She turns to me. "I'm not kidding. I want to hear what you have to say."

"I don't think that question is even worthy of a reply."

Cat inclines her head toward me, waiting for an answer.

"Ugh! I mean, you're not the first person to ever ask that question," I say, leaning back against the old headset. "My colleagues have been asked similar things. Humans just can't accept that someone can love an animal more than a human."

"See, you just said *more*."

"*More* than the average person. I don't love the average person."

"You're not going to answer me, are you?"

I turn to watch the rusty maple leaves waving their huge-veined hands in the breeze.

"Would you save me?" Cat asks again. "Would you? I would save you!"

I turn back to her. "Can't I save you both?"

"But who would you save if you could only save one of us?"

"Can anyone really know what they'd do in a fire before it happens? There's so much to factor in. Where are you both? How bad is the fire? Can I crawl through the rubble to reach you? Am I wearing a smoke mask? It would all make a difference."

"The details don't matter," Cat says. She pulls into the parking lot of the Flying Monkey Bike Repair Shop and Coffee Bar and turns off the ignition.

"You don't want to say it, do you—what you'd really do? Animals *are* more important to you than people."

"You know humans *are* animals, don't you? I don't know why people keep thinking that we're not," I say, exiting the car.

"You can't give me an answer, can you?"

We begin to walk across the gravel lot to the door of the coffee bar. Inside, I pause in thought, then turn to her. "What I *can* say to you is this: I love you. And I will always try to save you. But will I ever ask you to choose between me and your daughter if we were both in a burning building? No. I'll never ask you to do that."

51

NINE MILLION AND COUNTING

FISHERIES MINISTER GAIL Shea has announced a quota of 400,000 harp seal pups for the 2011 commercial hunt. It is the greatest TAC on record. Shea justifies it by claiming nine million harp seals are preying in the waters off the Northwest Atlantic consuming every fish in their sight. If hundreds of thousands of seals aren't killed every year, there will be no fish left in the ocean, she says. Despite the high TAC, fewer than fifty boats participate in the year's commercial seal hunt, and a mere 38,000 seal pups are killed, with a landing value of C$750,000. If the harp seal population is overabundant, why didn't the fishermen kill more?

Since I began working on the seal hunt, and decades before it, millions of harp seals have been slaughtered, though the DFO likes to call the slaughter *harvesting*. Most of the victims have been babies or young pups—not cobs of corn—who will never have the chance to reach sexual maturity or produce offspring. With so much killing, how could the harp seal population grow out of control? After all, mother seals only give birth to one pup a year.

I decide to meet a harp seal population specialist at the Red Brick Café downtown. The road there climbs a hill of Victorian homes and hundred-year-old maple trees, and elbows its way through town. I plop down at an outdoor table and wait. Minutes later, the specialist appears. I dive straight in. "How can there possibly be nine million harp seals when sealers have killed nearly three million in just over seven years?"

The specialist smiles. "Obviously, harp seals are copulating with added vigour." He empties his pipe into his palm and extracts a bag of fresh tobacco, pulling out bits of what's inside to stuff into his pipe. A nose-dazzling fruitiness wafts from the bag. I want to stick my nose inside, but I pull myself together.

"With a *total allowable catch* of 400,000, you'd think anyone who owned a fishing boat would be out clubbing seals, wouldn't you? But fishermen in 2011 had the smallest landing of seal pups since 1993, when they only landed 27,000."

The specialist sucks the stem of his pipe and puffs out, "Ah, yes."

"What evidence do they have that the population is increasing?"

"At this point, I'm not sure the government's data show the population *is* increasing, let alone increasing uncontrollably. Regardless, the TAC's increases, in my opinion, are for political rather than factual reasons. Raising the TAC alone won't have any impact on the population's trajectory. Nowadays, the TAC is often not reached, as you know."

"It hasn't been reached in the last four years," I say. "So how do they come up with the number nine million?" I know from working on the purchase slips that the DFO isn't all that good with numbers, but nine million! That large a number shoots credibility all to shit.

"That's the nine-million-dollar question, isn't it?" the specialist says.

"Is it just some number the minister pulls out of her hat?"

"A long time ago, my organization asked the DFO for its population model. We wanted to see how the department achieved its population figures."

"It would be interesting to see."

"Yes, it would have been, had they sent it."

I blow air through my lips. "But they didn't? Come on!"

"The DFO promised to send it, but never did."

"How long ago was that?"

The specialist rubs his thumb and forefinger over the hang of his beard. "Maybe fifteen years ago. We hired a population ecologist from the University of Guelph to reconstruct the DFO's model based on the formula the DFO published in its pup production report that year. No matter how he plugged in the numbers, he couldn't replicate the findings."

"So, the DFO's sound science isn't so sound."

"The DFO has never been able to accurately measure the harp seal population."

"But still, they keep pretending to."

"There's a study by a team at the University of Bristol in the UK on the DFO's seal management precautionary approach.[1] They found that the DFO's precautionary approach isn't so precautionary after all."

"What do you mean?"

"The Bristol team found that the DFO didn't count the deaths of harp seals from natural causes, such as illness or starvation or climate change. All they did was count the seals the fishermen landed during the hunt. They also didn't count the seals who were struck and lost or drowned in fishing nets during the other fisheries."

"I'm not sure I follow."

"Without knowing the mortality rate each year, the DFO can't know how many seals they can kill without crashing the population, which is why they crashed the population in the 1970s."

"That's crazy."

"Even the fisheries department's own scientists suggest the numbers of struck and lost seals could be double what the DFO officially claims."

"Wow. Basically, the DFO doesn't know how many seals are killed each year, either by natural causes or unnatural ones, like struck and lost."

"Reproduction rates have been declining ever since the 1970s, and there's also been a decline in the size of the pups." The specialist puffs on his pipe. "You're right," he says. "There should be fewer seals, not more."

"So, instead of nine million, there might only be five million or one million? How can anyone really know?"

"What it comes down to in the end," the specialist adds, "is that Canada's commercial seal hunt is not about science, or economics, or facts. It's a conflict over differing attitudes and values about animals, and differing views about right and wrong."

"Like people thinking *not* smashing in the head of a two-week-old seal pup is wrong. It makes you wonder how anyone could think like that."

The specialist puffs. The coffees we bought earlier remain untouched.

I lean back in my chair and cross my arms over my chest. "No wonder it's so hard to end the seal hunt with so few people really understanding seal science, and the ones who do aren't even employed in the Canadian government."

* * *

If Canada won't give its people a precautionary approach to save the harp seals, other countries will. In December, Russia, Belarus, and Kazakhstan inform the WTO they will no longer import or export seal products. The decision is another gut punch to Canada's seal trade as Russia has been seal fur's biggest fan. I don't think Canadians really understand how much of an animal lover Vladimir Putin really is.

52

MYSTERY IN THE SENATE CHAMBER

THREE YEARS AFTER his first attempt, Senator Mac Harb introduces a new bill in 2012 to amend the Fisheries Act to prohibit commercial sealing. Bill S-210 is read on May 2. It receives support for a second reading.

Conservative fisheries minister Keith Ashfield (2011–13) ties himself into a knot when he learns of Harb's treachery, but he also blames other political parties and animal rights groups for pulling the knot together: "We will not abandon this [sealing] industry at the behest of opposition parties or irresponsible and out-of-touch animal rights activists. We will continue to put the livelihood of hardworking Canadian families first."

What Ashfield fails to mention is that Newfoundland is neck-deep in an economic boom—so much so that province imports workers from the Philippines to do all the jobs Newfoundlers refuse to do.

Harb's bill gets its second reading. I pull out the Hansard transcript detailing it. *Hansard* is the chichi name for a parliamentary transcript, though a casual reading of it is like watching a documentary on how to eat raisins. If one reads slowly and savours every word, however, one can taste the drama, spectacle, and Machiavellian motives of the Senate's debaters. I like to think of Hansard transcripts on the seal hunt as Nancy Drew mysteries with better character development and dialogue. My coffee-stained BOYCOTT CANADIAN SEAFOOD T-shirt and plaid pajama bottoms are perfect for reading this genre.

Harb's opening remarks begin: "I have a taste for debating politically controversial issues [. . .] [like] banning commercial seal hunting. Not one single soul in this whole chamber has the courage, the backbone, or the ability to stand up and allow the debate."

It's exactly what Shakespeare would have written had he been alive today. I read some more, not surprised when the senators strongly object to Harb's characterization of them as cowardly. Yet it also seems that Harb has shamed them into allowing him to debate his bill. Up he gets, taking command of the Senate floor.

"International bans and seafood and tourism boycotts are hurting the C$1 billion East Coast fisheries," he begins.

Wait! What did I just read? I read it again and power-punch the air. Harb's mention of the seafood boycott is the Holy Grail of compliments. I hurry into the kitchen for a paper towel to wipe a tear of gratitude from my eye. When I return, I notice Harb is now widening his lens to show how commercial sealing is hurting all Canadians, not just East Coast fishermen.

"[It costs] the Canadian economy millions in lost revenue every year—all this at a time when we are struggling [. . .] [with] a serious global economic crisis," he says. (Of course, he means the bubble-bursting 2008 global recession.) "Let me remind you that in 2008, total trade between Canada and the United States exceeded C$650 million. Nearly two-thirds of Canada's seafood is shipped to the U.S., producing C$2.5 billion for the Canadian economy."

I stop reading the debate for a moment to contemplate what C$2.5 billion—or even a portion of it—could do for Newfoundland and the Magdalen Islands. More than the seal hunt no doubt, which was a little over C$8 million in 2007. The seal hunt has never and will never end poverty in rural fishing communities. The only thing it does is keep supportive MPs in office.

I return my focus to Senator Harb. There are no market for sealskins, he notes, and the pelts are piling up in warehouses: 50,000 in

Newfoundland, 140,000 in Greenland, he tells the Senate. Nor are they being sold at the major auctions in Copenhagen and Ontario.

"Already close to 630 million people and their governments from around the world are calling for the end of the commercial seal hunt in Canada. Canada's trading partners are letting us know that they are fed up with the commercial seal hunt." He further states that about 59 million people from the Netherlands, Germany, France, and the United Kingdom say they "will avoid buying Canadian products specifically because of the hunt."

In my mind, I can just see a group of Parisians sitting at a table Ernest Hemingway once frequented, smoking, moving their hands wildly, talking about great literature and the arts, and drinking Merlot. Then the conversation moves to their August holiday.

"*Où allez-vous en vacances?*" I hear one of them asking. (Where are you going on vacation?)

"*Canada!*" says one.

"*Non! Pas de Canada!*" another says. (No. Not Canada!)

"*Pourquoi pas?*" (Why not?)

"*Merde. Si vous allez au Canada, vous marcherez sur le dos de bébés phoques morts!*" (Shit! If you go to Canada you'll be walking on the backs of dead baby seals.)

I pull my ear away from Paris and return it to the Hansard manuscript. Reading it is almost like listening in.

"I disagree with my colleague [Senator Harb]," says one senator.

"I do not agree with a thing Senator Harb said," says another. "I, too, will be taking a position against him."

And the others? There is no need for them to speak. All link their philosophical arms around each other, like in a daisy chain, leaving Senator Harb the odd man out.

With that, I flip the Hansard transcript closed and sulk myself into a depressed nap, with a pillow over my head.

53

My One Precious Life

HOW DO I tell Ben about Murray without hurting him? I ask the Dop one summer day in 2012, as a breeze filters through my open office window. On a day like this, I shouldn't have a care in the world. But to be honest, I've never had a day when I didn't have a care. I'm just that type of person. But I'm grateful for the Dop. She seems to have all the answers.

You have one precious life, she tells me.

So?

So, how long will you walk on your knees? Will you take yourself through a bed of nails? Will you lie down on a riverbank and allow stones to be dropped on your chest?

Wow, I didn't know the Dop wrote poetry. She's good. Maybe I should write this all down.

Can you repeat what you just said, only slowly?

Love the one you love.

No, that's not it. Start from the beginning.

Sigh. She's gone again. However, the scent of summer sifting through my office window makes all things feel possible. *Forget poetry,* I say to myself. My life will be the poem. And I will love whom I love.

* * *

Ben is dressed in his neon fish sweatshirt and sweatpants, not in his usual hospital gown. He's lying on top of his bed, not underneath the covers.

His hair looks newly washed, glossy, and his eyes fluoresce with happiness to see me. It's too much. My heart drops like rain on a weeping day, and I want to turn and run. Just blurt it out. That's all I have to do. *Just blurt it out*, I tell myself.

I take a step forward. "Ben, I have something I need . . ."

"I'm so glad you're here. I have something to tell you!"

"Okay," I say, chewing on my bottom lip.

Ben inclines his head to the visitor's chair.

I sit and fold my hands in a prayerful position. *Breathe*, I urge myself.

"I don't want to hurt you," Ben says.

My eyes flash as wide as they'll get. "What?"

"I don't want to hurt you."

What does he mean by "I don't want to hurt you"? I'm the one who's supposed to say that. I bite on the puncture my teeth have made on my bottom lip. "Okay."

"It wouldn't be fair to you if I didn't tell you my truth."

I can feel a cocktail of worry being shaken and stirred in my belly.

"You're not going to tell me you're ready to die, are you?"

"No. It's nothing like that. Just the opposite."

"Phew!"

"I need to be free from our marriage. I need to be free to feel the kind of love you can't give me."

My eyebrows rise involuntarily. I cough. The word *what?* follows.

"I just can't go on like this. You'll always be my family. I'll always love you. But I have a hole in my heart that you can't fill." He's saying the words I couldn't think of saying, and he's saying them better. "You're the love of my life. But I'm lonely. You can't live here and I can't live at home. And to be honest, our marriage never was. . . . We're so different."

There's a sudden lump in my throat. I notice Ben has closed his eyes, just as I do when I'm trying to access a thought and the words to express it. When he opens them again, he says, "There's this woman who's started visiting me."

"What woman?" I ask.

"She's a nurse. She comes to the meditation group I've started."

I didn't even know he had started a meditation group. "Isn't there a 'no fraternizing' rule?"

"Her name is Nadia."

"Nadia? You mean *the* Nadia? The one who goes to sweat lodges and believes in spirit guides?"

"We're just friends. It probably won't go anywhere."

"You're in a chronic care hospital! Where can it go?"

"Just because I'm here doesn't mean I can't find love."

"I didn't mean that. I mean. . . ."

"I didn't plan on this happening. I don't want to hurt you."

"You're not hurting me," I say, feeling hurt.

"I just want to be happy."

"I want you to be happy, too." I feel like I've just taken a warm bath, maybe in a rainforest.

When he finishes telling me about Nadia, I tell him about Murray.

54

A Practical Guide to Debating the Seal Hunt

You can debate abortion, gun legislation, and the legalization of marijuana, but you can't debate the seal hunt.—**Liz White**, Animal Alliance of Canada

"TIME TO FACE the fact: the Newfoundland seal hunt is doomed," says Ryan Cleary.

Who the fuck is Ryan Cleary? I ask myself. A brief Google search fills me in. He's the newly elected Newfoundland MP for St. John's South and Mount Pearl, just one of the 338 MPs who sit in the House of Commons. I find it impossible to keep track of them all, which is why he's initially flown under my radar. *Ugh!* As I look further, I see he's a former Newfoundland journalist and president of the Federation of Independent Seafood Harvesters. Now I have another seal hunt–spouting politician to keep an eye on.

I become more and more interested as I read the headline of the article, "Time to Consider Ending Seal Hunt, MP Cleary Says," posted by CBC News on January 24, 2012.[1] Is he being incredibly brave or incredibly daft? My first thought is that he's daft, or let's say ill-informed. To tell the CBC, a Crown corporation, that the seal hunt is doomed and that no one wants seal products anymore, or to point out that "[part] of our history is also whaling [. . .] and the day came when the whaling industry stopped. Now, is that day coming with the seal hunt?" is political suicide. He might as well dive headfirst off Flatrock's cliff into the rock below. Has he not been following the news? Does he not know of the firestorm of vitriol that Senator Harb has faced from his own party as well as the opposition?

As I stare into the photograph of Cleary in the CBC News article, I see he has the kind of jockish features that must have made him popular with the College of the North Atlantic set. His shirt is open at the collar and tucked into dark pants. He wears a brown wool sports jacket, not the usual navy suit favoured by most Canadian politicians. He exudes a casual confidence, though perhaps not so much in his message, since he acknowledges he may be shot for his comments (not literally—we aren't the United States after all—but figuratively, politically). His confidence is in himself, which makes me think he's brave but naïve, and probably ignorant of just how bad it can get when one intentionally provokes a public conversation that shivs the seal hunt.

A few days later, the Liberals request that the NDP leadership come forward and state for the record their position on the seal hunt. Cleary steps up to the plate. He tells CBC News that he and the federal NDP still officially support the seal hunt. (Forget what he said earlier.)

Just to be clear, the Conservative Party wants Newfoundland, Québec, and Atlantic Canada to know that it supports the seal hunt unequivocally. Conservative federal Fisheries and Oceans Minister Gail Shea announces that sealers can take up to 400,000 harp seals during the 2012 seal hunt. She justifies her announcement because, she says, seven million harp seals are ripping the livelihoods out of the stomachs of fishing families. Interestingly, I note that Shea has recalibrated her estimate of how many harp seals there now are, down two million from the previous year's nine million estimate. What happened to the missing two million harp seals? Did they die by lightning? Did they transmute into starfish? Did they turn themselves in to the authorities and are they now rotting in a Newfoundland jail? Or maybe, just maybe, they never existed at all. Harp seal population science has never been a forte of the DFO.

By the end of the 2012 seal hunt, the portrait is clear. Despite the enormous TAC, only 680 fishermen participated in the hunt, and they were able to land only 69,175 harp seals.[2] A far cry from previous years. Activists aren't the only ones claiming the seal hunt's value is negligible. Now, thousands of licensed sealers are, too, simply by refusing to go out on the ice, despite the high sealing quota. Both activists and sealers know that Shea has set an impossible-to-reach quota—not to benefit sealers, who were finding fewer and fewer seals each year, but to benefit the pugilistic desires of a foiled fisheries minister to say "fuck you" to the EU, whose members banned her seal trade.

* * *

Before the seal hunt, in early March, Karma decides to go cod-fishing, not by way of a round-trip airline ticket to Newfoundland but by coming along with me to visit Ben at St. Mark's. His fishing escapade begins the moment we enter the lobby of St. Mark's. Jerking his leash from my hand, Karma accelerates zero-to-sixty through the lobby, weaving in between the wheelchairs of patients and the groups of visiting family members. He turns a sharp right, then sharp left, his nose on high alert, only slowing to a trot when he sees the cafeteria. Once there, he knows he must work quickly. He steps into the open space and begins sniffing around the tables and chairs, gobbling every crumb he sees on the floor. I'm just seven lengths behind him but already out of breath. I sputter down the corridor, my sneakers splatting on the linoleum, and propel myself into the cafeteria, where I skid to a stop, just barely missing a pushed-out chair.

"Karma! Karma! Get over here right now."

Oblivious, Karma sniffs and trots around the circular cafeteria, his nose vigilant lest he overlook a tasty morsel. Just a table behind him, I stretch out my arms, ready to grab his collar. But before I can reach him, he jumps up onto his hind legs and noses a plastic dinner plate to the floor. With nanosecond efficiency, he hoovers up the remaining cod fillet and is starting on the wax beans and mashed potatoes when I grab him.

"Sorry," I say to the cafeteria manager, a diminutive Portuguese woman with black hair and poison darts for eyes. Her arms are so firmly folded across her chest that they're probably stuck there permanently. She doesn't say a word, just stares, and I fear she may be calculating how to capitalize on Karma's tomfoolery to argue why dogs need to be banned from visiting St. Mark's, something the administration has already been looking into.

"Bad boy. Bad, bad boy! You should be ashamed of yourself," I tell Karma loud enough for the woman to hear. I make a big show of pulling him out of the cafeteria and down the corridor, scolding him all the way to Ben's room. That's when a thought suddenly occurs to me, as Karma and I step out of the way of a meal wagon. A nurse's aide moves from room to room, collecting trays of half-eaten cod from the bed tables of bedridden patients. I fathom that all the leftover cod that will soon find its way into the hospital garbage. Is this what the seal hunt is for? I mentally fume. So fishermen can sell cod fillets to nursing homes that feed them to patients who leave them half-eaten on their plastic plates? Fucking codswallop!

* * *

In late April 2012, I learn that Senator Harb will be debating in the Senate his new bill, Bill S-210, to amend the Fisheries Act to legislate the end of the commercial seal hunt.[3] Liz and Stephen have asked me to write a book on leading the Canadian Seafood Boycott, AAC's campaign to end the seal hunt. As part of my research, I convince Liz to send me to Ottawa to interview Harb.

As I sit on the plane, it hits me that the revolution I hoped for at the beginning of the Canadian Seafood Boycott is about to take place. I hum the Beatles' "Revolution" until I fear my row-28 seatmate might call a flight attendant. But all's good. Senator Harb has found a seconder for his reconstituted bill, which gives him a legal right to debate the seal hunt.

The viewers' gallery is high above the Senate chamber. Leaning over the edge of the balcony and looking down, I see a cornucopia of Canadian artifacts and images, almost too many to take in. A marble bust of Queen Victoria sits stonily above the Senate throne, while elaborate carvings and oil paintings depict Canada's early history and massive bronze chandeliers illuminate the vaulted ceiling, ensuring that Queen Vic is kept in the manner of chandelier finery she was no doubt accustomed to. I, who have not had the burden of such luxury, feel awed by the hallowedness. I want to fall to my knees and say a prayer to the animal protection gods and maybe to Victoria herself, though I don't know her position on sealing. But one can't fall to one's knees in the viewers' gallery of the Senate chamber while representing AAC.

Several colleagues from IFAW and HSUS trickle in and sit behind me. We chat until the door to the chamber opens and a train of dark-suited, white-shirted senators walks in. My eyes search for Senator Harb—I know his face from his seal hunt–witnessing photograph, taken just after the defeat of his first anti-sealing bill, Bill S-229. From high up in the viewers' gallery, however, all the senators look like penguins toddling to their seats. After the last senators straggle in, the Speaker calls the Senate to order. Several minutes of boring Senate business ensue. I'm just finishing my extended yawn when Senator Harb is called to rise and introduce his renamed bill: Bill S-210. Oddly, it is exactly three years to the day since he introduced the former bill.

I notice things I couldn't from the seal hunt–witnessing photograph I've seen of him. He is tall and slender and he carries himself with a sophisticated grace as he steps up to the podium on the floor below. I can see him clearly from where I sit and there's a heightened sensitivity in his eyes, perhaps to life's cruelties. It is as if he is in the room, but somehow above it. When he speaks, I lean over the railing so I don't miss a word:

> These are desperate times for sealers. They need actual and tangible government assistance and not the lip service they have been getting thus far. A sealer's licence buyout is the most effective and fair way to provide that tangible help to these hardworking Canadians and their communities. Science shows seals are not to blame for the depletion of the cod or their struggle to recover. It is government inaction and misguided action that is responsible. [. . .] Out of 14,000 commercial sealing licences issued in 2011, only 225 sealers

participated. [. . .] Workers in East Coast rural communities
[. . .] do not need to be patronized with handouts and hollow
promises that [. . .] all will be fine, new markets are around
the corner, and that the EU market will reopen once the
challenge to the WTO is successful. [. . .] The government
must tell [. . .] the truth. The market is dead.

My heart swells like water in a lock, filling me with gratitude. I want
to stand up and applaud, but Senator Harb has not finished.

"Instead of working against animal welfare groups and environmental
organizations, let us join hands with them to share ideas and resources
and find answers that will help the communities in Atlantic Canada and
in Canada's North."[4]

When he is finished, I expect other senators to raise their hands in
objection to his argument. It is their time to debate and defend the seal
hunt. After all, the purpose of a second reading is to debate the bill. Thirty
seconds pass, and then a minute. It is so quiet I could drop a tissue from
the balcony and the sound would reverberate from wall to wall. Yet, the
senators are so still and hunched that they resemble the round-shouldered
mountains in a Lawren Harris painting.

It's an awe-inspiring moment in Canadian history—a second reading
and debate of a bill to end the commercial seal hunt. Perchance the
senators have been equally awed and stymied for a response. After what
seems like hours of interminable silence, the Speaker calls for a vote.

"That's that," a colleague says behind me as we exit the gallery.

"So much for the Senate being the seat of sober thought," another says.

I feel sick to my stomach and ashamed at what I've just witnessed. Not
a single senator supported Harb's bill. I climb slump-shouldered down the
steps of Parliament. The air feels cadaverous; the earth has shriveled. I'm
glad it's raining. The drops hide the upsurge of emotion trickling down
my face.

At Tims, I choose a seat next to a window and drink two cups of black
coffee. I distractedly roll up the rim of my cup, hoping I will at least win
a car or a TV or any prize. But it's not Roll up the Rim to Win time. I've

missed it by two months, and my coffee rim holds nothing to roll away the loss I feel. I finish my coffee, then hurry to Senator Harb's office for my prearranged interview.

Senator Harb receives me in a room filled with law books. A plush couch and a high-backed Queen Elizabeth chair create a small island of wood and upholstery. On the wall are photographs of sailboats on Lake Ontario. He beckons me to sit across from him, at the far end of the room, and waits until he is sure I am comfortable. He then lowers himself into an expensive brown leather armchair and pushes his spectacles high up on his nose.

"I saw you this morning presenting your bill. I thought you did a wonderful job," I say. "Supporting the bill should have been a no-brainer, if they really cared about east coast fishermen." My sentences run together as I rush to assure him that I am on his side.

"Thank you," he says. He rests his elbow on top of his raised knee and steeples his hands. "The role of a democratic government is to be responsive to its citizens. But this government is neither responsive nor responsible, not when it comes to sealing."

"It is not easy being a lone voice in the wilderness," I say.

His eyes are kind but sad. "Thankfully, I'm not a lone voice. I know of senators who have received thousands of emails and letters and calls, asking them to help end the seal hunt. I've received more than 90,000 emails and I've filled wheelbarrows with signed petitions, and I've wheeled them right to the doors of Parliament." (I remember seeing a photograph of him doing just that.) "They've come from every single province," he says.

"Even Newfoundland?"

"Yes. Many from Newfoundland."

"Wow!" It takes me a second to recover from my surprise, and then another question leaps out of my mouth. "How do you explain what just happened in the Senate? Not a single senator raised their hand in support of your bill."

He shrugs his right shoulder. "My colleagues did what was politically expedient. For me, the Senate has been a disillusioning place. I came to the Senate with great hopes that I could promote ideas I believe in, express my views openly, and discuss them with my colleagues without reprisal. It has been the greatest disappointment of my career—in a place that is supposed to allow free thoughts and ideas and speech—to be shut down, to have my bill not debated. This has never happened in Canadian history." He pauses for a moment and stares at the knuckles of his hands folded in his lap. "When you shut down the ability of a senator to express views that are fundamental to him, then you are not living in a democracy. You are living in a friendly dictatorship."

"What happens next?"

He doesn't answer right away. His eyes stare at the wall behind my head, but it's as if he isn't seeing the wall at all. Instead, it seems that he is staring at the thoughts flowing through his mind. After a moment, he pulls his eyes away from whatever has given him a moment of respite. "The seals are going to survive because the people are supporting them. Animal protection organizations without exception, volunteers, and communities around the world are supporting them. It is only a matter of time. The seals will win. The people will win. We will win."

Before I leave, I share a quote so often used as a rallying cry by my activist colleagues: "First they ignore you, then they ridicule you, then they fight you, and then you win." He seems comforted by it and smiles, but his eyes have deep circles around them, as if he hadn't slept, as if he could see a future ahead of him that I cannot.

* * *

In the spring, one of the last seal-processing companies, NuTan Furs, shuts down. The remaining processing plant, Carino, is only squeaking by on three legs and can't afford to buy this year's pelts. The government gives it a C\$3.6 million loan to buy the pelts without any caveats that it must process them. With so many stockpiled pelts and no markets, Carino's purchase of the pelts is merely optics. How will it repay the loan if it has no customers to buy its sealskins?

Six months later, in my red swivel chair in my office, opening emails sitting in my inbox, and clicking on links to articles colleagues have sent to me, I read a CBC News article. An ice floe of chill runs down my spine. The Royal Canadian Mounted Police has charged Senator Harb with fraud and public breach of trust over questionable housing expense claims. As if I were an out-of-control elevator, my chest descends to the floor of my stomach. While I'm trying to catch my breath, Senator Harb resigns.

55

MICE RUNNING THROUGH THE CUPBOARDS

"Nancy now brought out the notebook, opened it to read the important page, and handed it to the men to read. When they finished, Mr. Jensen said, 'What a mystery!'"—**Carolyn Keene**, *The Secret of the Old Clock*

IT'S FEBRUARY 2013, and fifty seal pups have washed up dead on the frigid shore of Eastern Prince Edward Island. By the time I learn of the tragedy, veterinarians have autopsied ten of the seals and found their skulls were bludgeoned. Their last minutes were spent in agony as their bodies froze on the beach, one of the veterinarians says.[1]

I'm sitting on the sofa, my legs curled under me, my teeth gritted so tightly that I can almost hear the orthodontist's bill printing out. The killers are all boys: the youngest fourteen, the oldest eighteen. One of them, trying to justify his actions, says, "I've always thought of seals as mice running through the cupboards. . . ."

Later, when the sheriff speaks to reporters, he describes the three boys as "respectful young men" and gives them a two-year probation.

* * *

Fisheries and Oceans Minister Shea sets the TAC in 2013 at 400,000, with sealers only able to slaughter 90,318.

In September, Canada's Freedom of Information commissioner accuses federal officials of "dubious new tactics to thwart the freedom-of-information law" and gives the DFO a "D" in transparency.

On November 25, 2013, the Canadian government announces it is appealing the WTO ruling to uphold the European ban on seal products. My gut feeling says our government will lose.

I finish my report, writing a final sentence:

> Based on the systematic analysis of four thousand purchase slips from the years 2006 and 2007, and also based on the lack of data to identify the process and methods used to calculate the announced values, I am obligated to conclude that there is no legitimate, verifiable, evidence-based method that the DFO uses to determine the value of the seal hunt. The purchase slips are useless, in this regard.
>
> Keeping track of the fiscal benefits of an economically vital enterprise, as the DFO claims the seal hunt is, should be a priority. Poor data collection, improperly trained staff, and a lack of willingness to provide transparent economic data are evident and impede the validation of the economic importance of sealing. Such findings lead the author to surmise that either the DFO does not have the competency to extract the data or it does not have the motivation to do so. Given the many millions of dollars in subsidies propping up the seal hunt, which have been provided by diverse federal and provincial agencies, the author wonders if the betterment of poor rural fishermen is not the reason the government supports sealing. Could it be, the author wonders, that sealing props up politicians hoping for election in politically valuable areas, such as Newfoundland and Québec? The commercial seal hunt in Canada must end, not only because it is inhumane, but because it is a huge drain on the taxpayers of our country.

56

THE YEARS SHALL RUN LIKE RABBITS

"NOW WHAT WILL you do?" Murray asks at our favourite Indian restaurant, a glass of Pinot Noir in his hand.

The same question has been chewing at me. The report of my findings is sitting on my red swivel chair. I am so certain the government won't read it and the media won't report it that I hardly want to waste the postage to mail it. All the work—on the report, on the boycott, on becoming a fine seal-hunt detective—seems for naught.

"I don't know. The one thing I do know is I love you."

Murray is about to take my hand when my cellphone buzzes. It's Nadia at St. Mark's. The restaurant is noisy, so I press a finger against my left ear to block out the sound.

"Could you say that again? I'm having trouble hearing. . . . Oh my God. When? How is he?" I hang up the phone, stunned.

Murray leans in and takes both of my hands in his. "Whatever it is, I'm here for you."

"Ben has been transferred to Guelph General by ambulance."

Murray stands up and takes his wallet out. "Stay here while I pay the bill," he says.

The first thing I see is a tube snaking up one of Ben's nostrils and down his throat.

"Are you family?" a nurse asks before we enter.

"Yes, the wife. What's going on?"

"He came in around three this morning."

A buzzer sounds down the hall. The nurse puts her hand on my shoulder. "I'll be back in a wee bit, my dear," she says, then hurries away.

I move a chair beside Ben's bed. His exhale sounds like Darth Vader's. "Ben? Can you hear me?" His eyelids flutter. His head moves infinitesimally on his pillow. I call the office to tell Liz I'm at the hospital.

Murray is standing in the doorway in his navy pea coat, hesitant to enter. I wave him in. He takes his coat off, folds it neatly behind me on the back of a visitor's chair, and reaches for my hand. Ben's doctor enters the room just as Ben is waking.

"What's wrong?" I ask her.

"Your husband is very sick."

"I can see that."

"I need to speak to him alone," she says, tilting her head toward the door, indicating we should leave. Murray steps back into the hallway.

"Why? I'm his wife. Whatever you say to him, you can say to me."

"It's okay, love," Ben says, sounding as if he were emitting a cotton ball from the back of his throat.

Everything is so fucked up. Here I am in the acute ward of Guelph General, watching my husband knocking on death's door, while my lover—my love, the man whom I want to spend the rest of my life with— is standing right outside my door, listening to my husband—the man I don't love, the man who has abused me, the man who is dying—call me "love." I leave the room, but stay right outside the door, listening. No one is going to tell me I can't listen. The doctor's voice is so low I can barely hear. But when I hear the word *DNR*, I hear it clearly. DNR. Do Not Resuscitate. I step back into the room.

"What are you talking about?" I say, defiantly folding my arms across my chest.

"Your husband has a DNR. He's in a lot of pain." She mentally calculates how to describe the pain to me. "On a continuum, it's about a seven. While you were waiting outside, I asked him what he wants us to do if it gets to a nine or a ten."

"What do you mean *do?*"

"It's okay, Karen," Ben says, trying to calm me down. "We've talked about this."

I glare at the doctor. "He's not ready to die." I turn to Murray. *"He's not ready to die!"* Then I turn to Ben. "You don't want to die, do you?" Tears burn my cheeks. When he hesitates, I implore, "It's not time."

Ben's hospital gown has inched down his arm, leaving his shoulder exposed. The doctor steps closer to Ben and puts her hand on his bare shoulder. "It's his decision to make."

I inhale deeply, but I'm ready to spew dragon's breath because anger is better than tears. Anger gets things done because anger. . . . I burst like a wall of sandbags in the wake of a hurricane. Large, rib-wracking sobs. Murray puts his arm around me.

The doctor tilts her head and raises her chin. "You don't want to upset your husband, do you? Maybe you should wait outside until you get yourself collected."

The nurse appears out of nowhere and says to Murray, "Why don't you take her to the cafeteria, the wee dear?" She sounds like a compassionate drill sergeant with a Scottish accent. To me, she says, "Get yourself a coffee or a sandwich, lovey. They have lovely fruit—a nice apple or banana."

"I don't want a fucking banana," I scream, barely able to walk, my shoulders are so bent over my feet. My chest heaves.

"Come on, sweetie, let's sit down somewhere." Murray leads me from the room and walks me down the hall to an upholstered bench by the elevators. We sit and I bury my head on his shoulder and howl. By the time I stop crying, his shirt is sopping wet. But when I look into his eyes, I realize no one has ever looked at me with so much love and concern.

* * *

Ben dies on the same day as the 2014 seal hunt begins. Murray and I had gone home to rest after leaving the hospital the night before. I had cried myself into a stupor and didn't fall asleep until three in the morning.

But just as I was nodding off to sleep, without thinking I turned off my cellphone, so the buzzes and bleeps didn't wake me. Although I expected the seal hunt to start that morning, I didn't expect Ben's death would. When I wake and realize that I had turned off the phone, I grab it from my night table, turn it on, and listen to the single new message. I throw myself out of bed, grab yesterday's clothes, feed my four-leggeds, and run Karma down the stairs to pee. I lunge into Murray's car and we whip down the road to St. Mark's.

"Ben died early this morning," Nadia says.

Ben is laid out on his white bed sheets as if he were sleeping on a pan of sea ice. His body is still warm and his cheeks rosy, as if he would soon wake. The visitor's chair has been moved out of the room, so Murray and I sit together on the heating unit. Murray holds my hand. The only photographs taped to Ben's walls now are of rabbits, his totem animal: white ones, grey ones; some of them domestic, some wild.

A group of nurses joins Nadia just outside the door. They are the ones who changed his diapers, clipped his toenails, and turned him on his side when he couldn't sleep. In the end, they are his family, not me.

"It happened so quickly. He was fine last night," Nadia says, stepping into the room, her sorrow palpable. Two orderlies wheel in a gurney and hoist Ben's body onto it. Murray holds my hand as we walk behind it, Nadia following. A funeral home hearse is parked at the curb outside the front doors, its back door open. The orderlies manoeuvre the gurney in and close the door; the sound is soft and final.

* * *

Sometimes, a seal pup who has been injured but not yet killed manages to escape into the water and hides under a sheet of ice. There, having finally eluded her attacker, she suffers until she drowns or succumbs to her wounds. Scientists have given this consequence a label: *struck and lost.* The DFO estimates there are about 26,000 struck and lost seals each year. Scientists believe the numbers are in the hundreds of thousands.

* * *

A few days later, the auditorium at St. Mark's is packed with friends I never met, along with Nadia and the nurses I know well. Ben's mother sits at the far end of the front row, her metal cane resting on her knee. Ben's older brother, who has started having muscle weakness himself, sits beside her. On the other side of the aisle are my friends, some of the dog walkers, the people from my painting studio, my book club members, and Murray. Catarina, who now has cancer, couldn't come. The chaplain speaks about Ben's life at St. Mark's: the meditation group he started, his kindness toward other patients, his neon-orange hair. John Lennon's "Imagine" plays in the background. I wait until it finishes and then step to the podium. Instead of looking at the people in front of me, I address the back of the hall, as if Ben were somewhere seated, listening, just out of sight.

"Today, I say goodbye to you, Ben. You were a fighter in the very best sense of the word. In the end, you found your purpose. You lived deeply in our world, and now you will live in another. May the rabbit always be with you, and also a little bit with us."

Murray pulls into his driveway and we both get out of the car. It has snowed and our feet make tracks; mine indent the snow around the car and stop beside his.

"What are you looking at?" I ask.

He points down the road. A rabbit is hopping in the middle of it, leaving his own snow tracks. We turn to each other.

"Do you think it's. . . ?" I ask.

"No. . . . Maybe. . . ." Murray answers.

Is Ben telling us that death is just another journey down the road and he's okay? Before I take a step further, I look back down the road. The rabbit is gone.

57

ENDINGS

"We are going to let you go," Liz says over the phone.

I fall into my red swivel chair, all ability to stand gone. "Why?"

"We need to change direction and cut expenses. We're shutting down the seal campaign."

"Not the campaign."

"There are larger organizations with more money, more resources. Let them take over."

It may be good fiscal management, but all I can hear is that Animal Alliance is being ripped from me; the seals are being ripped from me. I had expected to stick with the seals to the very end, and I've even imagined what that end would look like. I'm survival-suited up next to Paul Watson, Brian Davies, David Lavigne, Rebecca, Sheryl, Liz, and Stephen, and all the other anti-sealing activists who came before me. We stand together, all holding our unbreakable, reusable glasses. We hear the pop of the cork, and see the rise of the champagne effervescing like frothy waves rushing onto an ice pan. When all our glasses are filled, we raise them, as high as we can, as if we could touch the clouds. Paul and Brian fight over who will make the first toast, and then Stephen makes one, and Rebecca, and we laugh, and the bubbles sting our nostrils, and we are filled with love, compassion, relief, and gratitude. We stand in our tight circle in the middle of an abandoned and bloodless seal nursery, because unlike every other year back through time, the babies this year have grown and learned to swim and feed themselves, and they will moult and migrate together—thousands of them—following the lip of the ice all the way to Greenland. This is what we will be celebrating: the end of Canada's commercial seal hunt. This is what the end will look like.

When the phone call ends, I walk out of my office and into the living room. Outside the window, I can hear children playing street hockey and dogs barking. I crumble onto the sofa and hook my legs into a fetal position.

What am I going to do now? How am I going to save the seals? I wait for the Dop to come and make me feel better, or at least pull me up by the shoulder straps. But she's uncharacteristically silent.

Hello? Are you there? The bitch remains silent. Fuck her.

I lay on my right side with my left arm bent and my hand held up in front of my eyes. I stretch my fingers wide, so I can stare through them, as I would look through a magnifying lens straight into the future. But all I can see is the anti-sealing movement carrying on without me. I squeeze my fingers tight to block out the sight.

I'm sorry I haven't appreciated you, I call to the Dop. *I really need to talk with you. You have helped me so much.*

I hear a key rattling in the doorknob.

What? The Dop doesn't need a key. I lift my head to see Murray in the doorway.

"I came as quick as I could. How are you holding up?"

"My heart is broken. I think I'm going to die!"

"Come on, sit up." He pulls my left arm and coaxes me into a sitting position.

"I had one big dream. . . ." He settles on the sofa beside me and takes my hand in his. "Animals are my life."

"Animals can still be your life."

"How?"

"You'll figure it out. But not right now."

I don't know how much time has passed, but Murray and I are walking Karma behind his house, on a path full of brambles and rabbit droppings, and the sun is high overhead. I scuff along in silence while Murray and Karma, his leash still in my hand, walk a few steps ahead.

The seals gave me a purpose. They helped me sharpen my outrage and polish my courage. They directed my fury and my hope, and they made me fight and break through the surface of what I thought I could do. But what have I given them?

My chin wobbles as I think about next year, and the year after that, and the year after that, and how they will be slaughtered.

Behind me, I hear something rustling as if someone is walking through dense overgrowth. Maybe it's the Dop. I turn to look, but no one is there. But the minute I hear her voice, I know who it is.

Life is filled with cruelty and you must breathe through it, my grandmother says.

It hurts too much!

Why do you think I took up painting?

Because you didn't love Grandpa? Because he killed someone and never owned up to it? Because he made you go to a mental hospital too many times and then Daddy made you go too, until you lost faith in yourself.

No. Because painting helped me breathe. And with enough breath, I could cope.

I step along the path, my legs brushing against the prickly gooseberries and highbush cranberries with their hard orange fruits. Soon, they will ripen to a pulpy purple and the sparrows and finches and cardinals will feed on them until the trees are bare. Karma pulls at his leash and I release it. He high-steps through clumps of sweet vernal grass and runs, his mouth slightly open, a silly, beautiful grin on his face. His black nose sniffs and his head turns, looking behind him to make sure I'm there.

Murray, who is up ahead, turns and points to the path in front of me. "Watch where you're walking." I notice the small pile of dog shit in front of me. I miss it by inches.

EPILOGUE

2015

- The DFO raises the commercial sealing quota to 470,000. Activists continue to call on Ottawa to support a licence buyout of the sealing industry without success, and 35,304 harp seal pups ultimately die.
- Without further hope of selling commercial seal products into the EU, Ottawa switches gears to support Inuit seal product sales into the European market. Its C$5.7 million allocation will create a certification and tracking system to ensure indigenous seal products can be marketed in Europe.

2016

- A newly released 2009 DFO document, acquired by the HSUS, reveals the government spends about C$2.5 million annually just to monitor the seal hunt. This doesn't include all the other government subsidies. Canada's commercial seal hunt is on life support. It has been for years. The humane thing would be to pull the plug. The government won't.
- Crown prosecutors admit they don't have a strong case against retired Senator Mac Harb and withdraw all criminal charges. The Crown exonerates him.

2017

- The seal hunt opens two weeks earlier than usual, while seal pups are still nursing. A video shared on Facebook shows a baby seal being teased and kicked on the deck of a fishing boat. Three Nova Scotia men are charged for Marine Mammal Regulations violations.

- Québec Senator Céline Hervieux-Payette introduces Bill S-208, marking May 20 as annual National Seal Products Day. It passes into law.

2018

- Commercial fishermen kill 80,000 harp seal pups, though demand for seal products is at an all-time low. Nonetheless, Canada's commercial seal hunt enjoys support from all 338 parliamentarians.
- India bans seal imports, becoming the thirty-fifth country to issue bans on commercial seal products. Other countries banning these products include the twenty-eight EU countries, the United States, Switzerland, Belarus, Kazakhstan, and Mexico.

2019

- The yearly audit of Canada's fisheries shows 70 percent of Canada's fish stocks are "critically depleted" and highlights the DFO's "disappointing lack of action on the continuing crisis."
- First Nations groups, commercial and sports fishermen are petitioning the DFO to reopen British Columbia's commercial hunts of harbour seals and sea lions to increase Chinook salmon numbers. BC's marine mammal experts warn such a move could destabilize the province's balanced ecosystem.

2020

- Canada's commercial seal hunt skids to a halt, not because of anti-sealing activism or climate change, but because of COVID-19. Under the threat of the virus, few sealers sail for the harp seal nursery. Only 390 harp seals are killed, the lowest number in Canada's commercial sealing history. At last, nearly a full cohort of baby harp seals survives and follows the sea ice north to their ancestral summer feeding grounds off the coast of Greenland.

Acknowledgments

I AM PROFOUNDLY grateful to everyone who has stood up for the seals. There are two people, however, who deserve my utmost appreciation and gratitude. Barry Kent MacKay, Born Free Canadian campaigner, naturalist, author, wildlife artist, and seal campaign mentor, I am so indebted to you for your encouragement, support, and friendship. You read, and reread, and then re-reread again my early drafts, and took seriously the vision I had for the book. Sheryl Fink, director of Canadian Wildlife, IFAW, you are a repository of seal hunt knowledge and expertise. You kept me from falling through the ice many times during the writing of this book, answering questions at the spur of the moment, and staying up late so you could read another chapter. Someday when Newfoundland builds a heritage museum to celebrate the glory days of Canada's anti-sealing movement, you will be front and centre.

Without Liz White, executive director of Animal Alliance of Canada and leader of the Animal Protection Party, and Stephen Best, founder, and chief agent of the Animal Protection Party of Canada, (formerly the Animal Alliance Environment Voters Party of Canada) there would be no book. Liz, when you asked me to write about my experiences running the anti-seal hunt campaign, I didn't realize how arduous or life absorbing or life changing it would be. Thank you for putting your faith in me. Stephen, thank you for sharing with me your seal hunt campaign expertise and political savvy. Speaking to you is always like taking a master class in seal hunt activism and electoral politics.

Many people helped inform or inspire parts of this book. Zoologist, wildlife biologist, and IFAW's former science advisor, Dr. David Lavigne, without your countless research papers and expertise, my knowledge about the harp seal species would be a mere carbuncle on the hull of a DFO research vessel.

Former Senator Mac Harb (2003–2013), you are bravery personified. You spoke truth to power with grace and resilience. Thank you for reviewing my accounts of your efforts to make sure they are accurate.

Former Minister of the Environment and Climate Change Tom McMillan (1985–1988) helped me fill in the holes in my understanding of the seal hunt and sealing politics during his time in office for which I am especially grateful.

Dr. Clive Southey, professor of economics and finance at the University of Guelph, patiently helped me understand in layman's terms how the Government of Canada creates the economic value of the commercial seal hunt. Professor John Livernois, University of Guelph's former Associate Vice-President of Research and former Chair of the Department of Economics and Finance provided answers to my questions about economic projections.

Animal Alliance's Lia Laskaris deserves a get-down-on-my-knees thank you for helping me fill out the Excel Spreadsheets with the 2006 and 2007 purchase slip information. If it weren't for Lia's tireless assistance, I might still be at it.

Fia Perera, Sue Hirsch, and the late Marie Schwartz were among the most persevering and impassioned team of Canadian Seafood Boycott specialists I could have ever wished for. Amazing is the word that bests describes you all. I also wish to thank the over seven thousand chefs and seafood purchasers who supported ending Canada's commercial seal hunt by joining the Canadian Seafood Boycott campaign.

I was extraordinarily fortunate to sit with members of the Animal Alliance of Canada board, including Anne Streeter, Georges Dupras, and Sinikka Crosland, and call upon their expertise which they generously provided at a moment's notice. I'd like to thank Shelley Hawley-Yan, and

Ann and Pete Wilson. Bless you for giving new life to fifty-two needy lab dogs. A big thanks also goes to Norma Jeanne Laurette of Puppy Power who trained me to train the beagles and walker hounds. Dozens of people, including veterinarians, lab techs, and veterinary students lent their services and assistance to the rescue. Thank you.

Rebecca Aldworth, now executive director of the Humane Society International, is an intrepid, Newfoundland-born, anti-sealing activist, who gives lie to the claim that all seal hunt activists are from "away." You are an inspiring leader, role model, and mentor, and it is unnerving that you are so much younger than I am.

Toronto lawyer Murray Teitel undauntingly compiled and then wrote in the *Financial Post* about the dozens of government's subsidies trussing up a seal slaughter that could not (and cannot) stand on its own.

Special thanks to Bridget Curran, the founder of the Atlantic Canadian Anti-Sealing Coalition, who knows everything there is to know about the Nova Scotia seal hunts, and who speaks out for Canada's seals at every turn.

Dr. David Hackett Fisher, Pulitzer Prize winning author, historian, and Earl Warren Professor of History at Brandeis University, taught me the nuts and bolts of investigative research. They are the same nuts and bolts I used to investigate the DFO for this book.

Dr. Susan Forbes Martin, former professor of American studies, at Brandeis University taught me that I could create something big out of something very small or non-existent. Lesson learned.

Dr. John Sorenson, professor of critical animal studies, globalization, and anti-racism, Brock University, read early chapters and provided sound advice.

Pearl Hotai, thank you for never saying *No!* when I asked you to read the manuscript just one more time. Mimi, thank you for all the delicious vegan meals that sustained me while I was writing. Lexi, thank you for your inspiring and boundless talent which never fails to inspire me. Paul, thank you for being a surrogate father to Karma when I needed to travel for the boycott campaign.

Cat Uhlin and Sy Silverberg, where would I be without you? Thank you for reading the manuscript and for every other thing on a list too long to mention. Lucky Budd, author, oral historian, and radio host, thanks for pushing me to get my manuscript out the door.

I want to thank Humber College School for Writers and its former director, author Antanas Sileika, for giving me a space in the program, and to author and filmmaker, David Bezmozgis, now its director, for your emails of support. It takes a village to write a book—forget raising children, that's a piece of cake—and I am so grateful authors Sarah Sheard and Maria Meindl were in my village, providing their literary and publishing insights and generous encouragement. I must also single out editor and friend, Carole Fleck, for reading chapters, and Jocelyn Roy, for reviewing my French. *Merci d'être un professeur de français extraordinaire.*

Shakespeare's quote "What's past is prologue" certainly fits when I think of all the activists who came before me to fight against Canada's commercial seal hunt. Those prominent among them are Paul Watson, Robert Hunter, and Brian Davies. If it weren't for them, I still might be writing advertising copy for laxatives, anti-depressants, and breast pumps.

During the writing of this book numerous people have passed along information and shared professional and personal observations about Canada's marine mammal management. Thank you for your tips, your data, and your trust.

Without the help of my chiropractor, Dr. Mike Weber, I would be contorted on the sofa, groaning in spine-twisted agony. Thanks for straightening me out.

Murray, my partner, never flinched from a last-minute chapter reading, or the double-checking of my math. If I'm not emaciated—which I'm not—it's because he cooked me vegan meals when I was too busy writing to think of food. My mother is a tough critic, so when I passed to her drafts of chapters to read, I did so with trembling hands. I knew I was on the right track when she said after one such reading, "Your book is a lot more interesting than I thought it would be." It was high praise, indeed. Thanks Mom.

I give abundant thanks to my wonderful publisher, Martin Rowe of Lantern Publishing & Media. Finding a publisher is a bit like standing against the back wall of a high school dance. One prays that the person who asks you to dance is not a serial killer. Thank the universe you are not a serial killer, Martin, and my book is alive and well (as I am). You were my first choice in this publishing dance, and I am forever grateful for your advice and vision.

NOTES

1. Bombs, Anyone?

1. Stephen Harper was prime minister of Canada from 2006 to 2015. Loyola Hearn was Canada's federal minister of fisheries and oceans from February 6, 2006 to October 30, 2008.

2. Dogs of the Sea

1. Fred Bruemmer and Brian Davies, *Seasons of the Seal* (Minocqua, WI: North Word Press, 1988).
2. K. Ronald and David M. Lavigne, "Sealing," *The Canadian Encyclopedia*, February 7, 2006, https://www.thecanadianencyclopedia.ca/en/article/sealing.

3. Just Breathe

1. Reports of how many seals are taken each year vary depending on the source. For a breakdown of how many seals were killed each year and whether they were under or over one year old, I have referred to "Allowable Catches and Reported Kills of Harp Seals in Canada" in *Seals and Sealing in Canada*, a 2007 report by IFAW (International Fund for Animal Welfare). For a more detailed breakdown by age class, I consulted "Exact Pup Kills Age Class," a spreadsheet compiled by Sheryl Fink, Campaign Director, Canadian Wildlife, IFAW.
2. Ibid.

4. I Will Always Protect You

1. Michael Harris, *Lament for an Ocean: The Collapse of the Atlantic Cod Fishery, A True Crime Story* (Toronto: McClelland & Stewart, 1998), 67–68.

2. "The Atlantic Seal Hunt: Defending the Seal Hunt," interview by Michael Maltby, *Weekend Program*, CBC, March 26, 1972, broadcast, 7:37, http://www.cbc.ca/archives/entry/defending-the-seal-hunt.

5. A Greener Shade of Pale

1. Rob Parker, "Seal Slayers vs. Seal Sprayers," *As It Happens*, CBC Radio, February 6, 1976, CBC Digital Archives, 6:45, http://www.cbc.ca/archives/entry/seal-slayers-vs-seal-sprayers.
2. Bryce Muir, "In Defense of Canadian Seal Hunting," *New York Times*, May 21, 1977, https://www.nytimes.com/1977/05/21/archives/in-defense-of-canadian-sealhunting.html.

6. Fanatics and Sanitary Napkins

1. "European Parliament Endorses Import Ban on Seal Skins," interview by Nick Peters, *Sunday Morning Program*, CBC Radio, March 14, 1982, audio, 10:45, https://www.cbc.ca/archives/entry/european-parliament-endorses-import-ban-on-sealskins.
2. "Ottawa Rejects Ban on Seal Hunt," *New York Times*, March 10, 1984, https://www.nytimes.com/1984/03/10/world/ottawa-rejects-ban-on-seal-hunt.html.
3. Douglas Martin, "Days of Clubbing Seal Pups Appear to Be Over in Canada," *New York Times*, February 10, 1985, https://www.nytimes.com/1985/02/10/world/days-of-clubbing-seal-pups-appear-to-be-over-in-canada.html.

7. Bookstore Dave

1. Numbers from "Exact Pup Kills Age Class," a spreadsheet compiled by Sheryl Fink, Campaign Director, Canadian Wildlife, IFAW.
2. Marie Thompson, "Ottawa Ends Large-Scale Seal Hunt," CBC, December 30, 1987, 2:25, https://www.cbc.ca/player/play/1606933367.
3. Brian Davies, *Seal Song* (London: Penguin, 1979).

8. The Dictates of Conscience

1. "Newfoundlanders Protest Cod Moratorium," CBC Digital Archives, July 1, 1992.

2. William Schrank and Noel Roy, "Commentary: The Newfoundland Fishery and Economy Twenty Years after the Northern Cod Moratorium," *Marine Resource Economics* 28 (1992): 397–413.

3. J. W. Lawson, G. B. Stenson, and D. G. McKinnon, "Diet of Harp Seals (*Phoca groenlandica*) in 2J3KL during 1991–93" (Scientific Council Meeting, Northwest Atlantic Fisheries Organization, June 1993), https://www.nafo.int/Portals/0/PDFs/sc/1993/scr-93-036.pdf.

4. Sealers purchase the spike ends commercially and attach them to regulation-sized clubs or wooden handles.

9. Blink

1. Evidence (House of Commons, March 28, 1996), https://www.ourcommons.ca/Content/archives/committee/352/ocea/evidence/05_96-03-28/ocea05_blk-e.html.

2. "Marine Mammal Regulations (SOR/93-56)," *Fisheries Act* (February 4, 1993), https://laws-lois.justice.gc.ca/eng/regulations/sor-93-56/fulltext.html.

3. Miguel Llanos, "Humane? Canada Seal Hunt Centers on Question," MSNBC, April 4, 2004, https://www.nbcnews.com/id/wbna4608053#.X3ciEpNKgSw.

10. Vacuums and Viagra

1. Peter Mansbridge, "Tobin Says Seals Slow Down Cod Recovery," on-the-ground report by Leslie MacKinnon, CBC, June 28, 1995, 2:17, http://www.cbc.ca/archives/categories/economy-business/business/pelts-pups-and-protest-the-atlantic-seal-hunt/tobin-says-seals-slow-down-cod-recovery.html.

2. Peter Mansbridge and Tonda MacCharles, "The Seal Hunt Makes a Comeback," CBC, December 18, 1995, 2:07, http://www.cbc.ca/archives/entry/the-seal-hunt-makes-a-comeback.

3. Maureen Brosnahan, "Video Prompts Calls for More Enforcement," CBC, February 10, 1997, 2:34, http://www.cbc.ca/archives/entry/video-prompts-calls-for-more-enforcement.

4. See "Letters," Politico, Lesley O'Donnell, coordinator, International Fund for Animal Welfare, EU office, Brussels, April 24, 1996, https://www.politico.eu/article/letters-23/.

5. Mansbridge and MacCharles, "Seal Hunt Comeback."

6. T. J. Kenchington, "Canadian Fisheries Management in the Twenty-First Century," a submission to the Standing Committee of the House of Commons on the Department of Fisheries and Oceans, January 1998.

7. "A Partial List of Canadian Government Sealing Industry Costs and Subsidies (1995 to 2001)," appendix to Access to Information (Atlantic Canada Opportunities Agency): 2.

8. Kenchington, "Fisheries Management Twenty-First Century."

9. Elizabeth Brubaker, "Unnatural Disaster: How Politics Destroyed Canada's Atlantic Ground fisheries," in *Political Environmentalism: Going Behind the Green Curtain*, ed. Terry L. Anderson (Stanford, CA: Hoover Institution Press Publication, 2000), 192.

10. "Dogs Mutilated in Viagra Test," *Special Report*, BBC News, 1998, http://news.bbc.co.uk/2/hi/special_report/1998/viagra/190800.stm.

11. Michael MacDonald, "Fur Institute of Canada Seeks to Revive Seal Penis Sales," The Canadian Press, June 8, 2015, https://www.cbc.ca/news/canada/north/fur-institute-of-canada-seeks-to-revive-seal-penis-sales-1.3103756.

12. Quoted in Elizabeth Brubaker, "Unnatural Disaster: How Politics Destroyed Canada's Atlantic Ground fisheries," *Environment Probe*, January 18, 2000, https://environment.probeinternational.org/2000/01/18/unnatural-disaster-how-politics-destroyed-canadas-atlantic-groundfisheries/.

13. "The Torment of the Beagles; World Exclusive: How Dogs Were Sliced Open, Had Needles Put in Them and Were Given Electric Shocks to Test Viagra—Then Were Put to Death," *The Sunday Mirror*, October 11, 1998.

14. Quoted in Brubaker, "Unnatural Disaster."

15. Standing Committee on Fisheries and Oceans, "Minutes of Proceedings," Fish Committee Meeting, House of Commons, April 15, 1999, https://www.ourcommons.ca/DocumentViewer/en/36-1/FISH/meeting-71/minutes.

14. What's Your Emergency?

1. Michael Dwyer, *Over the Side, Mickey: A Sealer's First Hand Account of the Newfoundland Seal Hunt* (Halifax, NS: Nimbus Publishing Ltd., 1999).

15. By Any Means Necessary

1. Rosemary Burdon et al., "Veterinary Report: Canadian Commercial Seal Hunt" (March 2001), 23–26, https://www.harpseals.org/about_the_hunt/ifaw_vet_report_2001.pdf.

18. Low-Hanging Fruit

1. Stephen Best, *Understanding the Political Reality Behind Canada's Commercial Seal Hunt* (International Fund for Animal Welfare, 2002), 3.

2. "Department of Fisheries and Oceans Newsreel," Department of Fisheries and Oceans, 2004.

3. "Trade Data Online," Government of Canada, 2003, http://strategis. gc.ca/sc_mrkti/tdst/engdoc/tr_homep.html; see also Gary B. Stenson, "The Status of Harp and Hooded Seals in the North Atlantic" (Scientific Council Meeting, Northwest Atlantic Fisheries Organization, June 2014), https://www.nafo.int/Portals/0/PDFs/sc/2014/scr14-026.pdf.

19. Good Karma

1. For sales between 2003 and 2005, see "International Trade," Fisheries and Oceans Canada, n.d., https://dfo-mpo.gc.ca/stats/commercial/cfs/2005/ section4-eng.htm.

21. Getting to "No"

1. Jeffrey A. Hutchings and Ransom Myers, "What Can Be Learned from the Collapse of a Renewable Resource? Atlantic Cod, *Gadus morhua*, of Newfoundland and Labrador," *Canadian Journal of Fisheries and Aquatic Sciences* 51, no. 9 (September 1994): 2126–46, https://doi.org/10.1139/f94-214.

2. L. Morissette, M. O. Hammill, and C. Savenkoff, "The Trophic Role of Marine Mammals in the Northern Gulf of St. Lawrence," *Marine Mammal Science* 22, no. 1 (January 10, 2006): 74–103, https://doi. org/10.1111/j.1748-7692.2006.00007.x.

3. R. A. Myers and B. Worm, "Rapid Worldwide Depletion of Predatory Fish Communities," *Nature* 423 (May 15, 2003): 280–83, https://www.ncbi. nlm.nih.gov/pubmed/12748640. The study found that about 90 percent of world fisheries are close to being or have already been depleted.

22. Girl Detective

1. George Wenzel, *Animal Rights, Human Rights: Ecology, Economy, and Ideology in the Canadian Arctic* (Toronto: Toronto University Press, 1991).

2. Stephen Best, "Three Epiphanies," personal reflections, n.d.

23. Power Must Be Taken

1. For an overview of seal reproduction rates and thinning sea ice over a decade, see Gary B. Stenson, Alejandro D. Buren, and Mariano Koen-Alonso, et al., "The Impact of Changing Climate and Abundance on Reproduction in an Ice-Dependent Species, The Northwest Atlantic Harp Seal, Pagophilus Groenlandicus," *ICES Journal of Marine Science* 73, no. 2 (January/February 2016): 250–62, https://doi.org/10.1093/icesjms/fsv202.

24. Seeing Red

1. On the Red Lobster website, the company identifies that the snow crab it purchases "comes from the cold, pristine waters of the Bering Sea off the coast of Alaska, and St. Lawrence, Nova Scotia, and Newfoundland." See https://www.redlobster.ca/our-story/seafood-with-standards/sourcing-our-seafood.

2. Red Lobster commercials boasted about "Endless Crab: A celebration of all the hot, steaming snow crab legs you can eat," and the seven-week deal enticed customers to plough through piles of snow crab legs with abandon. One dinner party of five "put away 18 pounds of the stuff," and another group had "THIRTY!! refills of crab legs." See Benita D. Newton, "All-You-Can-Eat Was Too Much: Red Lobster's Chief Is Ousted after a Crab Promotion Loses Money. The Parent Company Says That Wasn't the Reason," *St. Tampa Bay Times*, September 1, 2005, https://www.tampabay.com/archive/2003/09/26/all-you-can-eat-was-too-much/.

3. Kim Lopdrup, President, Red Lobster, letter to the campaign, 2005.

4. Newton, "All-You-Can-Eat."

25. Hakapiks and Heroes

1. International Fund for Animal Welfare, "Seal Hunt Observers Attacked on Ice by Sealers," press release, April 1, 2005.

2. All details of the attack by sealers on IFAW observers have been verified or added to by Sheryl Fink, a witness to the attack, as a member of IFAW's seal hunt observation team.

3. "A History of Violence Against Seal Defenders on the Ice: Canada Gives Green Light for Sealers to Violently Oppose Seal Defenders," *Sea Shepherd News*, March 27, 2006.

4. "Shots Fired as Sealers, Protesters Clash," CBC News, April 1, 2006.

27. A Tale of Two Polls

1. Bruce Smith, "Improving Humane Practice in the Canadian Harp Seal Hunt: A Report of the Independent Veterinarians' Working Group on the Canadian Harp Seal Hunt" (August 2005), http://www.cwhc-rcsf.ca/docs/technical_reports/IVWG_Report_EN.pdf.
2. Pierre-Yves Daoust et al., "Animal Welfare and the Harp Seal Hunt in Atlantic Canada," *Canadian Veterinary Journal* 43, no. 9 (September 2002): 687–94.
3. "Marine Mammal Regulations," 1993.
4. Guy Beaupré, "Seal Fishery Enforcement and Monitoring Summary: EFSA-EU Study on Humane Killing," International Fisheries, Fisheries and Oceans Canada, 2007.

31. Don't Mess with Ladies Who Lunch

1. Per Lars Tonstad, "Staten Betaler for Brenning av Selfangst [The State Pays for Burning of Hunted Seals]," *Dagbladet*, May 31, 2006, http://www.dagbladet.no/nyheter/2006/05/31/467752.html. In 2006, the Norwegian government put 2.5 million Norwegian krone (NOK) in direct subsidies into the seal hunt, and then proceeded to subsidize the burning of the seal pelts (which could not be sold) with another two-million-krone subsidy.
2. Halvard Johansen, Statement at the Stakeholder consultation meeting of the European Food and Safety Authority, in An Overview of the Economic Importance of Canada's Commercial Seal Hunt, IFAW (2007).

32. A Publix Forum

1. Interview with Newfoundland Fisheries and Aquaculture Minister Tom Rideout, CBC Radio, February 20, 2007.
2. "Report on Landing Data," Department of Fisheries and Oceans, accessed December 12, 2006.
3. "Seal-Hunt Supporters Counter Protests," CBC News, Mar 15, 2007, http://www.cbc.ca/news/world/seal-hunt-supporters-counter-protests-1.669408. Clifford Olson was a notorious child abuser who confessed to murdering eleven children in Canada in the 1980s.
4. Jani Hall, "Demand for Seal Products Has Fallen—So Why Do Canadians Keep Hunting?" Wildlife Watch, *National Geographic*,

April 5, 2017, https://www.nationalgeographic.com/news/2017/04/wildlife-watch-canada-harp-seal-hunt/.

5. CTV News. "Federal Fisheries Envoy Criticized Over Seal Hunt," Canadian Press, January 11, 2008, https://www.ctvnews.ca/federal-fisheries-envoy-criticized-over-seal-hunt-1.270733.

6. "Nunavut Joins Battle to Support Seal Hunt," CBC News, February 20, 2007, https://www.cbc.ca/news/canada/north/nunavut-joins-battle-to-support-seal-hunt-1.652464.

33. Ad Hominem

1. "Liberals Step Away from Senator's Criticism of U.S.," *Globe and Mail*, March 17, 2006, https://www.theglobeandmail.com/news/national/liberals-step-away-from-senators-criticism-of-us/article1096408/.

2. I have shortened and condensed the debate, choosing to touch only on what I, as a memoirist, consider the highlights and the drama of the scene. The full debate can be requested from Talk Ottawa.

3. "Senator Sees Defeat for the Seal Killers," Sea Shepherd Conservation Society, 2006, http://www.seashepherd.org/news-and-commentary/commentary/archive/canadian-senator-sees-defeat-for-the-seal-killers.html.

34. No More Mr. Nice Guy

1. Constant Brand, "EU Rejects Appeal for Total Ban on Canadian Seal Products," *Associated Press*, January 26, 2007.

2. Ian McLaren, Solange Brault, John Harwood, and David Vardy, "Report of the Eminent Panel on Seal Management," Fisheries and Oceans Canada, 2001.

3. Stephen Chase, "Five Ways Ottawa Stymies Access to Information Requests," *Globe and Mail*, January 15, 2011, https://www.theglobeandmail.com/news/politics/five-ways-ottawa-stymies-access-to-information-requests/article562031/.

4. Standing Committee on Fisheries and Oceans, transcript, June 15, 2006: 4.

35. Giving Me the Slip

1. Standing Committee on Fisheries and Oceans, evidence, November 6, 2006: 29.

36. Oh Shit!

1. "Sea Shepherd Farley Mowat Rammed—Seal Defense Campaign," Sea Shepherd Conservation Society, April 3, 2008, video, 3:40, https://www.youtube.com/watch?v=ZmCFKnBaTBw.
2. I have not included the location to protect the source.
3. "EU Official Criticizes Canada for Blocking Seal Hunt Observers," *Vancouver Sun*, April 17, 2008, https://www.harpseals.org/resources/news_and_press/2008/sealhunt08.php.
4. "Only Four in Ten (39%) Canadians Support Seal Hunt," Ipsos Reid, April 18, 2008, https://www.ipsos.com/en-ca/only-four-ten-39-canadians-support-seal-hunt.
5. Standing Committee on Fisheries and Oceans, minutes of proceedings, 1st sess., 39th Parliament, November 6, 2006.
6. US Fish and Wildlife Service, International Affairs, Marine Mammal Protection Act (1972), https://www.fisheries.noaa.gov/topic/laws-policies#marine-mammal-protection-act. President Richard Nixon signed the proposed legislation into law on October 21, 1972. On December 21, 1972, it took effect.

37. Mrs. Vespa

1. "Prices for Seal Pelts during 2007 Season," Carino Company Limited, May 23, 2007.

38. Lost and Found

1. According to Sheryl Fink, Campaign Director, Canadian Wildlife, IFAW, each purchaser is asked whether or not they want their company name listed on the purchase slip. It remains a mystery why Fogo Island's name remains.
2. "Sealers Will Be Charged for Hunt Violations: DFO," CBC News. May 14, 2008, https://www.cbc.ca/amp/1.769789.

43. Snakes Are People, Too

1. Elena Harris, "Rabbit Spirit Animal," https://www.spiritanimal.info/rabbit-spirit-animal/.
2. Elena Harris, "Snake Spirit Animal," https://www.spiritanimal.info/snake-spirit-animal/.

44. Blame Game

1. Mark Saigeon, memo to attendees of a June 4, 2001 meeting regarding the Inuit gaining access to the United States Marine Mammal Protection Act, Department of Foreign Affairs and International Trade, June 6, 2001, https://www.harpseals.org/politics_and_propaganda/canada_saigeon_memo_play_inuit_card.pdf.

2. "Defence of the Fur Trade," unpublished discussion paper, Department of External Affairs, Agri-Food, Fish and Resources Product Bureau (TAD), May 1985, in *Icy Battleground: Canada, the International Fund for Animal Welfare, and the Seal Hunt*, Donald Barry (Breakwater Books Limited, 2005).

45. Codswallop

1. Carolyn Keene, *The Hidden Staircase* (New York: Grosset & Dunlop, 1961).

2. Peter Stoffer, Standing Committee on Fisheries and Oceans, comment, 2nd sess., 39th Parliament, April 14, 2008.

46. State of Play

1. Charlie Smith, "Critic of Canadian Seal Hunt Urges Opponents to Back Sen. Mac Harb's Legislation," *Georgia Straight*, March 23, 2009, https://www.straight.com/article-209057/critic-canadian-seal-hunt-urges-opponents-contact-senators.

2. Regulation (EC) No 1007/2009 of the European Parliament and of the Council of 16 September 2009 on Trade in Seal Products (Text with EEA Relevance), EUR-Lex, Access to European Union Law, https://eur-lex.europa.eu/eli/reg/2009/1007/oj.

3. Kelly Burgess, "Canada's Seal Hunt Continues Though Hunters May Be Paid Little Money for Pelts," *Los Angeles Times*, April 6, 2009, https://latimesblogs.latimes.com/outposts/2009/04/canadas-seal-hunt.html.

4. Billy Canning, "Pelt Prices Keep Some Sealers Home," *Nor'wester*, April 24, 2009.

5. Richard J. Brennan, "'Disastrous' EU Seal Ban Casts Gloom Over Summit," *Toronto Star*, May 6, 2009, https://www.thestar.com/news/canada/2009/05/06/disastrous_eu_seal_ban_casts_gloom_over_summit.html.

6. "Canada to Fight EU Seal Product Ban," CBC News, July 27, 2009, https://www.cbc.ca/news/world/canada-to-fight-eu-seal-product-ban-1.832548.